D0048786

The Last Empress

The Last Empress

The She-Dragon of China

Keith Laidler

WILEY

Published in the UK in 2003 by John Wiley & Sons Ltd, The Atrium, Southern Gate, Chichester, West Sussex PO19 8SQ, England

Telephone   (+44) 1243 779777

Email (for orders and customer service enquiries): cs-books@wiley.co.uk
Visit our Home Page on www.wileyeurope.com or www.wiley.com

Copyright © 2003 Keith Laidler

First published March 2003. Reprinted April and June 2003.
This paperback edition August 2003.
Reprinted September and December 2003.

All Rights Reserved. No part of this publication may be reproduced, stored in a retrieval system or transmitted in any form or by any means, electronic, mechanical, photocopying, recording, scanning or otherwise, except under the terms of the Copyright, Designs and Patents Act 1988 or under the terms of a licence issued by the Copyright Licensing Agency Ltd, 90 Tottenham Court Road, London W1T 4LP, UK, without the permission in writing of the Publisher. Requests to the Publisher should be addressed to the Permissions Department, John Wiley & Sons Ltd, The Atrium, Southern Gate, Chichester, West Sussex PO19 8SQ, England, or emailed to permreq@wiley.co.uk, or faxed to (+44) 1243 770620.

This publication is designed to provide accurate and authoritative information in regard to the subject matter covered. It is sold on the understanding that the Publisher is not engaged in rendering professional services. If professional advice or other expert assistance is required, the services of a competent professional should be sought.

Keith Laidler has asserted his right under the Copyright, Designs and Patents Act 1988, to be identified as the author of this work.

Other Wiley Editorial Offices

John Wiley & Sons Inc., 111 River Street, Hoboken, NJ 07030, USA

Jossey-Bass, 989 Market Street, San Francisco, CA 94103-1741, USA

Wiley-VCH Verlag GmbH, Boschstr. 12, D-69469 Weinheim, Germany

John Wiley & Sons Australia Ltd, 33 Park Road, Milton, Queensland 4064, Australia

John Wiley & Sons (Asia) Pte Ltd, 2 Clementi Loop #02-01, Jin Xing Distripark, Singapore 129809

John Wiley & Sons Canada Ltd, 22 Worcester Road, Etobicoke, Ontario, Canada M9W 1L1

British Library Cataloguing in Publication Data

A catalogue record for this book is available from the British Library

ISBN 0-470-84881-2

Typeset in 11/13pt Photina by Mathematical Composition Setters Ltd, Salisbury, Wiltshire
Printed and bound in Great Britain by The Cromwell Press, Trowbridge, Wiltshire
This book is printed on acid-free paper responsibly manufactured from sustainable forestry in which at least two trees are planted for each one used for paper production.

Contents

Author's note

In the early 1980s I had the good fortune to be the first documentary film-maker invited to visit the People's Republic of China to research a television series on the wildlife of China. In the course of six weeks' intensive travel I journeyed across the length and breadth of that vast nation, from Tibet to Shanghai and from the snowy wastes of Manchuria to the southern rainforests of Yunnan.

This journey led to several programmes on China's wild places, to a lifelong fascination with Chinese history, and a continuing engagement with the Middle Kingdom that has lasted, in a series of yearly visits, up to the present. Much has changed since that time: China today is, in parts a least, a very modern country, one of a fortunate few with a strongly expanding economy, this century's coming superpower. But twenty years ago it was still the land of a million bicycles, of 'fashion' that offered a choice between grey or blue Mao suits (three sizes), of shrill loudspeakers on every street corner and in every railway carriage, stridently exhorting the masses to follow Maoist thought and the edicts of the Party. It was most definitely a 'less developed country' – still reeling from the Great Leap Forward (or as some of my more forthright Chinese friends delighted in naming it, the 'Great Leap Backward'). And 'backward' would be a more apposite term for the state of the nation at that juncture. I spent time in remote villages and towns – off-limits to other Westerners – that reminded me irresistibly of Medieval Europe: unpaved roads that turned instantly to mud at the first downpour; non-existent sanitation, with rubbish and ordure piled up in the streets; gangs of navvies man-hauling huge logs on flimsy barrows, their faces blank with exhaustion; hawkers, tinkers, shoemakers all noisily calling out their wares; street dentists extracting reluctant molars from groaning patients; and over and through it all a swirling, seething mass of humanity, numbers past counting, all hell-bent on their own personal goals but stopping briefly to gawp at the *Da Bizi*, the first Western 'big nose' they had seen in the flesh.

After four weeks of continuous travel and alien meals of snake, dog and camel-web, my companion and fellow film-maker, Mike Rosenburg, had had enough and flew back to the UK. The last two weeks were one of the hardest and yet most rewarding periods of my life. I was totally immersed in things Chinese, a lone Westerner in a deeply alien culture. But being alone forced me to look at this, to me, strange society with new eyes. Whereas China today has assimilated much of Western culture and mind-set, in those days, despite its veneer of Communist thought, it was still very much a Confucian society, its behaviour tied to the self-same traditions that have governed Chinese life for millennia. I was there to make wildlife programmes, but I learned much more about China than its zoology. I found that I got on very well with my Chinese hosts, they opened up to me and showed me aspects of themselves and their culture that, I believe, have helped me to understand and explain the seemingly irrational happenings in the lifetime of the Last Empress. In addition, my dealings with officials gave me insights into the sometimes Alice-in-Wonderland world of Chinese bureaucracy. There was in China (and to a lesser extent there still is) a general proclivity among officialdom for denying the obvious, for flying in the face of common sense and, with apparent conviction and sincerity, brazenly naming black 'white'. This was brought home to me most strongly in an interview with a Chinese forestry official in Sichuan. Outside the office trucks passed noisily down the track at a rate of one or two a minute, packed to the gunwales with huge tree trunks, cut from the forests near the Tibetan border and destined for some construction site in the provincial capital, Chengdu. Their passage shook the thin walls of the small office we sat in.

'Where exactly do these lorries deposit their timber?' I asked.

The official stared back, his eyes puzzled, 'What lorries?'

It became obvious later in the interview that Party policy said no timber should be cut from this region. Therefore, for the official, the lorries simply could not exist. Everyone knew the problem was not to be discussed, so everyone pretended it was not there. That way, in a typically Chinese solution, the business could go ahead, Chengdu could get its timber, and at the same time Party policy was adhered to – because nothing was happening! To me it seemed like madness.

At the end of a heated discussion I was given a very important piece of advice, a key of sorts to understanding much of the Middle Kingdom's history. 'You must understand,' the official told me earnestly, and with every indication of sincerity, 'facts are different in China.'

*T*o my many Chinese friends, for a multitude of privileged moments in the Middle Kingdom

Acknowledgements

The content and conclusions of this book on Yehonala are solely my own responsibility, as are any unconscious errors that may exist. But the work could never have been written without help and advice from numerous sources. Many Chinese friends provided information for the work, and opened up aspects of Chinese history that have thrown new light on the turbulent times Yehonala lived through; especial thanks are due to Mr Shen Zhihua for his zeal and commitment to unearthing information within China. In the United Kingdom, the staff of Durham University Library have been tireless in helping me obtain obscure books and manuscripts. At home, my wife Liz, and my children Rachel and Jamie, have endured my deadlines, and my doubts and conflicts in dealing with the enormously complicated events that compose the life of the Last Empress. Their enthusiasm and understanding have been an invaluable support. My editor, Sally Smith, guided me in numerous ways; her persistence and patience have added immeasurably to the style and content of these pages.

Cast of major characters

Pinyin romanisation of the Chinese names is given in parenthesis after each entry.

1. A-lu-te (A-lu-de) – Empress of Tung Chih Emperor. Possibly murdered on Yehonala's orders after the death of Tung Chih.
2. An Te-hai (An Dehai) – Grand Eunuch during early part of Yehonala's rule. Executed after breaking house-laws and (by Yehonala's command) leaving the Forbidden City to travel to Shandong Province.
3. Bruce, Frederick – Lord Elgin's (q.v.) younger brother, first British minister to China.
4. Burgevine, Henry – American mercenary, second-in-command of Ever-Victorious Army fighting for Imperials against the Tai Ping rebels. Later absconded to Tai Ping.
5. Cheng (Zheng) – Prince, Imperial family. After the Hsien Feng Emperor's death he conspired with Su Shun and Prince I to assassinate Yehonala and Sakota and to become regents for the infant Tung Chih, Yehonala's son by the Emperor. Sentenced to hang himself.
6. Chi Ying (Qi Ying) – Chinese mandarin, forced to commit suicide after failing to halt advance of Franco-British forces, 1860.
7. Ch'ien-lung (Qianlong) – Emperor of China. Considered one of the most successful and prestigious of China's rulers (1711–1796).
8. Ch'un (Chun) – Prince. A son of the Tao Kwang Emperor. He married one of Yehonala's sisters, by whom he had a son who became the reformist Kuang Hsu Emperor, whom Yehonala later imprisoned, and may have ordered poisoned.
9. Dorgun (Dorgon) – Manchu regent; oversaw the final victory of the Manchu over the Ming Dynasty in 1644.

10. Elgin, Lord – envoy of British government during Franco-British embassy to Peking (1860). Ordered the burning of the Summer Palace as reprisal against the Chinese torture and murder of allied prisoners.

11. Favier – Roman Catholic Bishop of Beijing. One of the first foreigners to warn that the Boxers intended a massacre of all foreigners.

12. Gaselee – British general, relieved siege of the foreign legation at Beijing 14th August 1900.

13. Gordon, Charles George – British army officer seconded to fight against Tai Ping rebels as leader of Ever-Victorious Army after F. T. Ward's (q.v.) death. Later famously killed in Khartoum by followers of the Mahdi.

14. Gros – Baron, envoy of French government during Franco-British embassy to Beijing (1860).

15. Hart, Sir Robert – head of Chinese Customs Service, a sinophile who lived in China for over fifty years and survived the siege of the foreign legations.

16. Hsien Feng (Xianfeng) – Emperor of China. Raised Yehonala from concubine, third rank, to position of power in the Forbidden City, following the birth of their son, the Tung Chih Emperor.

17. Hung Hsiu-chuan (Hong Xiuquan) – failed scholar and visionary, who believed himself the younger brother of Jesus and, in 1851, raised the standard of revolt against the Qing Dynasty as undisputed leader of Tai Ping rebellion.

18. I (Yi) – Prince of the Imperial clan. Negotiator (along with Mu Yin (q.v.)) during Franco-British embassy 1860. With Su Shun and Prince Cheng he attempted to eliminate Yehonala and seize power after Emperor Hsien Feng's death. Sentenced to hang himself by Yehonala.

19. James, Hubert – professor, beheaded by Boxers during the siege of the legations, and head exhibited in a cage over the Dong'an Gate.

20. Jung Lu (Ronglu) – sometime Head of Chinese Army, probable fiancé of Yehonala before she was taken as the Emperor's concubine to the Forbidden City; her alleged lover thereafter.

21. K'ang Hsi (Kangxi) – Emperor of China, 1662 – 1722.
22. Kang I (Kang Yi) – Yehonala's 'Lord High Extortioner' and conservative anti-reform minister, made a Boxer general by the Empress Dowager's command.
23. Kang Yu-wei (Kang Youwei) – leading light of reform movement; responsible for the content of much of the Kuang Hsu Emperor's 'One Hundred Days' reform.
24. Ketteler, von – German baron, murdered by Chinese at beginning of Boxer rebellion and the siege of the legations.
25. Kuang Hsu (Guangxu) – Emperor of China 1875 – 1908. Son of Prince Chun and Yehonala's sister. After the failure of his 1898 'One Hundred Days' reform attempt, he was held prisoner in the Forbidden City on Yehonala's orders. Poisoned by persons unknown, possibly Li Lien-ying (q.v.), Yuan Shi-kai (q.v.), or Yehonala.
26. Kung (Gong) – Prince, brother of the Hsien Feng Emperor, negotiated the Convention of Beijing with British and French, 1860. Later acted as chief adviser to Yehonala until he fell from favour.
27. Li Hsiu-cheng (Li Xiucheng) – Tai Ping rebel commander. Known as Chung Wang, or Loyal Prince. Captured after the fall of Nanking (1864). Wrote a history of the revolt before being beheaded.
28. Li Hung-chang (Li Hongzhang) – Chinese minister and sometime Viceroy of Chihli Province. Served with distinction in the Tai Ping rebellion, and proved invaluable as a negotiator with the French, Russian, British and Japanese powers. Perhaps the most intelligent and far-seeing of all Yehonala's advisers.
29. Li Lien-ying (Li Lianying) – Grand Eunuch in the Forbidden City following An Te-hai's untimely demise. Became chief confidant of Yehonala during the final decades of her rule.
30. Li Ping-heng (Li Pingheng) – Chinese pro-Boxer commander. Committed suicide after series of reverses against Western and Japanese troops, 1900.
31. Li Tzu-cheng (Li Zicheng) – leader of rebellion which toppled the Ming; declared himself Emperor of China, but was soon afterwards crushed by the Manchu.

32. Loch, Henry – secretary to Lord Elgin, captured and tortured by Chinese in 1860.
33. Lung Yu (Long You) – Empress of Kuang Hsu Emperor. Reputedly spied on the Emperor for Yehonala.
34. McDonald, Sir Claude – British Minister in Beijing during siege of legations.
35. Morrison, George – *The Times* correspondent during siege of legations and well into the twentieth century.
36. Mu Yin (Muyin) – President of the Board of War, chief negotiator (with Prince I) for Chinese during pre-conflict phase of Franco-British embassy, 1860.
37. Muyanga (Muyanga) – Uncle of Yehonala, who cared for her after her father's death.
38. Nurhachi – Manchu ruler, founder of Qing Dynasty which ruled China from 1644 until 1912.
39. Parkes, Harry – British Consul in Canton, acted as interpreter during Lord Elgin's Franco-British embassy to China, 1860; captured and tortured by the Chinese.
40. Pearl Concubine – concubine of Kuang Hsu, murdered on orders of Yehonala during flight from allied forces 1900.
41. Pichon, Stephen – French Minister to Beijing at the time of the siege of the foreign legations, 1900.
42. Pu Yi (Puyi) – son of Prince Chun the Younger and Jung Lu's daughter; chosen by Yehonala to succeed the Kuang Hsu Emperor. He was to be the last Emperor of the Manchu Dynasty.
43. P'un Chun (Punchun) – son of Prince Chun, appointed Heir Apparent to Kuang Hsu Emperor. Later fell into disfavour and was demoted by Yehonala to commoner status.
44. Sakota – Empress of Hsien Feng Emperor, known also as Niuhuru, and Empress of the Eastern Palace. Ruled as co-Regent with Yehonala until her death in 1880 (reputedly poisoned on Yehonala's orders).
45. Seng Guo Lin Sen – Mongol Commander of Chinese Army which defended Beijing during the Franco-British embassy in 1860.

46. Seymour, Sir Edward – Admiral, Royal Navy. Commander of relief force charged with lifting the siege of the legations in Beijing.
47. Su Shun (Sushun) – Chinese Minister, renowned for his corruption and vast fortune. Conspired against Yehonala after death of the Hsien Feng Emperor. Beheaded on Yehonala's orders.
48. Sugiyama – Japanese Chancellor, Beijing. Murdered by pro-Boxer Muslim troops at the beginning of the siege of the foreign legations, 1900.
49. Tan Ssu-t'ung (Tan Sitong) – reformist scholar, executed for planning coup against Yehonala and her conservative allies.
50. Tao Kwang (Daoguang) – Emperor of China 1821 – 1850, attempted unsuccessfully to suppress the opium trade.
51. Tseng Guo-feng (Zeng Guofan) – Chinese general who gained renown fighting against the Tai Ping rebels.
52. Tuan – Prince of the Imperial clan, noted pro-Boxer sympathiser. His son, P'un Chun, was first made Heir Apparent, then demoted to commoner status.
53. Teng Fu-hsiang (Dong Fuxiang) – Muslim rebel turned Chinese general. Prominent in the siege of the foreign legations, 1900.
54. Tung Chi (Tongzhi) – Emperor of China, 1861 – 1875. Son of Yehonala, died of complications following smallpox; infection possibly orchestrated on Yehonala's orders.
55. Wade, Thomas – interpreter, Lord Elgin's Franco-British embassy to China, 1860.
56. Ward, Frederick Townsend – American mercenary, founder of the Ever-Victorious Army, killed fighting against the Tai Ping rebels in 1862.
57. Ward, J. E. – American envoy to China, 1859. Regarded as 'tribute bearer' by the Chinese.
58. Weng Tung-ho (Weng Tonghe) – tutor to Tung Chih and Kuang Hsu Emperors, Grand Councillor, supported reform movement and was cashiered by Yehonala after her 1898 'coup'.

59. Wu K'o-tu (Wu Ketu) – Censor, committed suicide at Tung Chih Emperor's tomb in 1879 in protest at Yehonala's flouting of tradition.

60. Wu San-kuei (Wu Sangui) – Ming general who turned his coat and fought for the Manchu invaders against the Ming Dynasty. Later a satrap of the Manchu in south-western China until he rose in revolt.

61. Yeh Ming-Ch'en (Ye Mingchen) – Imperial Commissioner at Canton. Taken prisoner by British during the *Arrow* war, held captive in India, where he later died.

62. Yuan Shi-kai (Yuan Shikai) – Chinese army commander, betrayed reformist coup. Promoted by Yehonala and became Viceroy of Chihli. After fall of the Manchu in 1912 he tried unsuccessfully to establish a new dynasty with himself as Emperor.

63. Yulu (Youlu) – Viceroy of Chihli Province during siege of the foreign legations. Committed suicide 6th August 1900 after Seymour Relief Force defeated Chinese forces en route to Beijing.

Maps

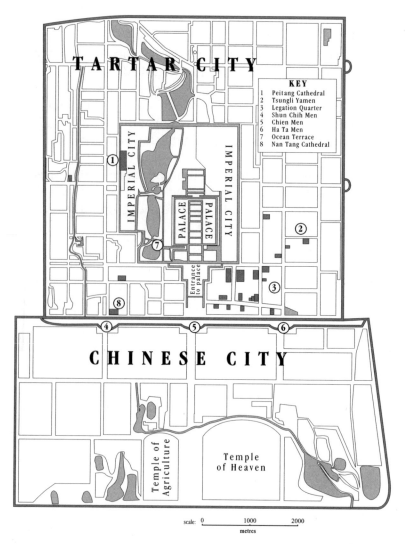

KEY

1 Peitang Cathedral
2 Tsungli Yamen
3 Legation Quarter
4 Shun Chih Men
5 Chien Men
6 Ha Ta Men
7 Ocean Terrace
8 Nan Tang Cathedral

TARTAR CITY

IMPERIAL CITY

IMPERIAL CITY

PALACE

PALACE

Entrance to palace

CHINESE CITY

Temple of Agriculture

Temple of Heaven

scale: 0   1000   2000
metres

Map 1   Beijing, 1900.

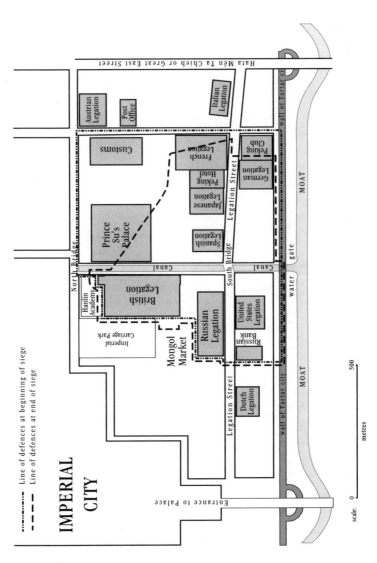

Map 2   Defence of the foreign legations, Beijing, 1900. (See also area 3, Map 1.)

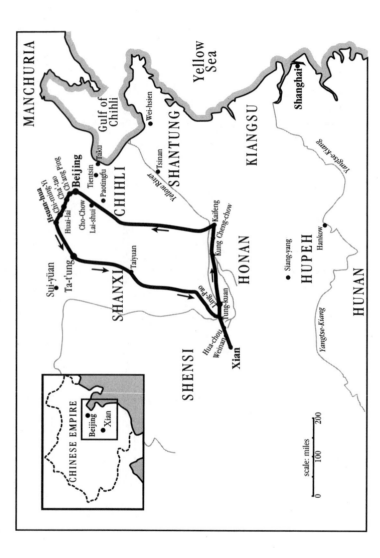

Map 3   The route of the Imperial journey, 1900–1901.

Introduction

*I*n 1618 the warrior hordes of the Manchu warlord Nurhachi swarmed through the northern passes into the plains of Ming China. By 1644 the power of the Ming Dynasty was utterly broken and Nurhachi's descendants soon established Manchu rule across the whole of the vast Celestial Empire, ruling as the Qing (Pure) Dynasty. Shortly thereafter an ancient marble stele was said to have been discovered in the northern forests of the Manchu heartland. Written upon it was a prophecy, a warning against a future Manchu female of the Yeho-Nala clan – were she to establish dominion over the Manchu, she would most certainly bring the nation to ruin and destruction.

It was only in 1912 that the prophecy was recalled. In that year, two hundred and sixty-seven years after its inception, the Manchu dynasty collapsed in chaos and violent revolution. The author of its destruction was Ci Xi (pronounced 'Sir Shee'), the Empress Dowager of China, nicknamed the Old Buddha. In her youth she had been known as the Orchid Lady, and later the Empress of the Western Palace. But the name she had carried with her when, in 1851, she had first entered the Emperor's harem should perhaps have been seen as a warning. For she was known then as Yehonala.

Yehonala's life covers an almost incredible swathe of history, for she reigned over the Middle Kingdom for almost fifty years. When she first joined the Imperial household as a 'concubine, third class' in 1851, the Emperor ruled supreme over a medieval – feudal society, secure in the knowledge that China was the very centre of the world, and that he alone, the Celestial Prince, swayed 'All Under Heaven'. All foreigners were 'barbarians', be they the *Xi Yang Guizi*, the 'Western foreign devils' of Europe, or the 'dwarf men' (Japanese) of the eastern seas. The ruling elite refused to acknowledge that any nation could engage with the

Middle Kingdom on terms of equality. They would allow no permanent alien presence in the Imperial City: the Chinese language contained no word for 'ambassador' – the representatives of all foreign governments were referred to demeaningly as 'tribute bearers'. The Chinese literati recognised no civilisation but their own: outside the Celestial Realm was only ignorance and squalor – the outer barbarians could have nothing to teach the rulers of the Middle Kingdom.

Just fifty years later, when as Empress Dowager all power lay in her own hands, Yehonala presided over a very different China, one in which 'treaty ports' allowed for the settlement of 'foreign devils' on Chinese soil, where trade and missionary work penetrated deep into the Chinese heartland, and where foreign soldiers guarded the legations of the Western Powers within the Chinese capital itself. In between, Yehonala had been at the centre of power throughout a multitude of historic events: the *Arrow* war with Britain, France's annexation of Indo-China, the Tai Ping and Muslim rebellions, the Anglo-French march on Beijing, war with Japan, the Boxer rebellion and the siege of the foreign legations in Beijing. Her personal odyssey through the twisted corridors of Chinese power reads like a history of Rome under the Caesars: intrigue, forbidden liaisons, betrayal, torture, summary executions and poisonings. Yehonala survived them all and triumphed, vanquishing her male opponents, proving her worth against the background of a culture that despised the feminine and held most women in contempt.

Strangely, there are substantial resonances between these momentous events and those close to our own time. In the 1860s China and the West faced each other in mutual incomprehension. China valued stability, respect for family and a reverence for ancient traditions that was religious in its devotional intensity. At the beginning of the twenty-first century, Islam and the West stared at each other with a hostility born of the same inability to recognise the other's point of view, much less its validity: Islam with its immoveable, time-honoured traditions *versus* the protean cultural values of the West and its obsession with the new.

Layered over this is a further compelling parallel. When the Europeans came to China it was to buy and sell. Britain and many another Western nation went to war to establish their right to 'free trade', the unrestricted ability to engage in commerce with anyone, anywhere in the world, provided a profit could be turned. These merchants and entrepreneurs were the forerunners, the advance guard, of late twentieth-century globalisation. 'Trade plus Christianity equals civilisation' epitomised their beliefs, and like them the prophets of globalisation preach a gospel of unrestricted trade as a panacea to all the world's ills – whether the world wants it or not. Nineteenth-century China revealed in no uncertain terms her dislike for this alien 'medicine', but was forced, at the point of a gun, to swallow the bitter pill. The World Trade Organisation spearheads globalisation with an almost religious fervour, and is not deterred even by the destruction of its headquarters and the death of nearly three thousand souls. Aid and economic assistance is made conditional upon the taking up of the standards and mores of the West. The trading *must* go on.

Whether globalisation will (or needs to) emerge as the sole, pre-eminent system in the world, or whether it will learn to coexist with other, less 'democratic' cultures, remains an open question. In the nineteenth century the Western push for free trade unleashed forces that produced the death of millions and destroyed Old China utterly. The story of Yehonala and the Middle Kingdom she ruled for over fifty years counsels caution.

Timeline

1644	Manchu Dynasty established
1850	Tao Kwang Emperor dies. Hsien Feng ascends Dragon Throne
1851	Yehonala enters Forbidden City Tai Ping rebellion begins
1852–53	Tai Ping revolt spreads. Fall of Nanking 20th March 1853
1855	Emperor 'knows' Yehonala
1856	April 27th Yehonala gives birth to son, to be eighth Emperor Tung Chih
1860	Franco-British embassy to Beijing. North China War Emperor and court flee to Jehol Summer Palace burned
1861	Hsien Feng Emperor dies. Tung Chih ascends Dragon Throne Court returns to Beijing. Conspiracy of Su Shun and the Princes Yehonala and Sakota joint Regents Frederick Ward establishes Ever-Victorious Army to fight Tai Ping rebels
1862	Ward dies. Charles Gordon leads Ever-Victorious Army
1864	Nanking falls to Imperial troops. End of Tai Ping rebellion
1869	Yehonala's favourite, eunuch An Te-hai, executed on Prince Kung/Sakota's orders
1872	Tung Chih reaches age of majority. Marries A-lu-te

1875	Tung Chih Emperor dies (poisoned by Yehonala?). A-lu-te's 'suicide'
	Tsai Tien, four years old, named as Kuang Hsu Emperor. Yehonala and Sakota re-assume the Regency
1879	Wu K'o-tu's protest suicide
1880	Sakota dies (poisoned by Yehonala?)
1885	Friction with Japan over Korea
1887	Kuang Hsu Emperor attains his majority. Yehonala retains control for further two years
1889	Kuang Hsu Emperor marries Lung Yu, Yehonala's nominee
	Yehonala 'retires' from government
1894	Sino-Japanese War. China loses.
1895	China signs Treaty of Shimonoseki, ceding Formosa, Port Arthur and Weihaiwei to Japan and paying a two-hundred-million-tael indemnity
1897	Germany occupies port of Kiaochow and environs on a ninety-nine-year 'lease'
	France occupies Kuangchowan in Canton on a ninety-nine-year 'lease'
1898	Russia occupies Port Arthur and port of Dalianwan on a thirty-five-year 'lease'.
	June/July/August: Emperor Kuang Hsu's 'One Hundred Days' reform; the Twenty-Seven Edicts issued
	September: Reformist plot against Yehonala betrayed by Yuan Shikai
	Yehonala's coup d'état; Kuang Hsu imprisoned; reformers flee or are executed
1899	China's new policy of resisting foreign aggression. Italian 'San Men Bay' fiasco. Boxer movement rises to prominence with slogan 'Support the Qing and Exterminate the Foreigners'
1900	Boxer movement attracts popular and government approval

	June: Ministers Sugiyama and von Ketteler murdered
	20th June: Siege of the Beijing foreign legations begins
	14th August: Siege of legations lifted
	Yehonala, Emperor and court flee Beijing in disguise; eventually settle at Xian
1902	7th January: Yehonala, Emperor and court return to Beijing
	Rapprochement with foreign community. Yehonala begins reforms
1904/5	Russo-Japanese war confirms necessity for China's modernisation
1908	Yehonala taken ill. Kuang Hsu Emperor mysteriously sickens
	14th November: Emperor dies (poisoned?)
	15th November: Yehonala dies (poisoned?)
1909	5th November: Yehonala buried
1912	12th February: Manchu Dynasty abdicates power

CHAPTER ONE

No joy shall be equal ...

When the Emperor Hsien Feng turned over a jade plaque on the ivory table next to his chamber the fate of the last Dynasty to rule the Middle Kingdom was changed irrecoverably in a single action. The plaque bore the name of a young concubine from his harem and indicated that she was to be his bed-companion for the evening. That night, as was the custom, covered only by a red silk sheet, the girl was carried on the back of a eunuch to the Emperor's stone-flagged room and laid naked at the foot of his bed, up which she had to crawl to the Lord of Ten Thousand Years, so symbolising her complete subjection to the will of the Celestial Prince.

The girl who was to become the Last Empress of China, was known to the Manchu as Yehonala, from her clan name, the Yeho-Nala. She was just sixteen when she was chosen as a concubine for the Emperor Hsien Feng's harem, and forced to leave her family home and her betrothed forever. But entrance to the Emperor's seraglio did not guarantee time with the Celestial Prince – his harem was well-stocked with beautiful women chosen from across the Empire and Yehonala was to languish there for five long years before she was summoned to the Imperial bedchamber. But once she had been brought to the Emperor's couch, she stayed and no one could usurp her place as the Imperial bed-partner. The Emperor was utterly besotted with his 'new' concubine and remained so almost until his death. He simply could not do without her.

No one can be certain of what passed between the Emperor Hsien Feng and Yehonala during that first night they spent together. But whatever occurred it can only have pleased the

Emperor, for it left an indelible impression upon him and set a
seed that would finally bear fruit fifty years later in the collapse
of a system that had governed China for over two millennia.
Perhaps the essence of that meeting is best summed up in
the words of the Chinese poet, Chang Heng, who almost two
thousand years before had written of a wife's desire:

> (So that) ... we can practise all the variegated postures,
> Those that an ordinary husband has but rarely seen,
> Such as taught by T'ien lao to the Yellow Emperor,
> No joy shall be equal to the delights of this first night,
> These shall never be forgotten, however old we may grow.
> Chang Heng (AD 78–139)[1]

While Yehonala was undoubtedly beautiful, she was not
exceptionally so, and (except for dynastic alliances) all the
women of the harem were chosen for their good looks. It was
in her sexual prowess that Yehonala's power over the Emperor
lay and it was this that brought her within reach of ultimate
power. For a woman in China, and especially one confined
within the sacred precincts of the Forbidden City, the bedroom
was often the only route to influence and authority. It was also
the means to obtain personal freedom. Deeply enmeshed in a
system that used women purely as pleasure-objects and child-
producers, Yehonala may have come to see sexual prowess as a
means of empowering herself, of taking control of an otherwise dull, preordained future and as offering her a chance to
be mistress of her own fate.

Like all the Imperial line, the Emperor Hsien Feng had been
schooled in pleasure from a very early age. His tastes were said
to be many and varied and, according to some, perverted.
While he may not have been an Emperor Yang Ti (who when
he travelled took with him a caravan of ten chariots, padded
with red satin, on each of which lay a naked beauty, awaiting
his attentions), it is certainly true that Hsien Feng was already
a dissipated roué long before he encountered Yehonala.
What sexual magic could this inexperienced girl of twenty-
one have to offer that made her superior to all the other beauties of his harem?

When she was inducted into the harem, stringent and intimate examinations ensured that Yehonala, like the rest of the new intake of concubines, had had no previous sexual contact with men. For the security and legitimacy of the Imperial line, all the Emperor's ladies had to be certified virgins. Once within the vermilion walls of the Forbidden City, with its 3,000 handmaidens and 3,000 eunuchs, the Emperor was the only intact male (other men were forbidden to spend the night within the Palace on pain of summary beheading). There therefore appeared to be very little chance of gaining the sexual experience necessary to hold an Emperor in thrall. How then, did Yehonala become proficient in these arts? It seems likely that it was what she did, and what she learned, in the five years *before* the Emperor was even aware of her existence in the Forbidden City, that set her apart from the other beauties of the harem.

What Yehonala's later life reveals is that nothing was left to chance in her bid to achieve and maintain power – and that whatever she needed to do was performed with dedication and application and energy. No doubt she would naturally have brought all these attributes to the Imperial bedchamber. But given her later lust for power, and the only route available for achieving such power, it seems likely that she would have dedicated much of the first five years of her time in the harem to practising every means at her disposal to please a lover: it is clear that, when the opportunity presented itself, it was mastery in the arts of love that was to single her out in the mind of the Emperor as exceptional.

Yin Daoism arose in the Eastern Han Dynasty (AD 25–220). Its adherents believed firmly in the importance of human sexual expression as an adjunct to mental and physical well-being. This branch of Daoism was responsible for numerous sex manuals, such as the *Yu Fang Mi Chueh* (Secret Codes of the Jade Room), the *Yu Fang Chih Ya* (Important Guidelines of the Jade Room) and the *Su Nu Ching* (Manual of Lady Purity). Anatomical details were hidden behind a code of poetical nomenclature. More than thirty love-making positions were documented, equally well camouflaged with elegant phraseology which included

'Approaching the Fragrant Bamboo', 'The Fish Interlock Their Scales' and 'The Leaping White Tiger'.[2]

Yin Daoism adopted a deeply aesthetic attitude towards sex; the emphasis was on the beauty and poetry of love-making, and its importance to health and longevity. The adherents believed that they could use sexual passion as a furnace in which to refine and concentrate their life energy, known as 'qi'. Properly controlled, in a species of sexual alchemy, the accumulated 'qi' could be directed from the generative organs along the meridians of the spine to the brain, achieving higher states of consciousness and, as a by-product, increased longevity, even immortality.[3] The philosophy was therefore no simple excuse for licentiousness – while the joys of love-making were there to be enjoyed, there was also a higher purpose and control was essential:

> The arts of the bedroom constitute the climax of human emotions and encompass the totality of the Dao. Therefore the ancient sages regulated man's external pleasures in order to control his inner passions, and they made detailed rules and terms governing sexual intercourse. If a man regulates his sexual pleasure, he will feel at peace and attain longevity. If, however, a man abandons himself to sexual pleasure without regard for the rules set forth in the ancient texts, he will soon fall ill and gravely injure himself.[4]

Certain techniques of feminine allure were closely guarded secrets, and at first taught only to those who were to become either the Empress or concubines of the Celestial Prince. A variety of tools were also used by young women, with the assistance of the palace eunuchs, to acquire sexual skills. A very ancient practice (at least two thousand years old) was the use of polished stone eggs to exercise the vaginal and pelvic floor muscles. Placed inside the body, the stones acted as a point of resistance against which these muscles could be stimulated in a series of complicated exercises. Recent excavations in the old Chinese capital of Xian have also brought to light skilfully crafted bronze prostheses of male organs dating from the time of the Han Dynasty (206 BC to AD 25).[5] Chinese authorities have concluded that the skilful and lifelike nature of these artefacts could only have been achieved by artisans dedicated to this craft. Other finds, from the 1800s back to the earliest discoveries of the Warring States period[6] have also been uncovered in female quarters of Imperial palaces or the houses of the nobility. Here then, would seem to be a possible source for Yehonala's skills.

Wherever Yehonala learned her skills, the events of her first night with the Emperor gave her the recognition she craved, and set in motion a train of events that would lead, ultimately, to the collapse of a Dynasty, to the fall of the mighty Manchu who, over two hundred years before, had ridden out from their dark northern forests to conquer the Chinese and to claim the throne of All Under Heaven.

CHAPTER TWO

The coming of the Manchu

The last Imperial Dynasty to rule over China was not Chinese, nor were they regarded as such by the Han people of the Middle Kingdom. They were foreign conquerors from the northern forests, whose original homeland lay between forested slopes of *Chang Bai Shan*, the Long White Mountain, and the featureless marshland of the Amur river. In China, this region is known as Dong Bei, but we in the West know it as Manchuria, after the tribal name of these doughty fighters, the Manchu.

The Manchu were known to the Chinese from a very early period, and their ancestors are recorded as bringing tribute of bows and arrows to the Emperor Shun as early as 2230 BC. Following the conquest in 1644, when the native Ming Dynasty was destroyed, the Chinese were pleased to portray the Manchu as rough, uncouth barbarians. No doubt this helped to assuage their feelings of hurt pride and to maintain their illusion of superiority over all other races – after all, a mugger is rarely regarded as morally or intellectually superior by his victim, merely more violent and brutal. This image of the Manchu as warlike ruffians has been taken up even by modern Western writers, but the truth is that the seventeenth-century Manchu were already at a high level of civilisation. Manchu monarchs gave themselves reign-titles, and ordered their courts in imitation of the Middle Kingdom's Celestial Prince, and their conversations and correspondence are peppered with quotations from the Sages and the Classics of China. Thanks to the influence of their vast southern neighbour, they had become almost completely sinicised.[1]

Not that they were for a moment considered so by the Ming Court. As non-Chinese they were, for the most part, beneath contempt. We have letters from the founder of the Manchu Dynasty complaining of the arrogant refusal of the Chinese Emperor to receive their ambassadors sent to negotiate peace: 'I desire peace, but only on a footing of absolute equality ... There must be no question of 'central' and 'outside' nations ... You Mings ignore my communications, and your Sovereign, in the fond belief that he is the Son of Heaven, displays contemptuous arrogance towards his equals ... .' A later letter repeats the criticism, 'You persist in asserting these exaggerated ideas of your own importance, and refuse to meet my envoys face to face, as if they were unworthy to enter your sacred presence'.[2] Given the Manchu Dynasty's almost identical attitude towards receiving representatives of the Western Powers some two and a half centuries later, there is no little irony in these words.

The Manchu would almost certainly have been content to maintain peaceful coexistence with the Ming Emperor, and would never have considered conquest, had it not been for the duplicity of a Chinese noble charged with administering the border region between the two nations. This official treacherously slew the father and grandfather of a young boy, Nurhachi. The Ming Court apologised for the murders, sent horses and silks in compensation, but steadfastly refused to hand over the miscreant to Manchu justice. Secure in their overweening pride, they felt that they had nothing to fear. But it was this one act, together with the boy Nurhachi's drive and intelligence, that was to set the seal on the Ming's destruction some forty years later. Incensed at the injustice, Nurhachi concentrated all his energies on gaining power to achieve his revenge. By the time he was twenty-seven years old he was acknowledged overlord of the five Manchu clans.

Nurhachi's army was organised under four banners, white, red, blue, and yellow, which were later expanded with the addition of striped banners of the same colours, to form a total of eight. Eight, to the Chinese and to the sinicised Manchu, symbolised good fortune. Later still, the Manchu's Mongol vassals,

and disaffected Chinese who had rallied to the Manchu standard, each formed a further eight banner regiments. Nurhachi's warriors were the Romans of the East: the men were
organised into well-drilled and disciplined units. Individual
heroism and initiative was frowned upon, and the emphasis
was solely on teamwork, each man a cog in a well-oiled, well-
maintained military machine. It worked. In 1586, the same
year he took command of the Manchu clans, the puissance of
Nurhachi's army was so highly regarded that the Chinese
court paid protection money (the Ming's face-saving term was
'subsidy') of fifteen dragon-robes and eight hundred ounces of
silver, to guarantee Manchu quiescence. Nurhachi took the
treasure, but continued to nurse his grievance and his plans
to extinguish the Ming bloodline. Over the final decade of the
sixteenth century, he ignored China and focused his considerable talents on subjugating the remaining Manchu tribes. By
1616, only the Yeho clan still defied his rule, but within a year
this tribe too had fallen before the combined might of his
armies. With the tribes united, Nurhachi formally took the title
of Heaven Appointed (*Tien Ming*) and the name 'Manchu' for
his new Dynasty.

Some years before this, the Yeho clan had themselves conquered a neighbouring tribe – a people calling themselves
the Nala. It was this combined group, the Yeho-Nala from
which Yehonala – the girl destined to rule China for almost
fifty years – derived her name. After they had been subdued,
and many of their warriors mercilessly slaughtered, it is
recorded that the head of the Yeho-Nala, Buyanggu, solemnly
promised upon his deathbed that 'even if only one woman of
our tribe managed to survive, she would certainly seek revenge
and the overthrow of Nurhachi's clan'.[3] The fierce indepen-
dence of this tribal group, and their defiance of the House of
Nurhachi, goes a long way towards explaining the prophecy
that a woman of the Yeho-Nala would bring the Dynasty to
ruin. It appears that Nurhachi realised how deep ran the hostility of the defeated clan: he sought to appease them with
promises of high position and intermarriage. From that time
forward, the concubines and wives of the ruling clan (the Aisin

Gioro, the 'Golden Race') were to be taken primarily from the Yeho-Nala tribe. But the proud Yeho-Nala could not easily forget the disgrace of their defeat, and the desire for revenge, for an opportunity to sweep away their dishonour, would undoubtedly have been carried down the generations. Given the strong blood-ties that linked all Manchu families,[4] such a secret, silent feud does much to account for the otherwise baffling indifference Yehonala displayed to the continuance of Nurhachi's Dynasty once she herself had attained supreme power.[5]

The conquest of the Yeho-Nala had other benefits for Nurhachi – it gave him the perfect pretext to attack China. The Ming, fearing Nurhachi's martial prowess, and seeing in the Yeho tribe a counterweight to the Manchu warlord's rising power, had ignored Nurhachi's demand that they maintain strict neutrality and had sent help to his foes. Nurhachi now revealed his true intentions. Before his assembled army he swore a sacred vow to exact revenge upon the Mings for the murder of his forebears and for their aid to the Yeho tribe. War had been declared. The Chinese responded with a determined effort to crush Nurhachi's growing strength. In 1619, four separate Chinese armies, supported by their Korean tributaries, crossed the northern border to crush the parvenu Manchu dynasty. Nurhachi destroyed them all with an army numbering less than fifty thousand men, scattering them to the winds, amassing much booty and taking thirty thousand men captive.

This reverse brought about a brief assertion of martial ardour in the Ming. While they shrank from invading Manchu territory, they did manage to find competent generals who (with the aid of Portuguese cannon obtained via the good offices of the Jesuit 'missionaries' retained by the Ming Emperor)[6] were able to hold the line against further Manchu encroachment. Some were able to hold on to strategic strongholds beyond the Great Wall, greatly hampering Nurhachi's freedom of movement. But such was the dissolute and dissipated nature of the Ming court that any benefits could only be temporary. The Emperor and his favourites were sunk in luxury, more interested in the latest songs or theatrical presentation than the grim verities of realpolitik. Funds destined for the army were diverted to more pleasing pastimes for the court. Eunuchs controlled access to the Celestial Prince, and they were able to suppress unwelcome news and at the same time portray rumour as truth. Without payment of large amounts of 'fragrant grease', these eunuchs could quickly and easily poison the monarch's mind against even the most competent of his generals. Most military men simply accepted their lot, but General Sun, a courageous and patriotic commander, was brave enough to write to the Emperor in person:

> Your Majesty's forces have lately been deprived of their necessary training and often of their pay. Instead of leaving the command in the hands of competent military officers, you dispatch ignorant civilians to train the troops. In battle, the supreme command devolves upon some high civil functionary, supported by a large and quite useless staff of literary men. The tactics which your armies are to adopt in the field are discussed at supper by your courtiers, or decided by a party of eunuchs in the intervals between their debauches.[7]

There is no guarantee that this courageous attempt to warn the Emperor was ever seen by the Celestial Prince. Rather the reverse. General Sun refused to vouchsafe the 'largesse' required by the chief eunuch, Wei Ching-hsien, a principled but ultimately disastrous decision. In a matter of days, the good general was demoted, and Kao Ti, who did provide financial support to Wei Ching-hsien, was set in his place. Even to the court literati this strategy (if we can grace these actions with such a term) must have been recognised as disastrous. Sun Tzu's *Art of War*, one of the military classics by which these men of letters set such store, had stated the case plainly: 'War is a matter of vital importance to the State; the province of life or death; the road to survival or ruin. It is mandatory that it be thoroughly studied.'[8] Unfortunately, by this stage in the court's evolution, an appreciation of eggshell porcelain was regarded as a far higher attainment than any martial pursuit.

Nurhachi took every advantage of such purblind folly. By 1625 he had consolidated his new capital at the strategic site of Mukden, from which he could threaten not only China but the vassal kingdom of Korea. A year later, at the age of 68, he led his men southwards towards the strategically important Chinese town of Ning Yuan. The Chinese court favourite Kao Ti immediately counselled retreat, but the commander, General Yuan, used his own blood to write out an oath, in which all his men pledged to die in defence of the town. When Nurhachi mounted his assault, he found the fortress defended by resolute warriors, and protected by European cannon, whose blasts ravaged his elite squadrons. For the first time in four decades, Nurhachi was forced to beat the retreat, and to leave a bastion untaken. He fell back with his army upon his capital at Mukden, and whether it was the shame of this defeat, his advanced age, or both, Nurhachi never again took the path of war. On 30th September 1626, this doughty warrior, the victor of scores of battles, died peacefully in his sleep.

Primogeniture was not absolute among the Manchu, and Nurhachi was succeeded by his fourth and most able son, who took the reign-title Tien Tsung (Heaven Obeying). Tien Tsung shared his father's dream of conquering China, but he was far-sighted enough to understand that it was only the debility and irresoluteness of the Ming that gave the Manchu the freedom of movement they had enjoyed for so long. Tien Tsung's strategic position was actually extremely weak. China was the acknowledged suzerain of Korea to the east, and in the west of the Mongol tribes (who had previously ruled China between 1206 and 1333 under the fabled Yuan dynasty of Kublai Khan). This posed a serious problem for any northern invader; as soon as the Manchu moved south into China, any competent administration in Beijing should have been able to rouse both tributary states to attack the aggressor in an east–west pincer movement that, together with a northward thrust by the Chinese armies would almost inevitably prove disastrous for the Manchu. Should the Ming come to their senses and organise a proper defence, China would be impregnable.

So concerned did Tien Tsung become with the strength and ability of his Chinese foe that his next major incursion was via Mongolia, circumventing a string of refurbished fortresses along the Chinese border. Tien Tsung led a substantial force of raiders to the very gates of the Ming capital. But the commander of the border fortresses, the formidable General Yuan, was more than a match for the Manchu: he led his men south by a series of forced marches, and surprised Tien Tsung at his encampment near the Imperial Hunting Park. Threatened with imminent destruction by a superior force, the Manchu monarch revealed again his *sang froid*, and his knowledge of the Chinese Classics.

A late Ming volume *The Secret Art of War: Thirty Six Strategies*, by an unknown author, expounded a number of ruses, based upon the most revered of all the classics: the *I Ching*, or Book of Changes. In this system, the number six, the primal Yin number, denotes secret military plans, and the thirty-six strategies of the title (six squared) indicates a whole bag of dirty tricks. Strategy Thirty-Three is termed 'Turn the Enemy's Agent's against Him':

> On detecting an enemy agent ... one may feign ignorance, expose the agent to false information, and allow him to return and report to the enemy commander. Taking the false information for facts, the enemy will make the wrong judgement.[9]

Tien Tsung had no enemy agents in his possession, but he did hold captive two eunuchs from the Forbidden City. He arranged for the pair to 'accidentally' overhear a council of war between himself and his generals, in which General Yuan was described as a traitor to the Ming, on the point of defecting to the Manchu cause. The following day, the prisoners were allowed to escape. As the wily Manchu hoped, the eunuchs made straight for the Ming Emperor and poured out their news, denouncing Yuan as a traitor. And the Chinese did indeed 'make the wrong judgement': General Yuan was immediately arrested and imprisoned. A court favourite was appointed in his place, an incompetent whose puerile manoeuvrings were no match for the battle-hardened strategems of Tien Tsung. In a combat fought just outside Beijing's Yung Ting Gate, the Manchu won a great victory, leaving the Forbidden City and its ruler defenceless. But instead of taking the Chinese capital, and the Emperor's crown that went with it, Tien Tsung ordered a withdrawal to their own territory. His men, his generals, even his own son protested. They were angry and confused – the road to the riches of the Forbidden City, perhaps to Manchu rule over China itself, lay open. Why refuse the God-given chance that their victory had earned them? But Tien Tsung was no mere freebooter intent on plunder; he was playing a long game. One contemporary chronicle records his words: 'To take the city would be easy enough, but the time is not yet. Their outlying defences are still untaken, we have established no terror in the heart of China proper. If we took Beijing today we would not be strong enough to hold it ... No; let us return to our own place and prepare for the hour of destiny, when God shall deliver the whole empire into our hands.'[10]

And so the Ming Dynasty was granted yet another reprieve; another chance to put its house in order and reclaim its days of greatness. But while Tien Tsung recruited expert founders and engineers to cast artillery of European design, the Chinese court fell back once again into an endless cycle of intrigue, debauchery and theatrical performances.

Slowly, Tien Tsung drew tight the net around the Ming. In 1635 all the Mongol tribes were brought within his rule, and in token of submission their leader handed over to Tien Tsung the Mongol Yuan Dynasty's Great Seal of China. Four years later Korea had fallen, the Korean king formally passing over to the Manchu monarch the Ming documents confirming his kingship. Tien Tsung's flanks were now secure and the Manchu were able to by-pass the Chinese defensive fortresses along the Manchu–China border and raid the rich lowlands with impunity.

One thing only remained: to establish 'terror in the heart of China proper'. This was accomplished by a series of raids, and by the slow destruction of China's remaining border fortresses. In November 1642 Tien Tsung dispatched an enormous force of men, under the command of his elder brother Abtai, into

China. The expedition was a resounding success: by the time the army returned to Mukden it had been victorious in thirty-seven separate engagements against the Ming, and had captured and put to death around a thousand members of the Imperial clan, including six Princes of the Blood. The spoil secured was staggering: 350 kilograms of gold, 348,000 kilograms of silver, 4,440 ounces of pearls, 52,234 bolts of silk and satin and innumerable quantities of furs, robes and deer horn. Almost 370,000 prisoners were taken (most destined for slavery among their Manchu captors) and over half a million camel, oxen and other stock.[11]

Once again it was not simply the superiority of Manchu arms that had carried the day. The cliques and factions, the intrigues and chicanery of the Ming court, especially the machinations of the eunuch cabal, made a coordinated policy impossible and emasculated the Ming defence. In the northern section of the Great Wall alone there were four viceroys, six governors, and eight generals-in-chief, all vying with each other for supremacy, and above them a eunuch commander-in-chief, who saw the purpose of his position solely in terms of personal advantage.

At the same time as the Manchu massed on its northern border, a second crisis of equal severity threatened the Ming Dynasty from within. Li Tzu-cheng, a one-time hunter turned brigand, had gradually drawn to his band numerous Chinese dissatisfied with their life under the Ming. From brigand, he had suddenly found himself at the head of a full-scale rebellion against the incumbent Dynasty. A natural general, his skills had won victory after victory for his troops. For more than five years he had marched across the breadth of China, from Hunan through Shaanxi and Shanxi Provinces, his force increasing in number and strength with every mile, and he had now set his face towards Beijing, threatening the Emperor's capital and giving out that Heaven had withdrawn its Mandate from the Ming. He would depose the effete Dynasty and place himself upon the Dragon Throne. Incredibly, at the same time as the nation was faced with this huge internal rebellion, the Emperor's advisers counselled all-out war with the Manchu, effectively committing the Dynasty to a war on two fronts.

By 1643 all seemed set fair for the Manchu; Tien Tsung's patient waiting game was about to pay off: he had no doubt that his army was a match for both the Ming and the rebel forces. In September of that year he enjoyed a strenuous hunting trip in the northern forests, then returned to his palace for a tiring day of audiences. That night, at 11 p.m., sitting in his chair of state as he readied himself for bed, he suddenly fell forward, and died. A heart attack is the most likely diagnosis. He was fifty-one, and for the 'Heaven Obeying' monarch, the dream of conquest was over.

Though not for the Manchu. The most able of Nurhachi's surviving sons, Dorgun, was barred by house laws from the throne, though not from a position as Regent. Using a combination of charm and intrigue, Dorgun placed a five-year-old youngster on the throne, with himself as Chief Regent. This went against all tradition and precedent, but it would have taken a hero or a fool to object: Dorgun's military prowess was undeniable, and he enjoyed the wholehearted support of the bannermen, the cream of the Manchu army.

With his authority confirmed for the foreseeable future, Dorgun continued his predecessor's plans for the destruction of the Ming. Just six months after the death of Tien Tsung, all the bastions guarding the route to Beijing had been captured save one – the impregnable fortress of Ning Yuan. The garrison there was commanded by a famous Chinese warrior, Wu San-kuei, and under his generalship the city had proved impregnable to Manchu arms, and looked set to remain so for some time to come. Then, suddenly, news was brought to Mukden that Wu San-kuei had abandoned this most strategic of fortresses and was marching his army on the Chinese capital. The news was disbelieved at first – it was inconceivable that Wu San-kuei could make such a monumental blunder – this was military suicide for the Ming.

What the Manchu did not know was that events had been moving swiftly to the south of the Great Wall. Li Tzu-cheng's revolt had prospered and he was moving rapidly north-east towards the capital, driving all before him.[12] He had lost his left eye to an enemy arrow during one of his many battles, but – as

an ancient prophecy claimed that the Ming would be conquered by a one-eyed man – he accepted the wound joyfully.
Li's whole rebellion was based upon superstition: Chinese his-
torians relate that, while a young man out hunting with two
close friends, he had suddenly driven an arrow into the ground
and stated that, if a snowstorm came that night, and if the
snow reached level with the top of the arrow, he would take
this as a sign from Heaven that he would eventually become
Emperor. The snow duly fell, and to just the right height,
leaving Li with a conviction that his rebellion would succeed.

The rebel leader combined superstition with cruelty – his
ruthlessness was legendary. When a captured Imperial general
refused to submit, Li had him fastened to a high beam and shot
at him with arrows until he was dead. When another captive,
Prince Fu, refused even to speak with him, Li decided on a grim
jest. The Prince's full name indicates 'good fortune'. Li had him
decapitated and mixed a cupful of his blood with cooked
venison, naming the dish 'red pottage of good fortune' before
eating his fill. But perhaps the most extreme example of
his bloodthirsty nature occurred in 1643, when his advance
through Hunan Province had been held up for almost two
years by the stubborn resistance of the city of Kaifeng.
Enraged, he imposed *corvée* labour on the farmers in the surrounding area in order to cut away the embankments of
'China's Sorrow', the Yellow River, and so flood the town. When
the river finally broke its banks it swept away over one hundred
thousand of these unfortunates (and took with them a further
ten thousand of Li's own men). But the scheme worked. The
destruction visited on Kaifeng was almost inconceivable: of a
population of over a million souls, less than one in ten survived
– more than nine hundred thousand lost their lives in the
flood, sacrificed to Li's ambition.

Li then led his men into Shanxi, to the ancient city of Xian.
Here, dressed in Imperial dragon-robes, on the first day of the
new year (1644) he proclaimed the inauguration of the 'Great
Obedient' dynasty and took upon himself the Imperial title of
Yung Ch'ang. As far as Li was concerned, his victories con-
firmed that the Mandate of Heaven, given by the gods, and

held by the Ming Dynasty for almost three hundred years, had been revoked – and given to him. In Beijing, the news of Li's rival dynasty, and his proximity to the capital was met with despair and fear. Yet even now it did not serve to shake the Ming and its courtiers out of their self-induced lethargy. Steeped in superstition and belief in auguries, they may have taken heart from the strangely titled 'Song of the cakes', a prophecy said to have been uttered by the first Ming Emperor, Chu Yuan-chang, concerning the fate of his Dynasty. It is claimed that this 'Song' tells of the coming of the eight banners of the Manchu, and the ultimate overthrow of Manchu power by the Japanese (which did in fact come to pass, but only after the Manchu had swept away the Ming). One line of the prophecy is striking. It states:

> Ten-mouthed women, with grass on their heads,
> once more carry a babe in arms
> to be Lord over the Empire.[13]

Remarkably, in Chinese, the first character of the name Yehonala, is composed of the symbols 'ten' and 'mouth' side by side; and above them ('on their heads'?) is the sign for 'grass'.

On this basis, then, the Manchu were the enemy to be taken seriously, with Li's rebellion nothing more than an annoyance, simply another of the periodic revolts which shook the peace of the Middle Kingdom. A Grand Secretary, Li Chien-tai, a man of great wealth, offered to fund the expenses of the army and to march at their head against the rebels. But while this disorganised Ming host searched vainly for the foe (and lost thousands of its own soldiers to starvation) the wily 'Emperor' Li Tzu-cheng and his army had slipped away northwards, before swinging east into Chihli Province, on the very doorstep of Beijing,

A second Ming army sent to oppose Li's forces was headed, not by a commander of vast experience, but by the powerful, and militarily ignorant, court eunuch, Tu Hsun. As Li's men converged on the next strategic town, Ta T'ung-fu, this same eunuch commander-in-chief refused to fight and, quickly turning his coat, abjectly agreed to the town's surrender. When the rebels finally appeared before the gates of the capital itself,

Tu Hsun fired a message in a quill into the city, in which he advised his late master that the rebels must win and that the Emperor's best course of action was to commit suicide.

Even this treachery did not bring the Ming Emperor to his senses. He appointed yet another eunuch, Wang Ch'eng-en, as commander-in-chief of the Beijing defences. The result was predictable. One by one the city's strong-points fell to Li's forces. But in the face of this disaster the court still could not free itself from the obsessive dream of Ming invincibility: on the day the first gate of the outer city fell, just two miles away (and with no line of defence between him and the rebels) a eunuch grandee was entertaining guests with a theatrical extravaganza.

Li's rebel troops surged forward and with very little fighting took the Chien Men, the main southern gate into the northern half of the city, making speedily for the last bastion of Ming power, the purple-walled enclosure of the Great Within. Suddenly realising the hopelessness of his position, the Emperor attempted to send his two sons to safety, dressing them in the ragged clothes of the 'stupid people' (the demeaning aristocratic term for Chinese hoi polloi). 'Today you are Heir to the throne,' he is reported to have told his eldest son 'tomorrow you will be ... a wanderer on the face of the earth. Reveal not your names and dissemble as best you may. If perchance your lives should be spared, remember in time to come to avenge the wrongs which your parents have suffered. Forget not these my words.' With that, the boys were spirited away out of the city. His daughters were to share an altogether different fate.

The Emperor now proceeded to get drunk, quaffing bowl after bowl of wine. Then, filled with the Chinese equivalent of Dutch courage, he assembled his harem and told the ladies bluntly, 'All is over. It is time to die.' His senior concubine, Lady Yuan, tried to flee, panic-stricken, but the Emperor cut her down with his sword. The Empress Consort was made of sterner stuff: she retired immediately to the Palace of Feminine Tranquillity, and there hanged herself. Altogether some two hundred of the Emperor's women committed suicide.

The Emperor's eldest daughter, the Princess Imperial, was waiting at the ironically named Palace of Peaceful Old Age.

Crying, 'By what evil fortune were you born into our ill-starred house?' the Emperor cut off her right arm and left her dying on the ornate tiles of the palace floor. He then made his way to the pavilion of Charity Made Manifest, and slew his second daughter.

Dawn was breaking. Some loyal follower, remembering palace routine, rang the bell for the morning audience, where in happier times the Emperor had received homage and reports from across his wide domain. No one arrived. Most of the palace servants had fled, but the Celestial Prince was attended by Wang Ch'eng-en, the one eunuch who remained faithful to him to the end. Frenzied and distracted, the Emperor changed from his Imperial robe into a short tunic with a dragon motif and, with a shoe on the right foot and his left foot bare, made his way to Coal Hill, a towering mound surmounted by pavilions, just to the north of the Forbidden City. Once again, his departure was not without irony, for he fled by way of the Gate of Divine Military Prowess. Mounting to the top of Coal Hill he stopped; and there in the Imperial Hat and Girdle pavilion the last of the Ming Emperors hanged himself. As custom demanded, his last act had been to compose his valedictory message. Lacking writing materials, he set it down on the lapel of his tunic:

> I, feeble and of small virtue, have offended against Heaven; the rebels have seized my capital because my ministers deceived me. Ashamed to face my ancestors, I die. Removing my Imperial cap and with my hair dishevelled about my face, I leave to the rebels the dismemberment of my body. Let them not harm my people![14]

Against all expectation, Li Tzu-cheng had won through to the Dragon Throne, and the former brigand was proclaimed Emperor of All Under Heaven. China was his. The prophecy had been fulfilled and a one-eyed man had toppled the once-mighty Ming. But as is usual in such cases, the prophecy revealed only half the truth – Li was Emperor, but his reign was to be measured not in years but days.

Just before the final attack on the city, the Ming Emperor had sent a desperate message to General Wu San-kuei, ordering him to bring his army of seasoned veterans to protect Beijing. It was this message that had precipitated Wu's sudden departure from his border stronghold, the same retreat towards Beijing that had so confused and bewildered the Manchu when they first heard of his baffling departure. Now, with the Ming gone, the new Emperor Li Tzu-cheng once again commanded General Wu's attendance in the capital.

Wu ignored the summons and continued to hold his position between the new Emperor and the Manchu Dorgun, whose forces lay like a wolf pack at the border, biding their time. Emperor Li, in exasperation, led an advance guard of more than one hundred thousand men against Wu's forces, but was heavily defeated. Chastened, he offered talks, and at a subsequent meeting, Li and Wu signed an agreement which effectively partitioned China. Li's 'Great Obedient Dynasty' was allowed to keep the treasures it had looted from the city, but agreed to relinquish Beijing to the Ming heir apparent (who was now a hostage of the General). Wu had proclaimed his 'guest' the new Ming Emperor, and intended to become China's *éminence grise* and the power behind the throne. Li's portion of China was to be all territory to the west of the provinces of Shanxi and Shaanxi. Both parties to the treaty promised to act jointly against the Manchu, should the Regent Dorgun invade.

The agreement was worthless. It gave Li the chance to escape from the catastrophic effects of a possible alliance between Wu and the Manchu, and granted him vast lands, the title of Emperor, and undreamed-of wealth. For Wu, the alliance allowed him to extricate himself from the possibility of having to fight on two fronts, against both Li and the Manchu. Even so, he knew his army was no match for Dorgun's forces. He schemed to extend discussions with the Manchu, to use sweet words to buy time, to amass sufficient power to withstand a Manchu assault.

But Dorgun was not to be fooled. On hearing of Li and Wu's meeting, he moved his forces through the Shanhaiguan Pass at the end of the Great Wall, and sent a stern message forbidding

Wu to enter Beijing with the heir apparent. He also reminded him of the Manchu's earlier offer, granting Wu the rank of feudal Prince should he agree to join with them. Wu now faced a stark choice: he could either ignore Dorgun's demands, set up the heir as a puppet Emperor, and face battle with a superior enemy. Or he could abandon the heir apparent, secure his future as a wealthy and powerful noble, and help Dorgun's attempt on the Dragon Throne.

Being a prudent soldier, Wu cast the heir apparent to the wolves, and threw in his lot with the Manchu. On hearing of this treachery, Li ordered the beheading of Wu's father and sixteen female members of his family, before setting out with two hundred thousand men to fight the combined might of the Manchu and his former ally. The combat began in a furious dust-storm with both sides scarcely able to distinguish friend from foe. But now he was Emperor, Li's luck seemed to desert him. His men broke before the united Manchu and Chinese banners, and he was forced to fly, escaping with as much booty as he could safely carry.

Still fearful of Wu's power, Dorgun set him and his formidable army on the trail of Li's forces as they made their way westwards. Ever efficient, Wu pursued and destroyed Li's 'Empire' for the Manchu and, ironically, having earlier sought to set up a new Ming Dynasty, he spent the next decade hunting down the four Ming claimants to the throne. Kuei Wang, the Yung Li Emperor and the last of the Ming line, was pursued as far west as Burma; once captured Wu had him strangled with a bowstring.[15] For thirty years he was the right-hand man of the Manchu and was granted a satrapy, ruling most of south-west China with an iron hand, and holding state like an Emperor. Despite this, he ended his days as a rebel, rising in revolt in 1674 upon hearing that the Manchu Emperor intended to curb his powers. His early offensives proved that he had lost none of his martial skill, and the history of China may well have been written quite differently had this formidable military genius not been cut down by a stroke in 1678, as he planned yet another campaign.

With General Wu pursuing the rebel Emperor, the way was open to the Manchu to assume the rights and prerogatives of the Dragon Throne. The Mandate of Heaven had been bestowed upon the Aisin Gioro. Nurhachi's dream had finally been achieved; the long-dead Manchu warrior had at last taken his revenge on the hated Ming. Fu Lin, the first Manchu Emperor of China, was now given the reign title Shun Chih. He was just five years of age when he attained the Imperial dignity. Dorgun was the effective ruler of China, acting as *primus inter pares* among the Regents.

Dorgun died in 1650, when Shun Chih was twelve, but already the child Emperor was revealing the serious and highly moral aspects of his character that were the marks of his short reign. The Manchu had despised the weakness and indolence of the Ming. And they knew their victory was due as much to their opponent's bondage to luxury, to the presence of sycophants at court, and to the ascendancy of the eunuch clique within the palace, as to their own skill at arms. They therefore took pains to remove those aspects of Ming rule that had contributed to their downfall. When Shun Chih died in 1661 he had set the foundations of a strong and stable monarchy: he had revised the corrupt system of examinations for the Chinese bureaucracy and instituted regulations governing admission to and training of the priesthood. But by far the greatest innovation, undertaken when he was still in his minority, was the suppression of the eunuchs as a clique in the politics of the Forbidden City. Had his strict regulations been followed by his successors, it is possible that a Manchu Emperor might still reign in the Forbidden City today.

In Chinese Daoist philosophy, the symbol known as Tai Chi encapsulates the cyclical nature of all material creation.

In this system, opposites are seen as complementary – and they succeed one another in an infinite cycle. The months of life, spring and summer, are followed by autumn and winter, the seasons of decay and death. But winter is once again followed by spring. Day follows night, and night day. The dot in the centre of the opposing colour symbolises the fact that within each day some anticipations of night occur, just as each night contains intimations of the coming day. All things contain the seeds of their own destruction.[16]

And so it proved with Manchu rule. Despite Shun Chih's able beginnings, within a few decades the Manchu too had been seduced by the cloying and voluptuous atmosphere of the Forbidden City, by the absolute power that they wielded over the world's most populous nation. The root of the problem was twofold. The very size of the Middle Kingdom made it seemingly impossible to govern; and yet, for centuries, the country had been held together by its formidable (though thoroughly corrupt) bureaucracy. Throughout its long history, when the Mandate of Heaven was given to a new Emperor, be he native sovereign or foreign conqueror, the wise course of action had always been to maintain this system essentially unchanged, for fear that the whole country might descend into chaos and schism. The second problem was just as intractable. The Manchu, like the Ming, believed that Imperial dignity (not to mention biological success) required that the sovereign possess a harem of immense size. The Ming emperors had maintained seraglios of enormous proportions (with as many as three hundred concubines being added en bloc in some years),[17] and their Manchu successors felt they could do no less. But the biological realities of this situation required that any male guardians of the Emperor's ladies should not be able to surreptitiously sire children on them. The first Manchu Emperor of China, Shun Chih, was said by many to have been the result of a liaison between the Emperor T'ai Tsung's favourite concubine and a Chinese hunter named Wang Kao, and the history of China is littered with stories of Emperor's 'sons' ascending to the Dragon Throne who were in reality the offspring of servants. The presence of eunuchs in the palace therefore became a necessary adjunct of the harem system, and once accepted in positions of power, these 'rats and foxes' could not help but aspire to more. No functioning male except the Emperor was allowed to reside within the Forbidden City. The Son of Heaven was thrown back upon the company of eunuchs, who, as his personal attendants, became also his confidants and friends. Graft and corruption sprouted like weeds, and the process of decline began anew.

When the European nations arrived in force on their borders, this process of degeneration was all but complete. Like the Ming before them, the Manchu had come to believe that they ruled the very centre of the earth, that China was *Chung Guo*, the Central Kingdom, surrounded by barbarian vassal states. They were convinced that their Emperor was quite literally a Son of Heaven. They knew that their system of civilisation, their Confucian code of ethics, was superior to all. Even when faced with proof positive of Western technological superiority, they acted towards the European envoys with the same insolent superiority and hauteur that had so enraged their own leader, Nurhachi, in his dealings with the Ming. The proud warriors had become an effete ruling class whose purblind arrogance was leading them to destruction. By a species of perverse alchemy, the Manchu had become the Ming.

Like the Ming, they were an 'apple ripe for plucking'. And as foretold in the prophecies of the first Ming Emperor, the final act in this drama was ready to begin. A 'ten-mouthed' woman was about to be invited into the very centre of Manchu power.

CHAPTER THREE

Concubine, third class

$\mathcal{T}$he girl who was to become the Empress of the Western Palace, and the greatest female autocrat the world has seen, was born into relative poverty in the southern province of Anhui, a warm, sensuous land of paddy fields and water oxen, and boasting the incomparably beautiful Huang Shan, the Yellow Mountains, sacred to the Lord Buddha.[1] Her father was Captain Hui Cheng, a Manchu officer in the Blue Bordered Banner regiment, who, like all bannermen, had been given a sinecure amongst the provinces of China. Hui Cheng's first posting, after the birth of his daughter, was to Luhan in Shanxi Province. From there he was transferred to Wuhu in Anhui, on the lower reaches of the Chang Jiang (Yangtse River). Here, close to the innumerable Buddhist temples of Jiuhua, Yehonala was to spend most of her childhood.

Some accounts relate that Yehonala's father died when she was three, others that he was cashiered from the army for cowardice when facing the feared *Chang Mao* insurgents of the Tai Ping rebellion.[2] But for whatever reason, we know that he proved incapable of supporting his family while Yehonala was still a young girl. Under the Chinese extended family system, this duty then devolved upon the eldest male relative, and Yehonala, her sister, and her mother, the Lady Niuhulu, were subsequently cared for by an uncle, Mu-fan, or Muyanga in his native Manchu language. Muyanga was head of the clan in the capital Beijing and, despite being afflicted with a painful stammer, was a high official at the Imperial Board of Works. It was through his good offices that Yehonala and her mother were transferred permanently from Wuhu to the capital.

They travelled to Beijing by barge via the Grand Canal, a man-made waterway completed in the seventh century AD to facilitate the transport of grain from Hangzhou and the Yangtse valley to the capital. According to one account[3] (which may have been devised and circulated by Yehonala's enemies to embarrass her) Yehonala and her family were very poor at this time, and travelling in the Chinese equivalent of steerage. As they passed through Tsing-kiang, one of the more wealthy travellers was visited by an old friend, the *tao-tai* (head mandarin) of the town. As is usual in Chinese society, even today, the two men spent the night gambling. The *tao-tai* lost heavily, and the next day, before the barge continued its journey northward, he sent a servant on board with cash to cover his debt. For some reason, the package went astray, and was given to Yehonala's widowed mother, who suddenly found herself possessed of, for her, a small fortune, compliments of the *tao-tai* of Tsing-kiang. When he discovered the mistake, the mandarin's first impulse was to demand the return of his cash. But his friend dissuaded him, pointing out that the girls were Manchu, and pretty, and might very well find themselves in positions of power, perhaps even in the Emperor's harem. 'At present they know you for a kind-hearted man who has befriended them in time of need. Why make enemies by giving them a grievous disappointment?' The mandarin took the advice, and many years later was said to have received numerous favours from the adult Yehonala, now grown more powerful than even the mandarin's friend had dared to predict.

Nothing in Yehonala's youthful experience can have prepared her for the moment when, standing at the prow of the barge, she first came in sight of the capital. Beijing was then the world's most populous walled city, a blatant display of Manchu power and skill. Standing four-square, the visual impact of the metropolis, with its forty-foot-high crenellated walls running a full four miles in length on each side, and massive roofed towers at each corner, must have been overwhelming. The city rose straight out of the low plain on which it stood, overpoweringly impressive: 'there was no other sight like it in the world'.[4] Apart from the walls, temples and palaces of the Emperor, Beijing lay low on the horizon, the citizens living in one-storeyed *pian-feng* 'bungalows'. Two-storeyed houses had long been prohibited, to prevent the sacrilege of ordinary folk looking down on the Emperor, should he pass in his yellow satin-covered sedan chair. The whole of the city was laid out on a grid pattern, established early in the fifteenth century. In all major towns the Manchu, ever mindful of their precarious minority position as overlords, had built walled 'Tartar cities' within the Chinese urban sprawl, as a precaution against rebellion. Beijing also had its Chinese city, straggling and overcrowded, the air of its narrow alleys pungent with a mixture of the wonderful spices of Chinese cuisine and the stench of ordure from open sewers, the walkways unpaved, dusty in the summer heat and ankle-deep with mud in the autumn rain. Lying to the north of this bustling mass of humanity was Beijing's Tartar city, secure behind crenellated forty-foot-high walls some sixteen miles in circumference, within which lay Manchu-only homes, and palaces. This enormous fortification had been built by the third Ming Emperor, Yung Le, in the fifteenth century, using more than two hundred thousand forced labourers. But here the similarities with other urban centres ended. Like a Chinese puzzle, with its boxes within boxes within boxes, Beijing was a nested set of progressively more sacred sites. At the heart of the Tartar city lay the Imperial City, a fifteen hundred-acre enclave which was the administrative and governmental centre of the nation. But there was more: at the centre of the Imperial City, squat and foursquare, its walls painted the dark purple of the Imperial potency, lay the Forbidden City, the Great Within, the home of the Son of Heaven. And within its sacred precincts, at the supposed centre of the earth, was the throne, the seat of Celestial Power.

The young girl of sixteen cannot but have been overawed by the size of this bustling, sprawling metropolis, and the brooding dignity of the purple-walled and gold-roofed splendour of the Great Within. What thoughts teemed through her mind as she regarded this symbol of apparently unshakeable power? The clan to which both girls belonged traced its descent in direct line to Yangkunu, a Manchu Prince of the Yeho tribe, whose daughter had been given in marriage to the great founder of the dynasty, Nurhachi. The Imperial family still took their principal wives from the clan of Yeho-Nala as a way of cementing the alliance of the two groups and soothing the humiliation of the proud Yeho clan's defeat at their hands. The eldest daughter of Yehonala's uncle had previously been chosen as consort of the Emperor, but had died soon after the marriage was consummated. Could Yehonala have dared dream that she too, might one day attain such an honoured and elevated position?

Whatever her possible dreams of grandeur, Yehonala's new home was far less exalted, but by no means humble. Uncle Muyanga lived in spacious accommodation, as befitted his high position. Protected from prying eyes, by the high windowless walls that faced the street and were normal in all Chinese cities, was a series of pavilions surrounding a central courtyard, green with willow and bamboo. The Chinese abhor grassy spaces, preferring water and rocky groves, and her new home would undoubtedly have possessed a water feature of some size, perhaps with an outcrop of the prized Tai-hu stone from Jiangsu.[5] Yehonala was raised in this commodious setting alongside her cousin, Sakota, a girl of the same age, and the two became firm friends.

When in 1850 the old Emperor, Tao Kwang 'mounted the dragon', his successor, the late Emperor's fourth son Hsien Feng, was a young widower of nineteen. His first wife, the elder sister of Sakota, had died soon after becoming his consort, and there had been no children. Following the demise of an Emperor, the Rites demanded that no new marriage be celebrated during the official mourning period of twenty-seven months. Soon after this, in June 1852, a decree was issued commanding Manchu officials throughout the provinces to present to Beijing a list of all eligible Manchu maidens. Such lists were always ready, and regularly updated with meticulous information on the girls' genealogy, the astrological alignments of their birth, their age, temperament and physical appearance and their education.

Of these, a girl's education was considered the least important. There was, quite simply, no need for it. *Li*, the precise description of social etiquette which governed the behaviour of the elite in both Manchu and Chinese society, demanded that the female sex follow the 'three obediences': to father, to husband and to eldest son. When she married, a woman was expected to conform to the wishes of her parents-in-law also.

The four greatest virtues of womanhood were first set down in the second century AD by a woman writer, Pan Chao. She cautioned all females:

> To guard carefully her chastity; to control circumspectly her behaviour; in every motion to exhibit modesty; and to model each act on the best usage. This is Womanly Virtue.

> To choose appropriate words with care; to avoid vulgar language; to speak at appropriate times; and not to weary others [with much conversation]. These may be called the characteristics of Womanly Words.

> To wash and scrub filth away; to keep clothes and ornaments fresh and clean; to wash the head and bathe the body regularly ... These may be called the characteristics of Womanly Bearing.

> With wholehearted devotion to sew and to weave; to love not gossip and silly laughter; in cleanliness and order [to prepare] the wine and food for serving guests. These may be called the characteristics of Womanly Work.

> These four qualifications characterise the greatest virtue of a woman. No woman can afford to be without them.[6]

In a word, Chinese women were to conform, to be passive. Man was *yang*, the active principle, woman *yin*, quiet and receptive.

This attitude reached its apogee in the practice of footbinding. The cruel and painful process of curtailing and distorting the growth of young girls' feet had a long history, beginning in the Sung Dynasty (AD 960–1126). It was widespread in the upper classes and in some provinces even peasant girls were subject to the implacable force of this barbaric custom.[7] At around the age of five or six the feet would be bandaged tightly, restricting normal growth and development and gradually forcing the foot into a bow shape, until heel and toes were touching. The resulting three or four inch deformities could barely support the weight of the owner's body. Walking became an ordeal, resulting in the 'lily walk' which Chinese gentlemen found so erotic. It also served to demonstrate the female's absolute vulnerability and dependence on the male for the necessities of life. In a grotesque parody of the Cinderella story, matchmakers would carry not a picture of a young girl, but the footwear into which her bound foot could fit. A mother seeking a wife for her son would often choose a prospective daughter-in-law solely on the basis of the tiny embroidered slippers that so aesthetically covered the deformities within. The smaller the slipper, the more desirable the girl.[8] As with the growing of the fingernails to prodigious lengths, footbinding also came to be regarded as a status symbol – only those who did not need to work could consider deforming their feet in this way – self-crippling thus became a statement of social caste.

Certain members of the Chinese intelligentsia rebelled against this restrictive view of womanhood and took a more enlightened position. The writer Li Ju-chen used his talent as a novelist to satirise society's contempt for female rights. His novel *Ching Hun Yuan* was enormously popular in its day and has strong resonances with Swift's satire *Gulliver's Travels*. Like Gulliver, the hero of Li's novel, Merchant Lin, undertakes a voyage to various realms. In one of these, the 'Country of Women', the sexual roles of men and women in Chinese society are reversed. Merchant Lin is chosen as a concubine for the Queen on account of his handsome features. But while Lin's beauty is admired, he is regarded as a rough diamond, uncouth and in need of training, a device by which the author distils into a few days the years of suffering endured by Chinese girls. 'He was made to wear feminine garments, his face was caked with make-up, his ears were pierced with great pain'. The final indignity is described in excruciating detail, the binding of Lin's rather large feet. 'Lin was in constant pain, walked with difficulty, and found it hard to eat or sleep ... he was no longer the master of his own fate. [Like countless girls throughout

China] he was given no choice in the matter; he was selected to be a concubine and the decision announced to him ... Lin was reduced from a man to an object to be adorned but not consulted, all for the pleasure of another. Escape was impossible, and suicide ruled out by constant supervision, so that Lin's spirit was soon broken.[9] Thankfully, footbinding was one of the few Chinese customs that the Manchu refused to copy.

At an even earlier date, the Ming philosopher Li Chih (1527–1602) had declared that the husband and wife relationship was complementary and equal, and had made the then-revolutionary statement: 'It is quite possible that a person could be a woman, but that intellectually she could be as good as any man.' Unfortunately, this surprisingly modern attitude to gender politics took an individualistic approach to the problem, and failed to challenge the essence of the Confucian system. As a result, it made little impact on Chinese society as a whole. 'Chinese women were circumscribed in their behaviour and activity because they were seen as different than men by nature, more acted upon than acting.'[10]

What Yehonala made of all this in her teens is not recorded, but her subsequent behaviour revealed that, while obedience, passivity, conformity and other such pious platitudes might hold for the majority of women, she did not believe that those same restrictions should confine her own freedom of action. Her favourite character in Chinese literature was Mu Lan, the young girl who usurped the male role of warrior, and proved herself as adept as any male in battle.

Among those eligible for the Imperial 'honour' of concubinage, any with obvious mental or physical impairments were winnowed out during a preliminary selection at provincial level. There were five million Manchu spread throughout the subject Chinese population of around four hundred million souls. Despite this, the shortlist that was forwarded to Beijing contained only sixty girls who were thought suitable for the Imperial attention. Sixty out of a possible female population of one and a half million, even allowing for the small age range considered nubile, would seem a minuscule proportion. No doubt the endemic corruption of the Middle Kingdom left some eligible maidens out of the list, but the answer may lie in the harsh vagaries of life in China at that time, which produced a multitude of minor and major disfigurements, even among the Manchu nobility. E. H. Parker, a former British Consul in the far east, reminiscing about his time in China during the 1860s, commented that in his experience all of China's elite, be they Manchu or native Chinese:

> ... seem to have a 'monstrosity' of some sort: either a fearful goitre; or one side of the face totally different from the other; or a strange squint or four or five teeth run together in one piece, like a bone; or a big dinge in the forehead; or a beard consisting of six long, stout bristles; or a set of eagle's claws instead of nails. In those days everyone was deeply pock-marked.[11]

Physical beauty was therefore at a premium, owing to its rarity. And there was no denying that the young Yehonala was beautiful. Although she was short for a Manchu, standing no more than five feet tall, her face, her winning smile and the perfect symmetry of her figure made her a worthy rival to the 'Round-Faced Beauty' of legend, a woman men could not look upon without desire, and that the ladies of court could not choose but envy. Add to this a quick intelligent mind, a mischievous sense of humour and a silvery, sensuous voice ('velvet' according to Sir Robert Hart, whose writings reveal him to have been another of Yehonala's 'conquests') and her presence in a room was guaranteed not to go unnoticed. And she knew it: 'A lot of people were jealous of me,' she was quoted as saying in her later years, 'because I was considered to be a beautiful woman at that time'.[12] Other, less praiseworthy aspects of her character – her unpredictable explosive temper and vindictive nature later became legendary – were no doubt carefully screened from her examiners during her first visit to the Forbidden City.

The fortunate sixty females received the summons to the Palace via the Emperor's own couriers. These heralds arrived with much pomp at each of the girl's homes in carts or sedan chairs of Imperial yellow (the colour symbolised the sun, and the Emperor's unique status as Son of Heaven). Notwith-standing the girl's own feeling on the matter, the arrival of Imperial messengers gave great 'face' to her family, and pro-duced an immediate rise in social status. The messengers were welcomed with every sign of humility, the elder of the house-hold kowtowing (from *kau-tau* – to knock head) as if the Emperor himself were present. While customary, this ritual symbolised the absolute power of the monarch over his sub-jects – the summons had arrived and there was no possibility of refusal.

There is little doubt that Yehonala would have much pre-ferred to decline the 'honour' given her. Prior to the Imperial summons she had been all but betrothed to another of her cou-sins, the tall and handsome Jung Lu. According to many accounts, the young couple were deeply in love, and would have married in due course. This affection was to last all their lives and, if the rumours current in Beijing were to be believed, it was to cast the ill-starred pair as an oriental Lancelot and Guinevere to the Emperor's King Arthur. Whatever the truth of this, Jung Lu was to play a vital and continuing role in his lost love's rise to absolute power.

The call to the Palace would have rocked Yehonala's world and her dreams of the future. It changed everything: there could be no marriage to Jung Lu if she were selected as a con-sort of the Son of Heaven. This shattering of her youthful dreams must have had a profound effect on Yehonala. She was sixteen, in love with a handsome military cadet who returned her affection and whom she knew she would marry. And then suddenly it was all taken from her, the vision shattered while it was still new and before time and experience had had a chance to sully the perfection of her emotions. It would have been less than human of her if she had not blamed the Emperor for this disaster. It is more than probable that this seismic shift in her fate left an indelible hatred in her heart, and (together with the tribal frictions and rivalry between the Yeho-Nala and the Aisin Gioro clans) does much to explain her subsequent indif-ference to and callous disregard of the fate of the Dynasty and the Imperial line.

Even to be successful in the selection process was no guarantee of Imperial favour. The harem was so vast that it was perfectly possible to be elevated to the rank of concubine and yet never be taken to the Imperial bed. As the Emperor's wives never left the Forbidden City, and the seraglio was staffed only with eunuchs, this amounted to a sentence of perpetual virginity. And should an Emperor die, custom forbade any of his wives to remarry, or to leave the precincts of the Great Within (consummation of the marriage was not required). They were imprisoned for life within its purple walls. When the remnants of the Manchu court were finally expelled from the Forbidden City in 1924, three old women, forgotten wives of long-dead Emperors, were discovered still living in obscurity in the warren of dilapidated apartments.[13]

On the day appointed, the sixty aspirants prepared their toilet with the greatest care. Like her rivals, Yehonala would have had her face caked with white-lead powder into a pale geisha-style mask, her cheeks daubed with twin spots of rouge and, as custom demanded, her lower lip reddened to resemble a rose or cherry. Dressed in the most sumptuous robes and jewellery their families could afford, the potential concubines were carried in sedan chairs towards the high walls of the Great Within. Cocooned in the musty, humid air of the enclosed palanquin, screened from all prying eyes, hearing nothing but the creaking of the wooden poles, the grunts of the bearers and the dull slap of their feet on the dusty road, Yehonala, like the others in her situation, can only have been in a high state of agitation. None knew what to expect, or what changes the next few hours might bring. Beyond the heavily embroidered silk hangings the sounds of the capital's street-life were muted, the cries of street vendors, the barber's rattling *huan tou*, the clack-clack-clack of hollow bamboo announcing the passage of a foot doctor, the charcoal seller's drum. As the procession approached the Tien An Men, the street noises slowly died away, and suddenly the comforting roll of the palanquin ceased as the sedan chair was deposited on the ground. The covers were drawn back, and Yehonala found herself in the shadow-filled outer precincts of the Forbidden City.

Here, her own servants were dismissed and, now on foot, she and the other girls followed eunuch guides deeper and deeper into the maze of yellow- and blue-tiled pavilions, palaces and apartments that formed the inner precincts of the Great Within. They were led finally to the Nei Wu Fu, a pavilion of the Imperial household, to await the arrival of the Empress Dowager, the wife of the late Emperor Tao Kwang and mother of the new Son of Heaven, who, according to the Confucian traditions of filial piety, outranked the Emperor. It was she, with advice from the Chief Eunuch An Te-hai, who decided which of the girls were suitable consorts for her son, the Celestial Prince. The reception room was hung with banners and multi-hued lanterns, and crowded with courtiers in their formal robes of vari-coloured silk, strewn with pearls and jade ornaments, and all anxious for a first look at the new potential additions to the harem. Although the Emperor was also present during the proceedings, sitting pale and weakened from years of dissipation next to the Empress Dowager, the monarch was allowed no part in the business of the day. Nor was he asked for his opinion.

Once assembled, each of the girls was called in turn to be presented to the Empress Dowager. The approach of each prospective consort allowed the matriarch of the royal family ample time to study her features and deportment. Once each had done obeisance before their majesties, tea was served, and the court could view and pass judgement on the grace or otherwise with which the girls performed this most basic ritual of Chinese society.

A Chinese princess, Der Ling, wrote an account of the years she spent with Yehonala in her old age. She relates that Yehonala claimed that, from that first meeting, the Emperor showed great interest in her and ignored the rest of the new arrivals.[14] Although unable formally to express a preference, he used this assembly to indicate his interest in the bannerman's daughter. Yehonala was invited to sit at the Emperor's table, and to converse with the Imperial family. Although education was not a prerequisite for the position of Imperial concubine, Yehonala was already well versed in the Chinese Classics and may have used this occasion to impress the young monarch with her intelligence as well as her beauty.

If true, it seems that the Emperor's admiration did not count for much in the eyes of the Empress Dowager. The Imperial concubines were separated into four classes of decreasing importance. The Empress Dowager's standards were high – of the sixty girls interviewed, none received the first rank of *Kuei fei*. Yehonala was one of twenty-eight aspirants chosen for the harem, but she was given a quite lowly grade (*Kuei Jen*). She was placed in the third rank, while Sakota her cousin (who by all accounts was both less attractive and less intelligent), was given the second rank (*P'in*). Yehonala and Sakota can only have been overjoyed that they would be entering the harem together. Life in the Forbidden City meant almost total isolation from normal family life. From the day the walls of the Meridian Gate closed behind them, each harem member was fated to live out her days within the Forbidden City, seeing friends and family but rarely. The two cousins now had each other to lean on and there was no doubt they would have need of each other. The world they were about to enter was dangerous in the extreme, one of the most debauched, capricious and cruel courts ever recorded in the history of Occident or Orient.

CHAPTER FOUR

The Great Within

The Forbidden City, the royal palace of the Celestial Prince, ruler of All Under Heaven, was built by Yung Le, the fourth son of the first Ming Emperor Chu Yuan-chang, a one-time Buddhist priest whose successful rebellion against the Mongol Yuan Dynasty had placed the Ming on the throne of the Middle Kingdom in 1368. It was Yung Le who in 1422 transferred the seat of government from Nanking (the southern capital) to Beijing.[1]

The main buildings of the Forbidden City were constructed between 1410 and 1420, and are laid out along a central north–south axis. The site contains more than ten major palaces, nine thousand rooms, three garden parks, and a lamaist temple, and occupies a total area of seven hundred and twenty thousand square metres, around two hundred and fifty acres.[2] The main temples and palaces are impressively ornate structures, built entirely of wood with vermilion-painted walls, and yellow-glazed tile roofs (yellow symbolising the sun and, by extension, the Emperor). Symbolism is everywhere in the Forbidden City: colours, names and shapes all had a meaning. Each palace stands on white marble terracing, beautifully carved with intricate designs, the most prominent being the twin sigils of Imperial Power, the dragon and the phoenix. The three main halls of the outer palace (the Halls of Harmony) stand on a three-tiered terrace of white marble which in plan view forms the Chinese character signifying 'the land'. Each door has nine horizontal rows of nails embedded in it, and each row has nine nails: nine is the biggest single odd number, and therefore represents the dignity of Emperors. The Chinese science of geomancy, *feng shui*, 'wind and water', was also integral to the construction of the complex. Just as the Emperor was known as *Nan Mien*, 'face south', so too did his capital Beijing. Backed by a semicircle of mountains to the north, to Chinese eyes the city looked south into the agricultural land of the eastern plains. At the very centre of the metropolis, in the Forbidden City, was the throne, around which the whole world was believed to revolve. In this way (in a Chinese version of the Hermetic axiom 'As above, so below, as below so above'), the organisation of the Middle Kingdom mirrored the celestial symmetry of the heavens, which move in perfect harmony around a central axis, the pole star. As a Chinese saying has it: 'All the stars in Heaven salute the North'; and 'All Under Heaven' paid homage to the Emperor, enthroned in the North.

The denizens of this city of symbols existed in privileged isolation at the apex of an enormous human pyramid, a land famed for its fecundity, and in Yehonala's time numbering around four hundred million people.[3] At its base were 'the stupid people', the peasants, merchants and artisans. Tradesmen and traders were the lowest class, small in number and treated with contempt (no Manchu would ever consider learning a manual skill, or engaging in trade). China was a largely agrarian society of peasants, using traditional techniques more akin to horticulture than agriculture (even in the last decade of the twentieth century, China was spoken of as being 'like one giant allotment'). Their task was, quite simply, to produce the food which was the foundation of the society. Capping the social pyramid were the elite of Chinese society, the scholar-officials, famous in the west as the mandarins. They possessed every privilege, owned the lion's share of all land, and enjoyed the greatest influence and prestige, having arrogated to themselves the most vital of tasks in Chinese society – that of governing the vast Celestial Empire. Each of China's provinces compares in size with a modern European nation state – Sichuan Province is larger than the British Isles and has a similar population, sixty million souls, and each province boasts its own dialect, each largely incomprehensible to its neighbours. In the 1800s, with communication and transport difficult, the Empire, this vast mass of disparate humanity, could easily have fallen into anarchy and schism. That it did not (and that it had, by and large, held together since its inception in 221 BC) was due in large part to the mandarinate. Although unproductive themselves, they performed the socially indispensable function of supervising and coordinating the work of others. They 'prepared the calendar, they organised transport and exchange, they supervised the construction of roads, canals, dykes and dams; they were in charge of all public works, especially those aimed at forestalling droughts and floods; they built up reserves against famine, and encouraged every kind of irrigation project. Their social role was at one and the same time that of architect, engineer, teacher, administrator and ruler.[4] Mencius (Meng-tse), arguably the ablest of Confucius' disciples, made their position plain:

> Great men have their proper business and little men have their proper business ... Some labour with their minds and some labour with their strength. Those who labour with their minds govern others; those who labour with their strength are governed by others. Those who are governed by others support them; those who govern others are supported by them.[5]

In contrast to Western ideas of specialisation, the mandarins recognised just one vocation: that of governing. They rejected careful study of agriculture, astronomy, architecture or any of the other myriad specialisations, believing that an education in the Classics and an appreciation of music, poetry and calligraphy would produce a more well-rounded and perceptive 'manager', one able to cope with the many and varied demands that their administrative duties demanded of them. In many ways this uniquely Chinese system was a palpable success: it can hardly have survived relatively unchanged for over two thousand years had it not possessed some merit. The Confucian ideals cherished honesty, reverence for the past and respect for parents and the Imperial line. It set out a stable net of societal relationships that should, in theory, have produced a well-ordered, well-fed and harmonious population of contented individuals.

In practice, a rather less admirable society evolved, a form of hereditary bureaucracy, in which everyone knew (or was told) his or her place. Upward mobility was theoretically possible via the examination system, where scholars were tested on their knowledge of the Confucian Classics, their calligraphy and their ability to create an essay (the 'eight-legged work') which showcased all aspects of their education. Those gaining the highest marks found the door to high appointment in government service open wide, irrespective of the student's purse or parentage. The mandarins made much of the populist/meritocratic nature of the examination system, but the truth was that such democratic levelling operated solely within their own class. Preparation for the examinations required years and sometimes decades of patient study with a mentor or tutor willing to instruct his pupils in the hidden depths of the Classics or the intricacies of a literary style. Peasants, merchants and artisans could not afford the onerous charges such an education demanded – only a well-placed mandarin could generate the required income. For all their high-flown rhetoric on truth and honesty, the mandarinate was, in effect, a self-perpetuating oligarchy. And like all oligarchies, when threatened it had no compunction in using the sternest measures to protect its vested interests.

Justice in nineteenth-century China was arbitrary, tyrannical and biased towards the ruling class The state's wrath fell not just on the individual, but on all his kin. The extended family or clan system – where each member of a clan was responsible for the well-being of any clan member – was turned on its head and used to instil terror – a family member's crime brought retribution on all his clan: whole families might be summarily executed, or exiled for life to the desert regions, solely on the basis of a single individual's misfeasance. Any accused person was presumed guilty, unless they could prove themselves otherwise, unfortunate at a time when judicial decisions were, for the most part, bought and sold like any other commodity. Torture was commonplace: an individual might be suffocated with weights, submerged to the point of asphyxiation or have slivers of bamboo driven beneath fingernails or toenails, in order to extract the 'truth'. And punishment for those found 'guilty' was swift and (even in the context of the harsh treatment meted out to criminals in Victoria's Britain) barbarous and horrible and specific.

Beheading was the most common form of capital punishment, but a highwayman might well be crucified instead near the scene of his crime; grave robbers were placed in a wooden cage and left until they died of starvation or heatstroke; captured brigands were forced to 'stand in the tub' – balancing on bricks in a vat filled with lime from which, each day, a number of the bricks were removed, the lime gradually eating through flesh and bone from the feet up; the cangue was a type of portable stocks, with the victim's head fastened into a wooden board so large he could not bring his hands to his mouth and so could neither feed nor drink for himself. The cangue was worn for a few days for minor offences; for more serious crimes the cangue was left in place until the offender died of thirst or starvation. Treason was regarded with horror (as a transgression against the Celestial Ruler, it offended the fundamental basis of Confucianism) and the most terrible punishment was reserved for rebels and traitors – slow dismemberment, the victim's body being disarticulated a joint at a time until death ensued.[6]

What makes such mandarin-inspired atrocities particularly frightful is the fact that the mandarinate itself was amongst the most corrupt and venal of all China's institutions. The same huge educational expenses that precluded participation by the 'lower orders' was also an enormous financial burden for many of the less prosperous mandarin families. A substantial proportion were forced to take out loans to complete their studies. In addition, the golden road to a government appointment would also require lubrication with 'fragrant grease' at several stages along the route, with 'squeeze' extracted by those in a position to help or hinder the appointment. Once secure in his new post, all such 'helpers' would demand repayment for their kindness, with interest, while at the same time the new official's extended family would look to him for financial support. Confucian doctrine taught that the interests of the family superseded those of the state, giving a rationale for and green light to nepotism.[7] On the basis of family ties, incompetents were raised to positions of power all over the Empire. Capping all these problems, the pay of a 'servant of the state' was proverbially low, and the required Confucian deference to superiors made it impossible to request any increase in salary.

Given the circumstances, there was only one alternative source of income available to the mandarin – extorting money and services from those he had been set over to govern. Bribes would be taken to turn a blind eye to illegal practices such as opium smoking or smuggling; and 'squeeze' would be exacted on legitimate businesses under threat of victimisation. Over time, sanctioned by custom, such practices became the norm and extended to every aspect of Chinese life. Such toleration allowed some officials to amass stupendous fortunes. When the infamous minister Ho Shen was finally brought to book in 1799, after twenty years in power, the property confiscated from him included nine thousand sceptres of solid gold, 288 large rubies, 4,070 sapphires and a solid gold table service of 4,288 pieces. Following his enforced suicide, Ho Shen's total wealth was estimated at over eight hundred million taels, a sum equivalent to almost sixty per cent of the total Imperial revenue for the same period. But his downfall did nothing to stop mandarin cupidity: in 1841, just nine years before Yehonala entered the Forbidden City, the Board of Revenue discovered that nine million taels of silver had been stolen, purloined by the same officials whose job it was to guard the treasure.[8]

China's social structure, its castes and classes, its customs and ceremony, and its system of rewards and punishments, had been set into the stone of Confucian mores for more than two thousand years. But since the victory of Nurhachi's descendants in 1644 a further stratum, a superstructure of Manchu privilege, had been layered over this ancient Confucian pyramid. The Manchu guarded their racial purity jealously: after the conquest they were forbidden to marry Chinese women (though this rule was often flouted as time went on); they were to dwell apart from the native population, in fortified areas, and be ever on their guard against rebellion; land was set aside throughout China for these descendants of the bannermen, and the choicest areas were reserved for the Manchu nobility, those lords that had supported Nurhachi's descendants in their attempt on the Dragon Throne. Their domains were vast and they were allowed a voice in the running of the Empire through various committees such as the Grand Council, where in time-honoured fashion the aristocracy intrigued and betrayed their way into the Emperor's favour and to the power and status that alone made life worth living.

Yehonala's new home, the Forbidden City, stood above even the Manchu nobility, serene and aloof from all worldly concerns – or so it was believed by the majority of the population. For the Chinese it was the omphalos, the navel of the world. It not only reflected the Celestial Order, it stood at the axis of Heaven and Earth and partook of both. The Great Within was a world within a world – China in miniature. The palace bureaucracy mirrored that of the state; there were forty-eight household departments responsible for every conceivable service, from finances and rent collection, through breeding the famous Pekingese 'lion dogs', to supplying the palace kitchen. But this correspondence between palace and nation broke down in one important regard. While the Middle Kingdom's population conformed to a normal fifty-fifty ratio between male and female, in the Forbidden City the presence of the harem precluded the presence of any adult male (except of course the Emperor) and the only 'balance' to the three thousand female servants and concubines was the existence of an equal number of 'half-men', the palace eunuchs, within its vermilion walls. Despite historical precedents to the contrary, the official Chinese view was that eunuch's were harmless 'creatures docile and loyal as gelded animals' according to one Emperor.[9] Males that could not sire children were believed less likely to commit treacherous acts in the hope of advancing their offspring. Maleness was *yang*, characterised by strength and action; the feminine principle was *yin*, symbolised by weakness and passivity. So it was believed that males deprived of their *yang* would tend towards *yin*; they would be forever accommodating and acquiescent and could therefore pose no threat. What they overlooked was another 'fact' of this quintessentially Chinese philosophical system: the association of the *yin* principle with evil.

Strangely, historical records of the eunuch begin in both East and West at the same time – in the eighth century BC. But the practice of employing castrated men in a king or noble's service is almost certainly more ancient. In China an ancient Yin Dynasty site during the time of the Emperor Wu Ting, yielded a bone inscribed with a two-element pictogram[10] and next to it another designating the Chiang people, a sheep-herding tribe and enemies of the Yin. The first double-character is made up of two separate signs, one designating the male genitalia and the second the verb 'cut'. Such bones, with a question written on them, were used in divination, and it seems that, some three thousand three hundred years ago, the Yin Emperor, Wu Ting, was asking the gods if he should castrate a Chiang captive.

The making of eunuchs advanced swiftly from the original brutal castration of enemies to become a refined surgical procedure. In ancient Egypt, one of the first civilisations to incorporate eunuchs as a class into its social structure, the wound was treated with ashes and hot oil to control blood loss, and the new eunuch buried in hot sand up to the navel and left for five or six days. Not surprisingly, the mortality rate was high – around sixty per cent of all those castrated died in appalling agony. In southern India the operation was taken to new heights of sophistication. The patient was seated on a special chair and given opium to control the pain. The genitals were clamped between two strips of bamboo and a razor-sharp blade slid down the wood to effect the amputation. The wound was washed with hot oil and covered in an oil-soaked cloth, and the patient kept supine and fed with milk until healing was complete.

By the time of the Manchu this fiendish operation had become something of a profession, with specialist castrators and their apprentices plying their trade at a *ch'ang tzu*, a small hut just outside the western gate of the Tzu Chin Palace in Beijing. The charge for emasculation was six taels.[11] Many refinements had been developed: the stomach and upper thighs of the candidate eunuch were tightly bandaged, to reduce blood flow to these parts and so minimise blood loss once the cut had been made. The genitals were washed three times in hot pepper-water to partially anaesthetise them; the patient was given anaesthetic tea and seated on a *k'ang*, a heated couch. Once settled in position, the apprentices held the patient firmly around the waist and thighs as the specialist approached, a small, curve-bladed knife in his hand. '*Hou huei bu hou huei?*' he asked ('Will you regret or not regret this?'). At the slightest indecision, the operation was abandoned, but if the man resolutely gave permission to go ahead, the knife did its work, severing both penis and scrotum. A plug was placed in the urethra and the lesion covered in water-soaked paper and bandaged. Unlike the practice in India, with the help of the apprentices the new eunuch was made to walk around the room for between two and three hours before being allowed to rest. No drink was permitted for three days, after which the urethral plug was removed. Should urine flow from the small hole in the wound then all was well – the operation had been a success. But a lack of urine indicated that the urethra had closed, and the man would certainly die in agony within a few days. However, so accomplished were the surgeons that George Stent, who gathered this information first-hand in the late 1870s, and spent many years studying Chinese archives, could find only one recorded fatality. The amputation took around one hundred days to heal, but it was not until a year after the operation that the new eunuch took up his duties in the Forbidden City.

Physical changes had occurred over this twelve-month period. Those emasculated after reaching puberty lost all facial and body hair (pre-pubertal castrati remained hairless) and their low masculine voices disappeared, replaced by a high falsetto. Muscle tone decreased and more fat was deposited on the body giving them a distinctly androgynous appearance. In addition, they had a characteristic gait, leaning forward as they walked, and taking short, mincing steps with their feet turned out. Some eunuchs did not appear to show these signs to any marked degree, and stories arose that the genitals of some grew back, albeit diminished in size. Other tales claimed that intact males occasionally bribed their way into the eunuch circle in the Forbidden City, and became the lovers of the Emperor's concubines, and even of the Empress herself. Several anti-Manchu pamphlets claimed that An Te-hai, Yehonala's favourite eunuch, was in fact her paramour. It may be that An Te-hai was both a eunuch *and* her paramour, and that he had been emasculated by the removal of his scrotum only. Such a castration technique, though rare in China, was reputed to produce lovers of prodigious endurance. An eighth-century Arab writer on the subject mentions that the Byzantines (whom he calls the Rum):

> do not harm the penis, and they only interfere with the testicles ... As for sexual pleasure and lust satisfaction, the Rum claim that they (the eunuchs) reach heights never reached by the unemasculated man. It is as if they claim that the eunuch draws out of the woman everything she has, because of his excessive ability to prolong [the sexual act].[12]

To forestall such affronts to the Imperial dignity, regular inspections were made of all eunuchs in the Great Within. The newly made eunuch was expected to buy back his genitals from his emasculator, and to preserve them in a hermetically sealed jar. The remains (known as *pao*, 'precious things') were treated with great respect and placed on the highest shelf in his quarters, to symbolise their owner's aspiration to rise in his chosen vocation. They were presented for inspection during an annual examination, and were mandatory whenever a eunuch was promoted to a higher grade within the palace. Nevertheless, rumours persisted that certain normal males had purchased or stolen the *pao* of genuine eunuchs and continued to pass themselves off as eunuchs within the confines of the Forbidden City. This not as unlikely as it first appears. Bribery was rife in the palace, and it is known that genuine eunuchs who had lost their *pao* would sometimes buy a new 'set' from the emasculator at the *ch'ang tzu* or hire preserved genitals from a eunuch acquaintance.

Eunuchs were held in contempt by intact males, who called them 'crows' because of their grating high-pitched voices, or 'rats and foxes'. In a society where any bodily mutilation was execrated, castration precluded participation in worship before the ancestral wooden tablets (upon which the souls of the departed descended to receive the submission of their descendants). The eunuch was excluded from those vital rituals which tied an individual to his family and clan, ever the centre of Chinese life. In addition, being unable to produce sons of his own, after death his own shade would remain forever without the solace of the ancestral rites. In this world and the next, the eunuch was an outcast.

As a result, the Imperial Palace eunuchs banded together in an exclusive brotherhood, forming a powerful clique in the tangle of human relations within the Forbidden City. In the 1800s most eunuchs were given a small rice allowance and just two to four taels per month on which to live, twelve taels being the official maximum salary. However, they were also entitled to 'squeeze' – a percentage 'tax' on all goods and services that passed through their particular department. Given the immense quantities of gold, silver, furs, ivory, horses, livestock, furniture, weapons and other commodities such as rice, wheat and timber that were delivered as tribute to the Son of Heaven each year, this percentage amounted to a tidy sum, not least because the eunuchs were in the habit of increasing their tax to truly onerous heights, sometimes demanding one-third of the value of the merchandise offered. In the hierarchical system of the Great Within, the lion's share of these riches fell to the Grand Eunuch, some of whom became immensely wealthy. At the end of the Ming Dynasty, a eunuch named Wei, by conspiring with the infamous Madame K'o, succeeded in dominating the Emperor and amassing such treasure that, according to one irate censor, he travelled '... in a chariot drawn by four horses, Imperial banners and insignia were carried in the procession. His bodyguard [strictly forbidden to eunuchs by the Dynasty's house-laws] surrounded him on both sides to screen his sacred person from the vulgar gaze. In every respect his

passing resembled a progress of Your Majesty!' Wei's under-
mining of the Imperial dignity was responsible in no small
part for the demise of the Ming, and similar scenarios had
been enacted during the reigns of the Chou, Ch'in, Han and
Tang Dynasties with equally dire results.[13] Despite this, and
the strict rules against meddling by eunuchs in state affairs
promulgated by the early rulers of the Manchu, at the time
Yehonala entered the Palace the eunuch clique was firmly
entrenched in most areas of Palace life, and they were
milking the Imperial milch cow for all they were worth.

A concubine of the third rank was a very small cog in this
immense machine of graft and corruption. Yehonala was given
lodgings in the Hall of Preserved Elegance, one of the six
western halls in the Inner Palace. From the small room that
the eunuchs had prepared for her in a row of blue-tiled, one-
storeyed pavilions, Yehonala was faced with a career choice of
immense importance: should she accept her lot as 'concubine,
third class' and live out her days in pleasant, if dull, obscurity
within the Forbidden City? Or dare she take her chances in the
'great game' that was played out behind its massive purple
walls, pushing herself to the very centre of things, gambling
for power and influence, risking everything, humiliation, torture and even death, to achieve her aims. Given what we know
of her temperament, it seems clear that she had very little
choice in the matter – obscurity would have been a living
death for Yehonala. She wore ambition like a diadem.

But even the ambitious need their share of luck. Despite
Yehonala's claim that the Emperor showered attention upon
her during their first meeting, it seems that her good fortune
deserted her shortly after she arrived at the Great Within.
Along with her cousin, Sakota, she was fated to languish in
the harem for five long years, while the Celestial Prince
bestowed his favours and his amours upon other, more fortunate, odalisques. It is during this period that she must have
absorbed everything she could learn of the arts of love, knowledge that was later to make her irresistible and indispensable
to the pleasure-sated Emperor. These must have been frus-
trating times for Yehonala, both sexually and politically. Her

surest, perhaps her only, means of enhancing her position was to find favour with the Son of Heaven. His immense power could be used as a reservoir of protection by those he desired to please. Under its shield Yehonala could pursue her own plans for advancement, all but invulnerable to the cunning of her rivals – while her influence over the Emperor lasted.

But there were other centres of influence in the Forbidden City. Even in her teens, Yehonala seems to have been possessed of an innate political compass which attracted her unerringly towards those with the power of life and death in Chinese political life. Denied access to the Imperial presence for the moment, Yehonala spent a great deal of time during the first few years of her confinement in the harem cultivating these alternative sources of authority, and establishing as large a power base as her lowly position would allow.

Yehonala's first action was to target the most important person in the Forbidden City. This was undoubtedly the Empress Dowager, the widow of the former Emperor, whose right to filial respect from the new Emperor was unquestioned in Confucian society. In all things domestic the Empress Dowager took precedence – the lower-ranked concubines were less the wives of the Emperor than they were servants of the Empress. But half a loaf is better than no bread and such access to a member of the Imperial household who, within the Forbidden City, enjoyed a rank superior to that of the Son of Heaven, could be used to advantage. Yehonala did all in her power to impress and ingratiate herself with the senior Empress: she was already much better educated than most of her peers, and she applied herself with enthusiasm to additional readings of the poets and classical authors, and further enhanced her status by revealing a natural talent for painting and, to a lesser degree, calligraphy, all of which was certain to raise her reputation in the tradition-bound eyes of the Emperor's mother and give her 'face' with the rest of the court.

She was also at pains to cultivate those most disparaged and yet most powerful of the court attendants – the eunuchs. Their greed for gain was legendary, but they exercised an even stronger – and at times baleful – influence at the very centre of the Chinese state. Normal Chinese society ridiculed and belittled the eunuch fraternity, but their situation within the Forbidden City was entirely different. The eunuch was an outcast, a pariah, banished to one pole of the societal spectrum, and apparently diametrically opposed to the position of Emperor, who occupied the opposite pole, a solitary figure of reverence and splendour. When the Emperor travelled outside the Forbidden City in his royal sedan chair, bamboo screens were placed along his route to shield his sacred personage from the eyes of the 'stupid people'. And yet, as revealed in the Daoist Tai Chi symbol, such distinctions were more apparent than real. For all his pomp and majesty the Emperor was still, *au fond*, a human being, full of hidden insecurities, needing above all the companionship of others of his species. But such companionship was denied him by his exalted rank – all must kneel in the presence of the Son of Heaven; no one (with the exception of the Empress Dowager) was permitted to speak unless spoken to, not even members of the Imperial family. During an audience with the Son of Heaven all kept their eyes decorously lowered, for none must gaze directly on the royal countenance. He was the peerless Celestial Prince and perhaps the loneliest man on the planet.

It was just this untouchable nature of the Emperor that made him approachable to the other 'untouchables', the eunuchs of the palace. Only half-men, creatures outside normal society, could attend upon the Son of Heaven, dress him, feed him, and see to those natural human functions of the mind and body that gave the lie to the whole Son of Heaven mythos, and betrayed the Emperor as just another member of *Homo sapiens*, whom history and chance had raised to this exalted position. The eunuchs became not merely guardians of the harem, protectors of the Emperor's honour and guarantors of the purity of the succession, they became his intimates, the counsellors of his darkest moments, those to whom he could show the face behind his Imperial mask. They became his friends. And in this and this alone lay all their power.

The Emperor came to rely upon these intimates, to the most powerful of whom he allowed unheard-of liberties. But this friendship had a darker side, especially for those Emperors who came to the throne as infants or in their early youth. As the eunuchs' hopes of advancement, power and a pleasurable life lay solely in retaining their sovereign's favour, most would stop at nothing, and would deny the young monarch nothing, in the hope of personal gain. They were in a unique position to mould the young monarch's personality, to alter his preferences, and to discover his deepest longings and anxieties and use them for their own advantage. In this they followed age-old custom: Han Fei-tzu, a minister of state in the third century BC wrote, 'Those who would control rulers first discover their secret fears and wishes.'[14] Anxious to please, and at the same time to find ways of manipulating their sovereign, time and again in Chinese history the Eunuchs of the Presence introduced their guileless young charges into enfeebling experimentation with perversion and promiscuity. The third son of the previous Emperor, Tao Kwang (and a brother of Yehonala's Lord, Hsien Feng), was infamous for his penchant for homosexual relationships with eunuch actors, some of whom he kept prisoner in his home to use as he pleased. Nor had the new Emperor, Hsien Feng, escaped the corrupting influence of his own eunuchs; stories of carousing and his bisexual tastes were common knowledge in the streets and alleys of Beijing, especially his infatuation with Zhu Lian-feng, a leading actor and female impersonator.[15] Given his debauched and dropsied condition when Yehonala first began to figure in his life at the age of twenty-one, there must have been much truth in these rumours.

But while the eunuchs were questionable friends to the Emperor, from Yehonala's perspective they undoubtedly had their uses. If she were able to cultivate friendships with those castrati close to the Emperor, they could provide her with an entrée to the Son of Heaven's presence, and hopefully to his bedchamber. The sheer number of concubines meant that, without influence, even the loveliest and most accomplished of the Emperor's wives might languish unnoticed until her beauty (and chance of power) had faded.

This was not a new problem. Yuan Ti, an Emperor of the Han Dynasty, had such a vast harem that he appointed a painter,

Mao Yen-shou, to produce portraits of his wives, so that he could use these paintings to choose a bed-partner. Naturally, many of the concubines were happy to pay the artist 'fragrant grease' for the privilege of being painted in the most flattering manner. However, one odalisque, the Lady Chao Chun, refused to advance the painter his accustomed 'fee', trusting that her natural beauty would win the Imperial favour. But Mao's talents for enhancing beauty could also be put to the opposite purpose. He produced a portrait that personified plainness and mediocrity – and so Chao Chun was ignored by the Son of Heaven.

A little later, the Great Khan of the Hsiung Nu (known in the West as the Huns) paid a state visit to the Chinese court. The Hsiung Nu made periodic raids into China and, in the hope of preventing these and increasing the ties of amity with a neighbouring state, it was deemed wise to give the visiting monarch a present most appropriate to the occasion – a lady from Yuan Ti's own harem. All unknowing the Chinese Emperor chose Chao Chun. When the lady was summoned, Yuan Ti was horrified – he had not realised that his harem contained a woman of such surpassing beauty. But his word had been pledged and, hiding his bitterness, he was forced to hand over the loveliest of his concubines to the Great Khan, and watch her leave his court forever. Almost as soon as the dust from the horses of his departing guests had settled Yuan Ti took his revenge. Mao Yen-shou, and several of the concubines who had paid to have their features enhanced, were dragged to the marketplace and publicly beheaded.[16]

In Yehonala's day no Mao Yen-shou plied his trade within the walls of the Forbidden City, but access to the Imperial Presence was still circumscribed and dependent upon payment of 'squeeze' – not to a painter but to the ubiquitous eunuchs. In the five years she spent in obscurity, Yehonala took pains to earn the gratitude and loyalty of the chief eunuch, An Te-hai, and he became her faithful retainer for over fifteen years, until his judicial murder by Yehonala's rivals in 1869. It was almost certainly by the wiles of An Te-hai that Yehonala came once again to the notice of the Son of Heaven. A story current in the late 1860s has it that Yehonala, now 20 years of age, was sitting forlornly in the Summer Palace, in a pavilion named 'The Deep Recesses among the Plane Trees', singing a plaintive southern folk-song from her native Anhui. It chanced that the Emperor too was walking in the garden and, hearing the sweet voice, he peered through the verdure to find its owner and was struck dumb by the beauty of the lovely girl he saw in the pavilion. Quietly, he slipped away and returned to the palace, but that same evening it was the jade plaque bearing Yehonala's name that he chose to display on the carved ivory table next to his chamber, indicating that its owner was to be his bed-companion for the evening. That night, a naked Yehonala was carried on the back of a eunuch to the Imperial bedchamber where she submitted to the will of the Lord of Ten Thousand Years.

Whether the story of their first meeting is true, or a more prosaic truth prevails (that Yehonala's cultivation of the chief eunuch resulted in his suggesting her name to the Son of Heaven), one thing is certain. During the passage of this fateful night she can only have pleased the Son of Heaven. From that time on, the Emperor was in thrall to Yehonala. And her inexorable rise to power began.

CHAPTER FIVE

Rebels and foreign devils

*T*hat the Emperor Hsien Feng should seek solace and oblivion in the arms of his favourite concubine was understandable. His kingdom was at breaking point, his realm beset with both internal and external enemies. There was every reason to believe that the Mandate of Heaven would be revoked, and that the proud Manchu, having reigned for over two hundred years, would soon go the way of the Ming, Han, Tang and all the other numerous ruling houses in China's long and bloody history – dynasties that had flowered in all their pride and then withered to nothing more than a memory. 'Look on my works, ye Mighty, and despair!'[1]

By the year that Yehonala finally found favour with her Lord, 1855, the Manchu were hard-pressed fighting one of the periodic revolts that had convulsed the Empire since the beginning of the dynastic system two thousand years before. The roots of these rebellions were legion: extortionate taxes, corvée labour, religious oppression, drought, famine or simple brigandage that fed upon popular resentment of the regime and snowballed into full-blooded insurrection, as with Li Tzu-cheng's almost-successful challenge to the Ming Dynasty. But this new revolt was fundamentally different: it was led not by disgruntled minorities, starving peasants or simple brigands, but by a much more dangerous phenomenon – a mystic visionary with the power to convince his followers of his direct contact with the Almighty, and to persuade them to die willingly for their chance of Paradise.

Its fuse was lit by a short, seemingly innocuous book distributed in Canton in 1836 by the Religious Tract Society of China, under the title *Good Works to Admonish the Age*. Its author was Liang Fa, a Chinese Christian convert, who had been assistant pastor to the British missionary, Robert Morrison, the first Protestant missionary to work in China. There is no doubt that this small book, the size of a modern-day paperback, was printed and distributed with the highest of motivations – to bring the benefits of the 'true religion' of Christianity to the Chinese masses. Instead, the tract became a supreme exemplar of the axiom that the road to hell is paved with good intentions. Unwittingly, the author of the book had lit a long fuse, priming a time bomb that was to explode fifteen years later, unleashing not the joys of Christian fellowship on the people of China, but the bloodiest civil war the world has known.[2]

Good Works to Admonish the Age is also an instructive example of the evolution of religions and the manner in which the culture and personal inclination of the adherent can colour the portrayal of his chosen path to enlightenment. In the book Liang Fa gives a reasonably tolerable précis of some of the major events in the Old and New Testaments, including Noah, the Exodus, the Sermon on the Mount and the life of St Paul. He enunciates the doctrine of an omniscient and omnipotent God, who had formed the whole of material creation in six days and under whose rule all humanity, regardless of race or nation, are equal. But Liang is also a man of his time and society, and he includes elements of Daoism, Buddhism and Chinese folk-tales in his work. Nor is he averse to simply making bits up, allowing his imagination free rein and having Jesus appear in the sky in broad daylight to produce the conversion of unbelievers. In other parts of the work Jesus and St Paul attend a baptism together, where Jesus relates that 'from ancient times there has never been anyone who has ascended to Heaven and seen heavenly things; I alone, who descend to the world from Heaven, know celestial matters, and thus I alone can talk about them'. St Paul then puts his hand on the head of the baptised man and the man 'talks in a strange voice and is able to predict the future'. One curious innovation (presumably taken from the Confucianist past that Liang Fa affects to abhor) is the notion that Jehovah chastises his sons. God whips his son Jesus because, it is explained, this is one way in which the Deity shows his love and corrects faults. Liang's prose is extremely repetitious and, in addition to these flights of fancy, he manages to give the impression that both God and Jesus commute between Heaven and earth on a regular basis.

Most Chinese recipients of the book, had they read it all, would simply have rejected its theology as that of the religion of the 'foreign devil'. A few would have embraced the new faith, and been given the disparaging title 'secondary hairy ones' by their non-Christian countrymen. But for one man, a schoolmaster of the south China *Hakka* minority named Hung Hsiu-chuan, the contents of this book became the basis, the seed-atom, of a completely new religion, a seminal text that would eventually result in the deaths of over twenty million souls.[3]

Hung first had sight of *Good Works* when he attended Canton for the official examinations that were the first step in his hoped-for career as a mandarin. He failed. He returned to teaching and the following year he attempted the examination again, but met with no better luck. Bitterly disappointed, he appears to have suffered a nervous breakdown, lapsing into delirium in an illness that was said to have lasted a biblically correct forty days. He was vouchsafed numerous visions during this time, in which the God of the Christians appeared and ordered him to repudiate Confucius and all the traditional rites of Chinese society. According to the official account of his followers (who knew Hung by the title 'The True Lord'), when he was:

> ... twenty-five years of age [twenty-four by Western reckoning], on the first day of the ting-yu year [5th April 1837] between 11pm and 1am, he saw numerous angels come down from Heaven to escort him aloft .... On his arrival at the Gates of Heaven he was welcomed by a bevy of lovely maidens standing by the roadside .... He was received by a number of people dressed in dragon-robes and wearing three-cornered hats. An order was given to cut open the True Lord's body and to replace his old bowels with new. Books too were placed at his side for him to read.[4]

When he recovered from the worst of his delirium, Hung – complete with his new bowels, and the knowledge from the heavenly books – became convinced that he was a second saviour, a son of God, and the younger brother of Jesus Christ.

Hung remained in his home village for the next few years, earning his living as a teacher. But his thoughts were elsewhere. The Middle Kingdom's disastrous confrontations with the Western powers at this time convinced him that the whole of Qing China was corrupt and required 'cleansing'. Secure in the knowledge of his position as Son of God, he resolved to overthrow the Qing Dynasty. It must have appeared a hopeless dream to all but Hung Hsiu-chuan – a failed scholar, an impecunious teacher, a member of the despised *Hakka* minority, eking out a precarious living in an insignificant village in a southern province remote from the centres of power, deciding to take on the might of the Manchu and destroy them. The arrogance of his ambition is breathtaking even now. The wonder of it is that he almost succeeded.

But Hung's powers of persuasion and oratory were phenomenal. With his cousin, Hung Jen-kan, and classmate, Feng Yunshan, Hung established a group known as the *Pai Shang Ti Hui* (Society for the Worship of God). People were impressed by their sincerity and by the moral transformation of those joining the Society, and many converts were made, especially among the peasantry. Over the next six or seven years Hung's triumvirate travelled widely in the south, establishing groups of *Pai Shang Ti Hui*. Despite his punishing schedule, Hung felt that the real work of his life had not yet begun. He wrote: 'At the moment I am idle like a fish leaping in a deep pool as I bide my time for men to congregate.'

By the beginning of 1851, he felt he was ready. Ten thousand members of the *Pai Shang Ti Hui* were ordered to gather at Chintien village in the foothills of Tzuchingshan in Guanxi Province. They pooled all their resources, money, clothing and food, and trained together as a fighting unit. In defiance of Manchu edicts, which required that all their Chinese subjects shave the front of their heads and wear the remaining hair in a queue or pigtail, the rebels grew their hair and wore it unbraided, glorying in their soubriquet *Chang Mao*, the 'long-haired warriors'. On 11th January, Hung solemnly announced the uprising of the *Chang Mao* against the Manchu and proclaimed the establishment of the *Tai Ping Tien Guo*, the 'The Heavenly Kingdom of Great Peace'. The great Tai Ping rebellion had begun.

Alarmed by these events, the Qing government transferred troops from Hunan, Guizhou, Yunnan and other provinces in an attempt to encircle and crush the insurgents. But the imperial troops, the descendants of Nurhachi's 'Romans of the East', had been softened by years of comfortable existence in their sinecures. The Tai Ping's disciplined army, hardened by the rigours of their previous peasant existence, and strengthened by faith in their leader's divine origin, destroyed all that were sent against them.

While the Dynasty's prospects were shaken by these reverses, in the Forbidden City Yehonala's personal fortune was in the ascendant. Thanks to her abilities in the bedchamber, she had already begun her rise to prominence: soon after spending their first night together Hsien Feng had promoted her one grade to the rank of *P'in* concubine. But even better fortune was to follow, for by September 1855 Yehonala knew she was pregnant by Hsien Feng. The news could only have inflamed her ambitions. Although several of the Emperor's ancestors had sired male heirs by the time they were fifteen years old, Hsien Feng, now in his mid-twenties, had still not produced the longed-for son that would guarantee his tottering Dynasty some measure of stability. Were Yehonala to present the Emperor with a son, her position in court would be assured, unassailable. To the mother of the heir many previously closed doors would fly open. The months of her confinement must have dragged by in an unbearable *mélange* of elation and fear. Nothing was said openly, but everyone knew that miscarriage, or a female child, would disappoint the Emperor, shame Yehonala before the whole palace, and return her to the obscurity she loathed. The climax of this quiet drama came in the spring of 1856, on 27th April, when all her dreams were realised – Yehonala gave birth to a healthy man-child, a

baby boy who was destined to become the eighth Emperor of
the Manchu Dynasty under his reign-title Tung Chih. The
Emperor was delighted beyond words. Yehonala was now
further advanced in the hierarchy of the seraglio – she was
immediately elevated to the rank of Kuei Fei, and given the title
of Empress Hsiao Ch'in. So pleased was the Emperor that his
favourite had produced the long-sought heir, he took the new
Empress completely into his confidence, and taught her to
classify his memorials, so that there was good reason for her
to be constantly at his side. And so the young concubine
obtained her first inside view of the workings of the Manchu
regime, and took her first taste of power. Such a position made
her privy to most state documents, a position she was not slow
to exploit. She read avidly, devouring everything that came
within reach and was soon acting as an unofficial adviser to
the Emperor.

During 1856, as Yehonala began her work of classifying the
memorials sent to the Emperor, she would have quickly realised just how great a threat the Tai Ping rebels had become.
The insurgents were now well ensconced in Canton, Guanxi
and Guelin Provinces and had held the southern capital of
Nanking against all-comers for the past three years. During
this time the nature of the rebellion had changed out of
all recognition. Once again, as in all China's rebellions, the
'imperial infection' had blighted the revolutionary purity of
the Tai Ping revolt. Hung Hsiu-chuan and his close confederates, the defenders of women's rights, the champions of
equality and the scourge of privilege, had been seduced by
power and had begun to reap the personal rewards of victory:
Hung had taken to wearing yellow dragon-robes in imitation of
the Emperor, calling himself The Heavenly King. His allies had
given themselves equally grandiose titles, styling themselves,
The King of the East, or The Loyal Prince, and they had all
begun building elaborate palaces and pleasure parks where
they each held state like the Emperor himself. All had procured
for themselves harems of fabulous proportions: Hung's own
stable of beauties numbered three hundred 'wives', and on certain of his birthdays he graciously increased the number of

odalisques each of his allies was allowed to possess. At the same time, the Tai Ping rank and file were subject to draconian discipline: all goods were held in common, and men and women were strictly separated, with sexual relations even between married couples punished by beheading.[5] Despite the obvious discrepancies between rhetoric and practice, many of Hung's followers retained a Messiah-like belief in their leader, and were willing to fight and die for him on a scale not seen among the Manchu forces, who laboured under the weight of centuries-old corruption. The vigour of the revolutionaries brought them more victories than defeats and slowly, but inexorably, their sphere of influence expanded. At the Beijing court it was whispered that if the Tai Ping successes continued, Hung Hsiu-chuan might bid fair to be the next occupant of the Dragon Throne.

Yehonala, true to her pugnacious temperament, counselled the Emperor and stiffened his resolve in the face of these setbacks. She was said to be responsible for the appointment of a capable general, Tseng Guo-feng, as commander-in-chief against the rebels. Tseng travelled south, provided with adequate funds to reorganise the Imperial troops, and to raise additional forces in Hunan Province. In the same year that Yehonala gave birth to the Emperor's son, Tseng Guo-feng's reforms began to bear fruit when he won a number of minor victories against the *Chang Mao*. These successes made Yehonala's stock rise even higher at court, much to the chagrin of those Manchu nobles who had heretofore been the bosom friends of the Celestial Prince.

These worthies, along with his eunuch servants, had encouraged and accompanied Hsien Feng on 'secret' visits outside the Forbidden City where, like Nero in Rome, a disguised Emperor had for several years indulged in the life of a libertine, visiting peep-shows, opium houses and brothels with their store of 'lily-footed' Chinese females, forbidden fruit to any Manchu, much less the Emperor. If rumour was to be believed, transvestite actors (men played almost all female roles in Chinese theatre) were also an important part of Hsien Feng's nocturnal adventures. As a result of these excesses, Hsien Feng had lost much of his former health (he had been a gymnast in his youth). European emissaries generally described him as an unprepossessing individual with a wispy moustache worn above his small mouth, though some remark on his stately, dignified bearing during their audience. By the time of his infatuation with Yehonala he was decidedly unwell, suffering from dropsy and the effects of his previous debaucheries. His illnesses (and his rumoured over-indulgence in the sensual charms of Yehonala) had left him exhausted, and it had been easy to persuade the Emperor to transfer control of the affairs of state to four Grand Councillors and four adjutant-generals. The most powerful member of the Council was an Imperial clansman of the blue-bordered banner, Su Shun, who derived much influence from being a half-brother of Prince I. Su Shun was greatly feared within and without the Forbidden City. As Assistant Grand Secretary he had contrived the murder of his chief, persuading the Emperor to order the beheading of the the honest and uncompromising Grand Secretary, Po Sui, who had thwarted the schemes of his confederates. Yehonala had intervened in a vain attempt to save the condemned man, a move which signalled the beginning of a deadly feud between herself and Su Shun. As he rose in power Su Shun engineered the arrest of all the Secretaries of the Board of Revenue, holding them prisoner himself and extorting from each of them an enormous ransom for their release.[6] This fortune formed the basis of his power at court and made Su Shun a dangerous man to cross.

As effective rulers of the Empire, the Grand Councillors, and Su Shun in particular, were an enormous obstacle to Yehonala's own ambitions. They, in turn, were resentful of Yehonala's power over the Emperor, and the weight Hsien Feng gave to her opinions on matters of state (the Emperor's agreement was still required on all major decisions taken by the Council). Yehonala found a natural ally in her cousin, Sakota, the Emperor's consort, and she joined forces with Prince Kung, sworn enemy of Su Shun and his faction. While the silk-robed courtiers enacted their ceremonious rites within the ornate palaces of the Forbidden City, a silent manoeuvring for power began between the competing cliques, all the more urgent when it became clear that the Emperor's illnesses were more serious than previously believed, and that the Lord of Ten Thousand Years was unlikely to survive even the next ten months. The question of who would rule the Middle Kingdom during the minority of the heir, Yehonala's son, loomed large on the political horizon of China. It was no longer a matter of 'face' between the factions, of currying favour with the Celestial Prince, and jockeying for position at court. The scene was set for an internal power struggle that would lead to the disgrace, and perhaps death, of one of the factions. That the growing power of the Tai Ping revolutionaries might mean that there would soon be no dynasty to fight over seemed to worry neither camp.

If the outlook for the dynasty within China was bleak, the view from without was, if anything, worse.

For millennia China had prided herself on being *Chung*, 'Central', the Middle Kingdom, with the Emperor at its heart, who swayed All Under Heaven, and around whom the whole world revolved. Successive dynasties had nurtured this Sino-centric view of the world, and even the Manchu could not withstand its seductive power. As outsiders the Manchu ridiculed the egocentric pomposity of the Ming; as possessors of the Dragon Throne themselves they were soon persuaded of the truth of the previous dynasty's position.

And in terms of the Chinese *umwelt* during the seventeenth and eighteenth centuries, such an elevated opinion of themselves was entirely justified. All nations and states surrounding China did acknowledge their suzerainty – and Chinese architecture, literature, technology and ethics were all arguably superior to that of their smaller neighbours. Knowledge of the West and its civilisation was limited and distorted through the lens of China's confidence in its own superiority. Even in the mid-1800s there were maps extant showing China as a nation of enormous proportions, with other states such as Britain and the United States represented as tiny islands at the very edges and the African continent rating no mention whatsoever (present-day maps of the world in the People's Republic continue the tradition by placing China centre-stage). One commentary names Great Britain the 'Red-Hair Nation', and allows it second place after China, owing to the people's 'sharp practice' and shrewdness: 'Its people are mostly clever, proud by nature and unwilling to be subordinate.'[7]

The Chinese had known of the existence of nations and empires far to the west of their borders for more than two thousand years. News of the Roman Empire (or at least its eastern segment), known to the Chinese as Ta-tsin and, later, Fu-lin, was carried via Parthia to the Middle Kingdom around the time of Christ.[8] Nestorian Christians later brought their version of the faith to China via the Silk Route, followed by merchants and priests like Marco Polo, Michel Roger and Matteo Ricci.[9] But these were all individual travellers, welcome for the curiosities of Western culture that they carried with them, and as curiosities themselves. Later arrivals, such as the Jesuits, proved the superiority of Western mathematics and astronomy, and their knowledge was avidly incorporated into the Chinese corpus. When the sea-borne nations of Europe, Portugal, Britain and France arrived to trade in larger numbers at the beginning of the nineteenth century, the Chinese were at first disdainful. For the scholar-officials, merchants were beneath contempt, and trading not an activity from which status or even wealth were to be drawn. As a kindness to the Western barbarians, and like the Indian and Arab traders who had preceded them, they allowed the Europeans access to Chinese markets via the port of Canton, but only under very restrictive ordinances. They were not allowed to enter Canton proper, but as traders, or factors, were confined to 'factories' in a small compound set aside for them outside the city walls. No official contact was permitted: the Westerners were forced to use 'compradors', specially assigned Chinese merchants who acted as go-betweens, doing business in China proper on behalf of the barbarians. In this way, what little benefit the Chinese could obtain from the Westerners was extracted while they themselves were kept at arm's length. By such means the mandarins insulated their nation from outside influences. China remained essentially unchanged and unchanging, self-sufficient, and secure in its ignorant self-confidence. Even as late as 1816, during Lord Amherst's embassy to the Forbidden City, the Emperor could still be shocked and surprised at the bickering that resulted from the Englishman's refusal to perform the kowtow (kneeling and 'knocking head' nine times in token of respectful submission). Presents brought by the British as symbols of friendship between one monarch and another were viewed by the Chinese as tribute from a vassal state. The edict issued by Emperor Chia Ch'ing at the end of the embassy is a wonderful example of this surpassing arrogance:

Imperial Mandate to the King of England

Whereas your country, lying far beyond the wide seas, was sincerely desirous of attaining the blessings of civilisation … you sent a special mission to pay homage.

You live at such a great distance from the Middle Kingdom that these Embassies must cause you considerable inconvenience. Your envoys, moreover, are wholly ignorant of Chinese ceremonial procedure, and the bickering which follows their arrival is highly displeasing to my ears. My dynasty attaches no value to products from abroad; your nation's cunningly wrought and strange wares do not appeal to me in the least, nor do they interest me.

For the future, O King, … pray do not trouble to dispatch missions all this distance; they are merely a waste of time and have their journey for nothing. If you loyally accept our sovereignty and show dutiful submission, there is really no need for these yearly appearances at our court to prove that you are indeed our vassal.

We issue this mandate to the end that you may perpetually comply therewith.

It was a culture clash of prodigious proportions. On the one hand were the industrial revolutionaries of the West, awash to the gunwales with manufactured goods in need of a market, and avid for tea, lacquerwork, silk, enamel and the many other aspects of chinoiserie then in vogue in Europe. Like the adherents of 'globalisation' at the end of the twentieth century, the

Europeans believed in 'free trade', in the free movement of goods around the world (controlled only by appropriate regulations and tariffs). Traders, provided they paid reasonable tax and customs duties, must be allowed to trade where and when they pleased, unfettered by too much 'red tape'. Free trade plus Christianity were seen as the shock-troops of civilisation, spreading the blessings of 'progress' to benighted natives across the globe.

Set against them was the agrarian-scholar society of Confucius, supremely confident in its own superiority and neither valuing nor needing any 'blessings' from the West. Trade was not seen as the lifeblood of the nation, and merchants were ranked towards the lower end of the social scale. The idea of commercial or mercantile law was foreign to the Chinese mind. Trade was looked on with suspicion, its only value lying in the 'squeeze' that could be extorted for the government (or for unscrupulous officials) from the mercantile class. China was self-sufficient, uninterested in innovation and, as Emperor Chia Ch'ing had stated, 'attaches no value to products from abroad'.

But the Emperor was wrong. There was one product to which the Chinese attached great value.

Opium.

CHAPTER SIX

The Emperor flees

S trangely, while we all conceive of opium as a drug of the exotic East, it was first discovered and domesticated during prehistoric times in the Mediterranean Basin. Opium was traded regularly between Cyprus and Egypt in the second millennium BC, and is listed in Greek medical texts between 300 and 400 BC. As the drug does not appear in Chinese pharmacopoeiae until the eighth century AD, some eleven hundred years later, it is believed that Chinese knowledge of opium came from the West, via established trade routes through the Near East to India and thence to the Middle Kingdom.

While the medicinal properties of opium were well understood, it was not until the 1400s that its 'recreational use' was first discovered, in either Persia or India. And as use of the drug was addictive, the commercial possibilities were soon recognised. During the reign of the Mughal Emperor Akbar (1556–1605) vast areas were placed under cultivation in the Ganges valley in Bengal, and in western India at Malwa, close to the city of Bombay. These two regions were still growing the 'best' opium when Yehonala entered the Forbidden City and would continue to produce the drug long after she had died.

In China, recreational use of opium was almost unknown, and the drug remained primarily medicinal until the arrival of the first Europeans, the Portuguese. These daring sailors, and the Spanish and Dutch who followed them, were eager to find a commodity other than gold or silver to trade for the Chinese silk they had travelled so far to buy. These products had made China a 'tomb of European moneys' since Roman times.[1] In the sixteenth century, as much as twenty per cent of all silver mined in Spanish America came directly across the Pacific to Manila and thence to China to pay for silks and porcelains. No less than 345,000 kilograms of silver were brought to the Middle Kingdom in 1597 alone, more silver than China herself could produce in fifty years.[2] In desperation, the Spanish and Portuguese carried tobacco half-way around the world from their Brazilian colonies in the hope that the heathen Chinese would become addicted to the dubious pleasures of nicotine. The plan failed, but the pipe that was introduced along with tobacco proved to be the key: when the Chinese tried smoking tobacco in combination with Indian opium they were quite literally hooked, and suddenly they could not get enough of the 'Western smoke'. The opium habit spread rapidly throughout the Celestial Kingdom, causing the authorities such disquiet that in 1729 the Emperor Yung Chen issued an edict banning the drug and condemning the practice as barbarous.

But neither the Indian merchants (who held a monopoly on the Bengal opium supply), nor the European mercantile fleets (who carried the drug from India to China) would allow the Emperor's commands to hold them back from such rich pickings. The Dutch soon joined the Portuguese in these tropical waters and, once they had established a permanent presence in Indonesia, at Jakarta, they began feeding opium to Java's newly addicted populace, realising enormous profits of four hundred per cent on each shipment. They also discovered that native ships would visit Jakarta to buy opium for distribution in China and elsewhere along the coast. Between 1660 and 1685 the Dutch East India Company's imports of opium rose from 0.6 metric tons to 72.3 metric tons, an astonishing 12,050 per cent increase in just twenty-five years. Sales to China were especially high in later years, prompting the Emperor Yung Chen's ban on the drug in 1729. In retrospect, the ban may well have been a mistake. It merely made the product harder to obtain and so drove up the price, which in turn made it more profitable for the Indians and Europeans to flout Chinese law and smuggle more opium into the Middle Kingdom. Some scholars believe that it might have been better to legalise the drug and to allow it to be grown within China (as was later done on a massive scale). That strategy would have reduced prices, destroyed the incentive for continued smuggling, and perhaps maintained opium consumption at bearable levels.[3]

The British changed the face of the opium trade when 'John Company' (the British East India Company) sent troops inland from Calcutta and, in 1764, conquered opium-rich Bengal. Within nine years they had ousted the native cartel, and set up their own monopoly in the trade, controlling opium farming, merchandising and international trade in the product. But the British East India Company at least limited exports to 4,000 chests (280 tons), which brought in just enough revenue for them to purchase China's tea crop – and so make a further handsome profit selling 'cha' to the caffeine-addicted British.[4] This commercial paradise lasted for more than fifty years. But once the Company's monopoly lapsed, in 1834, there was a further explosion in the trade, up from around four hundred tons to a staggering 2,558 tons in 1840. The profits were enormous. Throughout the 1800s, opium provided between six and fifteen per cent of British India's tax revenues, and helped finance the establishment of the British 'Raj'. The British government needed this source of wealth. It stopped at nothing to encourage the sale of opium to China, and well into the nineteenth century Britain can rightly be accused of state-sponsored drug trafficking.

In 1838, when Yehonala was still a babe in arms, the incumbent Emperor Tao Kwang, fearful of the haemorrhage of silver bullion from his nation's coffers, and the growing inventory of Chinese addicts, launched an anti-opium crusade that for a while seemed capable of halting illicit import. He charged his most honest and forthright commissioner, Lin Zexu, with the task of cleaning up Canton, the most intractable of the opium-importing areas. Lin confiscated over twenty thousand chests of opium, confined the barbarians in their 'factories' on the outskirts of the city, and demanded that each provide a signed document swearing that they would never again smuggle opium into China. The British responded to this reasonable request for foreigners to respect Chinese laws by dispatching six warships to the region, bombarding and capturing Canton in May 1839. Negotiations on a peace treaty dragged on between the two sides for years, with the Emperor refusing in 1841 to sign the first treaty that had been drawn up. The British fleet was then moved to threaten Nanking, the 'southern capital', at which point the Chinese capitulated. This First Opium War ended with the Treaty of Nanking in 1842, China abjectly agreeing to almost every British demand. Hong Kong was ceded to Britain 'in perpetuity', the British were paid a huge indemnity, and five more coastal towns were opened to 'free trade'. The Chinese were forced to accede to 'extraterritoriality' (foreigners accused of crimes in China were to be tried by their own countrymen) and to recognise the concept of 'most favoured nation' (where any agreement between China and one of the European Powers immediately applied to all of them). But still the Emperor refused to rescind the opium prohibition. Nor would he agree to meet any foreign representatives or ambassadors in Beijing.

This last European demand was considered by the Chinese as a great affront and of much more moment than the opium question. For the foreigners were adamant that they would not perform the traditional obeisance, the three prostrations and nine *ketau* (kowtows), before the Son of Heaven. This refusal verged on the blasphemous for the Chinese and it had been a point of contention between the Middle Kingdom and other nations for more than a thousand years. As early as AD 713 an Arabian envoy from the Caliph Walid asked to be excused from prostrating himself before the Tang Emperor Hsuan Tsung, stating[5] 'In my country we only worship Heaven, we never do a Prince.' He was instantly handed over for execution 'for seeking to commit an unpardonable breach of the usages of the country'. While the unfortunate envoy was later pardoned and sent back to his own country, the incident reveals the depth and gravity with which the Chinese viewed the question of the kowtow. Just as a single sun presided over the sky, so a single prince, their Emperor, held sway over all terrestrial creation. To their mind, it was simply right and fitting that emissaries from subordinate kings and princes should kowtow to the Celestial Prince. Such obeisance was a logical and natural extension of a culture where each layer of society kowtowed to those above. They simply could not abandon this principle, which acted as the glue holding the whole of Chinese society together.

For their part, the Western nations were equally adamant. Their *umwelt* was based upon the concept of nation states, sovereign and equal. And, for reasons of economics and of principle, they were determined that their ambassadors, the representatives of the Western heads of state, must meet with the Emperor on equal terms – there must be no talk of kowtowing.

In southern China, far from the Forbidden City and the true centres of power, the Western traders remained unperturbed by this recondite diplomatic brouhaha. Nor were they concerned that opium trading was still illegal. Demand was brisk, and they soon discovered ways of shipping their product to their customers. It was carried from India to the Chinese coast in European ships, and transferred, just below Canton City, in the estuary of the Pearl River, to Chinese smuggling boats nicknamed 'fast crabs' and 'scrambling dragons', whence, via myriad Chinese trading networks and with the connivance of bribable mandarins, it was carried far into mainland China. Business blossomed after the Treaty of Nanking, with opium shipments climbing to a peak of 4,810 tons in 1858.

Long before then, in 1850, Emperor Tao Kwang had died, and the Hsien Feng Emperor had ascended to the Dragon Throne, setting in motion the long train of events that would lead to Yehonala's fateful call to the Forbidden City. Yehonala's ignorance of the foreigners was profound, but like most of the Manchu elite, this did not prevent her from regarding them with contempt. Once she had attained the title of Empress of the Western Palace, and had secured her power base and rid herself of her enemies, she would become one of the most vociferous advocates of abrogating the unequal treaties. Nor was she afraid of the consequences. If the Western barbarians continued with their unreasonable and sacrilegious demands, then in her arrogance and conceited naivety, she believed that the Chinese forces would inevitably sweep the 'long-noses' into the sea.

Another of the periodic crises between the Middle Kingdom and the West occurred in 1856 when Chinese sailors boarded the *Arrow* and arrested twelve Chinese members of its crew for piracy, ignoring the fact that the vessel was British-registered and captained by a British national.[6] This relatively minor incident was seized upon as a pretext by the British government: despite the fact that the *Arrow*'s registration had lapsed eleven days before the incident occurred. Harry Parkes, the British Consul in Hong Kong, demanded an apology. Yeh Ming-chen, the stubborn and intransigent governor of Canton, refused, and dug his country an even deeper political hole by denying that the British flag had ever been flown on the *Arrow*. For the British this response was a godsend: gunboats were immediately dispatched to avenge the insult to Queen and Country. They 'opened' Canton to free trade by bombarding the city into submission and carrying off its governor to India, where he subsequently died.

But the British were not satisfied. Aided by the French (who had a pretext of their own in the murder of a French missionary in Guanxi Province) Palmerston sent James Bruce, the eighth Earl of Elgin, to demand reparations and to force revisions to the recent treaty, giving the European powers even greater advantages within the Chinese mainland. The French emissary was the nobleman Baron Jean-Baptiste-Louis Gros, whose slow progress from France caused Lord Elgin much frustration. But finally, in October 1857, a full year after the *Arrow* incident had taken place, the combined fleet of Britain and France were ready to sail north to Tientsin, the coastal port guarding the approaches to Beijing and the Emperor. The red barbarians were coming to demand an audience with the Solitary Prince within his sanctum of the Forbidden City. And they had no intention of kowtowing.

In Beijing, this news was heard with mounting apprehension. The Chinese had wanted the *Arrow* incident treated as a provincial matter, but the Europeans had blown it up into an event of international importance. Despite this, the Manchu still chose to see the whole affair as the intransigent behaviour of far-off vassal states who were unwilling to bow to the lawful will of the Son of Heaven. Yehonala was foremost among the ranks of the war party, counselling the Emperor to show no mercy to the barbarian 'rebels'. By contrast, Prince Kung, the Emperor's brother, felt that the *Arrow* affair was of no real moment. He was more concerned with the Tai Ping 'bandits', referring to the still-blazing rebellion as a possible fatal disease of China's body. The Russians, greedy for land and threatening the Middle Kingdom from the north, he considered a threat to the bosom; while the sea-borne nations, and especially Britain, he regarded as merely 'an affliction of the limbs', an annoyance and an irritation, but nothing more. 'Therefore we should suppress the ... bandits first, get the Russians under control next, and attend to the British last.'[7] The Manchu elite continued to cling to their dreams of barbarian inferiority – they still had no real conception of what they were facing in the eastward push of Western imperialism.

In May 1858 the combined British and French fleet, numbering twenty-six gunboats (and with the Americans in tow ostensibly as disinterested 'observers') dropped anchor before the Taku forts, four squat crenellated bastions sited athwart the mouth of the Baihe River, guarding the principal waterway to the Chinese capital. In Beijing, Yehonala and the war party were pushing for the mounting of a strong defence against the European powers, whom they still affected to regard as presumptuous tributaries. On 20th May the allies stormed the forts and to general surprise, both Chinese and European, the defences immediately collapsed. There was consternation in Beijing. Yehonala still called for war to the knife against the barbarian, but Hsien Feng heeded wiser counsels and immediately sent two high-ranking mandarins, Kuei Liang and Hua Sha-na to Tientsin to negotiate. Their brief was ostensibly to come to a 'reasonably and mutually advantageous peace' and 'to agree nothing detrimental to China', but in reality they were there to stonewall and delay and to do everything in their power to prevent the arrival in Beijing of the French and English 'ambassadors'. The Manchu knew that the Western emissaries would refuse to kowtow to the Son of Heaven, and that they would demand the right of residence in Beijing. Both were anathema to the Chinese: nothing would so irretrievably destroy the myth of Imperial omnipotence upon which the whole of Chinese society (and their own oligarchical privileges) depended.

After days of negotiation, while Lord Elgin worried and chafed, and Baron Gros affected an air of unconcern, the Chinese grudgingly conceded all the demands of the Powers save two, which the Dynasty regarded as non-negotiable: the right of residence in Beijing and permission for foreign merchants to trade freely on the Yangtse River and in the interior. But the British were unmoved by the numerous concessions and continued to press for total capitulation on all points. So desperate did the two mandarin negotiators become, they showed the American and Russian emissaries their death warrants, claiming the documents would be enforced immediately should they grant any further British demands. Baron Gros was later approached and asked to intercede on their behalf. Elgin's reply, on 26th June, was to declare that he was ready to march on the capital and install the ambassadors at gun-point. The Chinese begged more time while they sent desperate messages to Beijing informing them of the ultimatum. Despite the continuing resistance of Yehonala and other die-hards at court, the more realistic ministers realised that, with their modern equipment and training, the British were quite capable of carrying out their threat. Negotiations were over. It was concede or fight.

Wisely, the Chinese conceded. The Treaty of Tientsin was signed on 26th June and now, it seemed, everyone agreed that the red barbarians were coming to the Forbidden City where they would be received in audience by the Son of Heaven *without* the obligatory kowtow. For the Manchu elite, this one disastrous fact overrode all other considerations. It struck at the heart of their self-esteem, and they twisted like snakes to avoid the destruction of their carefully orchestrated charade of world hegemony – the myth of earth-encircling supremacy that had awed the 'stupid people' of the Middle Kingdom and maintained their power, and that of former dynasties, for

millennia. After further delays the two sides met again and
the Chinese played their final card. It was suggested that the
ambassadors waive their right of residence and in return the
Chinese would annul all trade duties on foreign goods. This
was an enormous concession – trade duties contributed much
to the Chinese exchequer – and bore witness to the overriding
importance the Manchu Dynasty attached to the ritual aspects
of their rule. To general relief and not a little surprise, Lord
Elgin agreed, stipulating only that the *theoretical* right of residence be upheld. In private, this was a great relief to the British
– now that it finally looked as if they would get everything
they wanted, they had suddenly realised how dangerous was
the position of a British resident in Beijing: 'Peking would be a
rat trap for the envoy if the Chinese meant mischief'.[8]

For their part, the Chinese were elated and relieved. From
the Manchu vantage point, victory had been snatched from
the jaws of defeat. True, they had agreed to a Beijing ambassa-
dorial visit the following year to ratify the new treaty, when the
question of the Imperial kowtow would again arise. But the
Chinese ruling class were masters of prevarication, and like
all good politicians, knew that nothing was certain in this
world, and much might happen in the space of twelve months
to alter or even cancel the planned visit. The Emperor and his
ministers breathed easier, and the disconsolate spirit of the
court revived to wallow in its accustomed vainglorious and
insolent ignorance. Once again, Chinese wisdom had kept the
barbarian from the gates of the Middle Kingdom.

And so, the Manchu courtiers were granted another brief
respite from the unwelcome attentions of the foreign devils.
They must have realised that time was not on their side, that
there was a very good chance that the *Ying-guo-ren* and the
Fa-guo-ren would return in their huge ships with their modern
guns and weaponry. Yet like the Ming nobles before them, as
soon as the threat had receded, the Manchu returned to their
traditional pursuits, following the rites and traditions of their
ancient culture, acting out the charade of world hegemony
and, seemingly, in some way still believing it. Slowly, the year
turned, and while the Tai Ping rebellion flamed across much of

southern China, no great international drama erupted to turn the attention of the Western Powers elsewhere. As 1858 passed into 1859 word arrived that the British and French were again on the South China Sea, and preparing to sail north to ratify the previous year's treaty in Beijing. The Chinese were running out of time. Their demands that ratification take place in Shanghai were ignored. Towards the middle of the year, on 18th June 1859, the British and French fleets, led by Frederick Bruce (Lord Elgin's younger brother) and Emperor Napoleon III's minister, M. de Bourbulon, hove into view at the mouth of the Baihe River. American gunboats, again ostensibly neutral, accompanied the fleet under Commodore Josiah Tattnall.

Nothing went according to plan. Instead of striking their colours when faced with superior Western technology, the Chinese batteries in the forts brought a heavy fire to bear on the allied gunboats. Four ships were sunk, and one, the *Plover*, suffered terrible casualties, with thirty men and her commander killed out of a crew of forty. Despite the carnage around them, the remaining nine seamen refused to give up, and continued to fire their guns against overwhelming odds. Commodore Tattnall, supposedly neutral, felt that he could not watch the slaughter of such brave men and sailed in under fire to offer his help and take off the British wounded. Later that day he discovered several of his own sailors black with powder smoke. 'What have you been doing, you rascals?' he demanded. 'Beg pardon, sir,' was the reply, 'but they were a bit short-handed with the bow gun.' Tattnall was equally direct when stating his reasons for committing this diplomatic gaffe: 'Blood,' he said bluntly, 'is thicker than water.'[9]

This Chinese victory over the Western barbarian 'rebels' was greeted with jubilation in Beijing. At long last the big-nosed curs had been sent packing, scurrying homewards with their tails between their legs. It was just the fillip that Yehonala and the 'war party' of hardline Manchu councillors needed. The civil war against the Tai Ping rebels had been going badly, but now the Dragon Throne had struck back against its enemies with a vengeance. The barbarians would think twice before again confronting the might of the Middle Kingdom.

For a while it appeared that the Chinese reading of the situation was correct, and that this defeat truly had left the British and French with little stomach for further Chinese adventures. The less bellicose Americans had fared much better at Chinese hands during the fracas, at least in the beginning. They had landed, as requested by the Chinese, at Pei-t'ang and been received with the polite dignity that custom demanded. But from there matters went rapidly downhill. The Americans had been required to suffer the humiliation of travelling the hundred and fifteen miles to Beijing in rude, springless carts. It was an opportunity to show the populace how humble and servile were these emissaries from the 'flowery state' and the mandarins played this card for all they were worth. But the American's journey, while less bloody than the European's ill-starred attempt to see the Son of Heaven, proved just as fruitless. The Chinese, puffed up with pride, demanded that the visitors kowtow before the Celestial Prince. The republican US envoys were incensed: they had fought a revolution to avoid bending the knee to an English king; they were in no mind to prostrate themselves and 'knock head' to a Chinese monarch. Nothing daunted, when the Americans finally left their shores, the Middle Kingdom chroniclers recorded the event as the departure of 'tribute bearer Ward'.

Nothing, it seemed, had changed.

But in the empire-building British, the denizens of the Middle Kingdom had found a nation which was perhaps even more sure of their God-given superiority than the Chinese themselves. For three-quarters of a year there was a welcome silence from the red barbarians. Then, in July 1860, they returned in force, landing a combined British/French army of eighteen thousand men at Pei-t'ang, just to the north of the redoubtable Taku forts. In charge were the two old China-hands, Baron Gros and Lord Elgin, come to repair the loss to European prestige, to demand even greater reparations from the Middle Kingdom (sixteen million taels, more than five million pounds), and determined this time to force ratification of the Treaty of Tientsin in Beijing, before the Son of Heaven himself.

The Europeans had learned from the fiasco of their defeat the year before. The main armaments of the Taku forts faced the river, but the landward side was far less well protected. It was here, against the most vulnerable sector of the two bastions on the northern bank of the Baihe, that the British and French forces mounted their attack. The assault was preceded by an artillery barrage that lasted two-and-a-half hours. 'The marines had the honour of forming part of the assaulting party ... The French attacked at a different point and the emulation among the troops to see who, French or English, should be first on the wall was very great. It is difficult to say who was first. Our flag was the first *hoisted*, but a Frenchman had waved a minute or two previously a French flag as he got on the wall, but was shot down ... At 2 or 3 minutes past 8, that is after a stiff engagement that lasted just 3 hours, the fort was won.' Harry Parkes and the rest of the allied command were '... full of admiration for the way in which the Chinese fought their guns. At 6.30 their magazine blew up with a dreadful explosion that for some time hid the whole fort from view and caused a lull in the battle; and yet for an hour after they remained steadily at their guns.' Once inside the forts, they discovered the reason for this suicidal courage. 'The horrors of the scene defy description. No one had been suffered to run from the fort by the Chinese – men being told off to cut down any who attempted to run: indeed all escape was prevented by the fort being barricaded; so they fell where they fought.'[10] At the end of the battle almost fifteen hundred Chinese combatants had lost their lives, for the loss of just thirty-four allied soldiers. The southern forts raised the white flag without a fight, and the Taku forts were once again in the hands of the foreign devils.

At first, the mandarins tried to keep knowledge of this disaster from Beijing's population, but like all 'secrets' in the city, news of the defeat leaked out and was passed by word of mouth through the numerous inns and tea-houses of the capital. One Beijing mandarin, Wu K'o-tu, a member of the prestigious Hanlin Academy, kept a diary during this time of turmoil;[11] it details the personal tragedy of his mother's imminent demise, interspersed with a priceless account of the Chinese view of the conflict and of the rumours sweeping the capital. Especially noticeable is the manner in which Yehonala's ascendancy is taken for granted by Wu K'o-tu, indicating that, by this time, her dominance in the Emperor's counsels was well established and a matter of common knowledge.

In August 1860 Wu noted that 'His Majesty was seriously ill, and it was known that he wished to leave for the north, but the Imperial concubine Yi [one of Yehonala's titles] and Prince Seng dissuaded him from this and assured him that the barbarians would never enter the city ... During the next few days, people began to leave Beijing, for the report was spread that our troops had been defeated at Taku, and that a brigadier-general was among the slain; the garrison had fled from Pei-t'ang and the forts were in the hands of the barbarians ... Nothing was known as to the real cause of our defeat, and the people, being kept in ignorance, gradually got over their first alarm.'

Had they known the full story, the citizens of Beijing might have been more concerned. The Westerners were even then en route to the walled town of Tungchow, where they planned to meet with representatives of the Emperor and conclude the terms of their entrance into Beijing. The Emperor, apparently at Yehonala's behest, sent a new envoy, Chi Ying, on a forlorn assigment to request the barbarians to withdraw. The mission was foredoomed, and all Chi Ying's powers of persuasion failed to move the allies. After he had reported his failure, the unfortunate envoy received a silken cord, symbol of Imperial magnanimity: rather than being beheaded like a common criminal for his failure, Chi Ying was allowed to hang himself. Three new negotiators, all senior mandarins, were now given the task of holding back the barbarians, using the age-old Chinese techniques of bluster and prevarication. This triumvirate also received short shrift from the impatient Western Powers. The advance towards Beijing continued.

An Imperial edict was promulgated soon afterwards which, in its fiery tone and blatant disregard for the truth, again bears the stamp of Yehonala's influence:

Last year the barbarians endeavoured to force the entrance of the Baihe, but in the twinkling of an eye

their ships were sunk and thousands of their bodies
floated on the water for a distance of one league from
shore. I thought that this lesson would have rendered
them more circumspect. But a year after their defeat
they have returned, more numerous and more insolent
than before. Taking advantage of the low tide, they dis-
embarked at Pei-t'ang and then attacked the Taku forts.
But, like true barbarians, they attacked from the rear.
Our soldiers, being accustomed to meet their enemies
face to face, did not expect so much cowardice and perfidy. Proud of a success that ought to make them blush
for shame, they have now attacked Tientsin. My anger is
about to strike and exterminate them without mercy. I
command all my subjects, Chinese and Manchu, to hunt
them down like savage beasts. Let the villages be abandoned as these wretches draw near. Let all provisions be
destroyed which they might secure. In this manner,
their accursed race will perish of hunger, like fish in a
dried-up pond.

On 6th September a new edict again excoriated the barbarians for their perfidy, this time putting a price on the head of
every rebel: '... for the head of a black barbarian, 50 taels [the
British had brought Sikh troops with them from India]; for the
head of a white barbarian, 100 taels.' Still labouring under
the delusion of omnipotence, the edict ended with a promise
of imperial clemency: '... and whensoever the British and
French repent them of their evil ways and return to their allegiance, we shall be pleased to permit them to trade again, as of
old. May they repent while there is yet time.'[12]

Next day, a further pronouncement summarily rejected the
additional reparation the allies had demanded. Much of this
stiffening of Hsien Feng's backbone was undoubtedly due to
Yehonala's reproaches. The Emperor still longed to escape the
crisis by fleeing over the Great Wall to his palace at Jehol,
secure in the heartland of his people. As a conquering race,
the Manchu had always felt insecure in China, and had long
viewed their old home as a safe haven. Up until the reign of

Hsien Feng's father, regular visits had been made to the region, to worship at the shrines of the dynastic ancestors. Even before the coming of the Westerners, the Manchu had laid plans against a successful uprising against their rule. Priceless treasures of all kinds, furs, silks, jades and gems were all hoarded at Mukden, the old Manchurian capital. Astonishing amounts of silver were stored in the old wells of the palace: the precious metal was melted in a clay furnace built over the top of each well, and poured down in a continuous stream until the massive silver cylinder reached the top of the shaft. Once full to the brim, it was capped with cement and a new well selected to repeat the process. They were known as 'silver cheeses', where an ousted Manchu Emperor could nibble away contentedly, paring off his wealth to fund and plan his revenge.[13]

To Yehonala and the war party such thinking was sacrilege. The barbarians would be defeated, what was needed was time to prepare a proper defence. And so the Chinese negotiators procrastinated and delayed, finding endless excuses to hold the Westerners from Beijing and their planned meeting with the Son of Heaven. Elgin's chief negotiators in these interminable discussions, Harry Parkes and Thomas Wade, engaged in endless verbal jousting with the Imperial envoys, slowly stripping away the onion skins of deception until they finally extracted from the three mandarins the confession that, in reality, they were not empowered to agree anything of substance with the Westerners. Exasperated beyond endurance, Elgin ordered the march on Beijing to recommence, advancing his forces rapidly to the amazement of the Chinese, whose huge unwieldy armies could take weeks to complete such a manoeuvre. Fear and consternation once again seized the court. Emperor Hsien Feng vacillated between his duty to his ancestors and his urgent desire to put as much distance as possible between himself and these inconsiderate barbarians who resolutely refused to acknowledge his suzerainty. And yet even Hsien Feng could admit the need for someone to negotiate with the advancing 'rebels' and to attempt to bring them back within the fold of Chinese authority; for despite all evidence to the contrary, the Emperor and the court still clung to the comforting illusion of Chinese world supremacy and continued to view the allied army as recalcitrant subjects who had for the moment slipped the yoke of the Manchu. The throne authorised new, higher-ranking envoys, the Emperor's own cousin Prince I, and Mu Yin, President of the Board of War, to replace the hapless negotiating trio who had been recalled in disgrace, but who, fortunately, in the confusion of the moment were not served with silken cords.

The choice of negotiators signalled a hardening of the Chinese attitude. Prince I was most certainly of the war party, and in firm agreement with Yehonala that no concessions should be made to the Westerners. The allied force was tiny compared to the Manchu army, said to number *in toto* almost half a million men. In addition, the Chinese were led by a capable and agressive general, Seng Guo Lin Sen (who, anglicised as 'Sam Collinson', became something of a mascot to the British squaddies). Moreover, the Westerners were far from their nearest base and with extended supply lines, while the Chinese were fighting for hearth and home. To the Manchu elite and the Chinese literati it appeared inconceivable that the Franco-British forces could prevail. In an attempt to lull the 'rebel' commanders, Prince I and Mu Yin sent placating letters to Lord Elgin, insisting that everything could be settled to his satisfaction. Elgin was having none of it. His forces would continue to advance, to Tungchow, where they might then negotiate the final entry into the city and the audience with the Emperor. This was the last straw for the Chinese: Tungchow was strategically sited, just twelve miles from Beijing, with road and water routes direct to the capital. With Tungchow under their control, nothing could stop the Westerners rolling down to the northern capital and the Great Within. This simply could not be allowed to happen. There was no alternative. It had to be war.

Continuing their strategy of lulling the suspicions of the allies, the Chinese affected to capitulate. Elgin and Baron Gros might ratify the treaty in Beijing they conceded; the Dynasty asked only that they visit the capital with a small honour guard, leaving the bulk of their army where it lay. Elgin shot back with a proposal that his forces halt their advance four miles before Tungchow, at the village of Chang Chia-wan. He and his French counterpart would then travel to Beijing with a one-thousand-man escort, still an impressive number of men, but not sufficient to panic the Chinese population into believing that a conquering army intent on pillage and rapine was advancing on them. Elgin added that, as well as ratifying the treaty, he carried a letter from Queen Victoria to the Chinese Emperor which he intended to hand personally to the the Son of Heaven. In most nations in the nineteenth century, such a letter would have been considered a compliment (indeed it was intended as such, to convey the high regard of the British 'Queen Empress' for her fellow sovereign). In China 'facts were different', and the missive, together with the very personal manner in which it was to be delivered, was construed as the grossest insult. No barbarian, royal or not, could ever be placed on a par with the Celestial Prince. It was unthinkable and intolerable. If the Chinese had entertained second thoughts about the coming conflict, Elgin's reiteration of his intention to deliver this letter wiped all further doubts from their minds. Had the British been actively seeking a confrontation, they could have done nothing better to steel their opponents' resolve for war.

Despite their anger, the Chinese continued to 'hide a dagger in a smile', the tenth of the Classic Thirty-six Strategies: 'reassure the enemy to make it slack, work in secret to subdue it; prepare fully before taking action ... This is the method of hiding a strong will under a compliant appearance.'[14] Prince I and Mu Yin affected agreement to everything, but as September progressed the Chinese Dragon began to move, mobilising its immense army: Mongol and Manchu cavalry, tiger soldiers in black and yellow uniforms, musketeers, jingalmen, cannoneers, and warriors from a score of provinces, all determined to stop the barbarian and prevent loss of face and humiliation of the Son of Heaven.

Had the confrontation occurred twenty years earlier, the issue could hardly have been in doubt. In those days, the weaponry of the two sides would have been far more closely matched and superior numbers would certainly have carried the day.

Until the late 1850s the British army had still been equipped with smooth-bore, muzzle-loading cannon virtually unchanged from the Napoleonic wars. The range and accuracy of these weapons were appalling: the cannon could barely manage to shoot accurately beyond 500–700 metres. The British infantry carried 'Brown Bess' muskets of similar vintage. While their effective range was said officially to be two hundred yards, tests showed that a trained infantryman shooting at this range under perfect firing conditions could hit a 1.75-by-3-metre target with only three out of ten shots. The reason was that the spherical musket-ball was made loose-fitting (to increase firing rate) with the result that it bounced its way down the barrel, the final bounce effectively defining its trajectory. Accuracy was quite simply a matter of luck. If Lord Elgin's embassy had taken place even four years earlier, Chinese numerical superiority would have easily overwhelmed enemy troops equipped with such slow-firing, inaccurate firearms.

But in the few years prior to the 1860 China campaign, something of a revolution had occurred in European weaponry, beginning with the introduction of the Delvigne-Minié bullet, which could be loaded quickly but which, on firing expanded to completely fill the musket barrel, drastically reducing loss of power from the propellant gases and increasing the range of the weapon. There was a second advantage: a missile in contact with the barrel of the gun allowed for 'rifling' (the cutting of a spiral groove in the barrel), so that the bullet emerged from the weapon with a spin that held it on target. The result was innovative and deadly.

Against this, the Chinese were equipped with firearms that were hopelessly obsolete. Many of their cannon were of ancient design, and fired stone shot; their muskets were for the most part matchlocks, having a burning taper which ignited the gunpowder when the trigger was pulled – a design which had not been seen in Europe since the early 1500s. Some of their cavalry still boasted plate armour – excellent protection when facing spears and arrows, but of no avail against the high-velocity Enfield rifle or the metal shards of the Armstrong gun's exploding shells.

On 18th September a joint Franco-British party, headed by Harry Parkes as interpreter and Henry Loch, private secretary to Lord Elgin, rode to Tungchow to settle with Prince I and Mu Yin the final details of the allies' 'visit' to Beijing. All seemed to be going smoothly, until they came to the question of Queen Victoria's letter to the Emperor. This was a sticking-point with the Chinese and the meeting went rapidly downhill, Prince I screaming, 'There can be no peace!' and 'It must be war!', all pretence of amicable discussion thrown to the winds. Unsettled, the Europeans left the Chinese camp. But as they returned to report the new Chinese position to Lord Elgin, they suddenly became aware of cannon batteries hidden in the man-high fields of millet surrounding Chang Chia-wan, where the allied army was to make its camp and await the return of Elgin and Baron Gros from their audience with the Emperor. On closer inspection, Manchu bannermen and Chinese infantry were found to have been deployed in great numbers all around the campsite. The Chinese general Seng Guo Lin Sen had made Chang Chia-wan a killing ground.

Incensed by this treachery, Parkes immediately fashioned an improvised flag of truce, fastening a kerchief to the lance of one of his Sikh *sowars*, and with his escort around him turned once more and pressed forward through the Chinese troops in an attempt to find 'Sam Collinson' and defuse the situation. The mood was ugly – the Emperor's edict offering a reward for every barbarian head had already been promulgated. Seeing the white flag, a Chinese officer intervened and volunteered to escort them to General Seng for an official safe-conduct. Parkes readily agreed, and together with his men rode confidently into the general's camp. But while the allies saw themselves as under a flag of truce, and as envoys of a foreign power due all the protection of diplomatic convention, to Seng they were simply rebels; and against such men all means were just. Parkes and his entire entourage were subjected to a torrent of verbal abuse from Seng, before being dragged from their horses and trussed up with their arms behind their backs and their wrists tied to their ankles – the traditional method of binding captured rebels. Seng ordered them thrown on carts and carried off to Beijing. There seems to have been a concerted plan to capture as many 'barbarians' as possible. In all, some thirty-nine allied prisoners – twenty-six British and thirteen French – were taken within the space of a few hours, all of them bound and transported in carts to Beijing.

It does not seem that the Emperor had given direct orders to detain any of the Europeans. News of their capture produced panic in the ailing, vacillating monarch and his entourage, and it was only the steadying hand of Yehonala that kept the ship of state afloat. According to the diarist Wu K'o-tu:

> ... our troops captured the barbarian leader Pa Hsia-li [Sir Harry Parkes] together with eight others, who were imprisoned in the board of punishments. Thereupon the whole city was in an uproar, and it became known that His Majesty was preparing to leave on a tour northwards [i.e. flee the city]. But the Concubine Yi persuaded some of the older officials to memorialise, urging him to remain ... All the Manchu and Chinese officials were now sending their families away and their valuables, but the large shops outside the main gate were doing business as usual.

At the time, the extent of the ill-treatment of the allied prisoners was not realised. But the very fact that they had been treacherously taken while under a flag of truce was enough to galvanise the Franco-British forces into action. They moved forward swiftly towards Beijing. Between them and the capital lay Seng's Chinese army, some thirty to fifty thousand strong, buzzing with hatred for the foreign devils and eager for combat.

The decisive encounter took place at Ba Li Gao ('Eight Li Bridge', three 'Li' being approximately one English mile). The bridge straddled the main waterway that ran from Tungchow to the capital, and it was here that the Chinese arrayed their forces and awaited the onslaught of the allied army. Seng Guo Lin Sen was a capable commander: his artillery had been deployed in the woodlands and on the heights, and his infantry were drawn up in serried ranks, their multi-hued dragon and tiger banners fluttering above them, barring the way to Ba Li Gao. But the Mongol general's main hope rested with the mass of veteran Tartar cavalry that he planned to use as a mailed fist to drive through the heart of the allied ranks. When, to the sound of bugles and the skirl of pipes, the British and French had advanced to within two miles of the bridge, Seng launched his phalanx of Tartars at the 'rebels'.[15] The Tartars charged in silence, changing formation skilfully by means of flags and without the use of shouted commands. The allied artillery (which ironically included rockets, first invented by the Chinese) cut swathes in their ranks but they closed and came forward relentlessly, ignoring the massed rifle fire from the lines of infantry. Had the Tartars been supported with accurate artillery to suppress their opponent's fire, the outcome may well have been different. But the Chinese gunners fired high, and did not bother to correct their aim. In terrible contrast, the allied artillerymen struck with fatal precision, cutting down the horse soldiers and sweeping away the ranks of infantry behind them. 'We could see deep furrows opening within the enemy's dense masses of men and horses. The attack gradually turned into a retreat, and the cavalry fell back towards the bridge.'[16] General Sheng Pao, the Chinese commander on the bridge, was among the casualties. A shell from an Armstrong gun blew away his jaw. Howling for revenge he had two of the European prisoners, Abbé de Luc and Captain Brabazon of the Royal Artillery, pulled out of their temporary jail, dragged to the parapet of the bridge, and summarily beheaded. The Chinese later gave out that the pair had died from natural causes, but several months later, two headless bodies were discovered in shallow graves. One body retained traces of British army-issue cloth; the other, black silk identical to that worn by the unfortunate French priest.

The Tartars held together for seven hours of desperate fighting before Ba Li Gao. But under the relentless, withering fire of the allied guns they eventually broke and fled northwards over the bridge, following the rest of Seng's army, which had begun to draw off into the fastness of the Chinese countryside.

But even as the remnants of the Chinese army fell back towards Beijing and the embattled Emperor, a more sinister, silent battle continued to rage around the Dragon Throne. The Manchu Dynasty might not survive the onslaught of the red barbarians (no one at court was sure if their apparent desire only to trade merely masked a desire to conquer the Middle Kingdom). But assuming that the regime did survive, or was forced into exile in its Manchu homeland north of the Great Wall, the question of who would rule after Emperor Hsien Feng was yet to be decided. Would supreme power lie with Yehonala and her allies, or with the cabal of nobles headed by her arch-enemy, Su Shun?

It is possible that Yehonala's strident anti-foreign rhetoric and her insistence that the Emperor remain in Beijing was motivated far less by patriotic fervour than simple self-interest. While the Emperor remained in the capital, the strict etiquette of the Great Within made it difficult for other males to gain an audience with the Son of Heaven. By contrast, as the Emperor's favourite and mother of his only male heir, Yehonala enjoyed almost unrestricted access to the Presence. She could use all her feminine wiles to persuade and cajole the ailing monarch into siding with her faction and opposing her rival Su Shun. It followed that Yehonala's position was immensely strengthened by Hsien Feng's remaining in the city, while her influence would be greatly weakened, perhaps fatally, should the Emperor move to a less formal residence beyond the Great Wall. At all costs, he must be dissuaded from leaving the capital.

When the allied soldiers reached the outskirts of Beijing there was an engagement outside the Chi Hua gate of the city, which resulted in another defeat for Chinese arms. According to the diarist:

> Many were trampled to death ... our men fleeing in every direction and the barbarians pressing on to the city walls. Certain Princes and ministers besought the Concubine Yi to induce the Emperor to leave on a tour, but the Concubine Yi persuaded two of the Grand Secretaries to memorialise against his doing so, and in response to this a decree

was issued stating that under no circumstances would the Emperor leave his capital. Another decree was put out by the Concubine Yi offering large rewards to any who should slay the barbarians It was generally thought that the Emperor would now forgo his intended departure.

Early the next morning another battle was fought outside the Chi Hua Gate, and again the Emperor's troops were bested. This final defeat of the Chinese forces, combined with the astonishingly rapid advance of the 'rebels' on Beijing had changed everything. Hsien Feng's backbone dissolved, and Yehonala's pleas to defy the barbarians fell on deaf ears. Worse, by identifying herself so strongly with the policy of 'no surrender' against the foreigners, a stratagem that had failed so conspicuously and so grievously as far as Hsien Feng was concerned, Yehonala had gravely weakened her influence over the dying monarch. As soon as the news of this second defeat reached the Summer Palace, where Hsien Feng had set up his court, pandemonium ensued: 'His Sacred Majesty, attended by all his concubines, the Princes, Ministers and Dukes, and all the officers of the Household, left the city in a desperate rout and disorder unspeakable, affording a spectacle that gave the impression that hordes of barbarians were already in close pursuit. As a matter of fact, the foreigners were still at a considerable distance …' (Wu K'o-tu).

The court's journey northwards must have filled Yehonala with shame and foreboding. Her careful and increasingly desperate schemes to keep the Emperor in Beijing lay in tatters. Notwithstanding her status as mother of the heir, Yehonala's once unassailable position as the Emperor's favourite was now seriously in question. Her influence over Hsien Feng was waning rapidly. She had counselled defiance of the barbarian and disaster had ensued. Hsien Feng's blatant lack of courage and shameful, ignominious flight reminded everyone of the dishonourable departure of an Emperor of the Chou Dynasty, who fled the capital 'his head covered with dust'. That the Yi Concubine had been foremost in outspoken condemnation of the flight into Manchuria made many think, as one European diplomat later commented, that Yehonala 'was the only man in China'. Such sentiments did nothing to endear her to the weak and vacillating Emperor, whose loss of face increased in proportion with her continuing demands for resistance. Nor were her enemies slow to take advantage of her reverses.

Compounding her misery, the court had fled in such haste and disorder that Yehonala suddenly realised that she had lost possession of her most precious asset, her son the heir. As the unwieldy dragon's tail of covered carts and palanquins lumbered northwards along the highway, turned to mud by the autumn rains, Yehonala's trusted eunuchs and servants searched desperately for the boy, at the same time her only child, and her surest passport to safety. If Su Shun or any of his faction had managed to secure possession of the heir, Yehonala's room for manoeuvre would be severely curtailed. After what must have seemed an age, word was brought to her that the boy was safe. His aunt, the Empress of the Eastern Palace, Yehonala's cousin Sakota, had him safely with her in her royal litter.

With the heir safe, Yehonala could take stock of the situation. There was no doubt that her position became more perilous with every additional mile they marched from Beijing. But she had the heir. And there was one additional asset she could rely on. By chance, in the escort selected to accompany the Son of Heaven on his 'northern tour' (as it was euphemistically termed later) was a substantial proportion of bannermen from the Yeho-Nala clan. Their loyalty could be counted on, to the death. So too could the fidelity of their commander. The leader of the escort was a tall young captain: Jung Lu, Yehonala's betrothed, before her call to the Great Within.

CHAPTER SEVEN

Acts of barbarism

*A*fter their victories against the Chinese army, the main allied force circled to the north-east of Beijing, hoping to regain contact with the retreating enemy. For a while, the British advance lagged behind the French forces who, on the night of 6th October, fetched up against the imposing walls of some large enclosure, with the needle-like silhouette of three large pagodas limned faintly against the night sky. It was too dark to see much more but, as they bivouacked close to the wall, the shadowy forms of Chinese peasants were observed using ladders to break into the land behind the wall. Intrigued, the French investigated, following the Chinese and finding themselves unexpectedly in fairyland, in the *Yuan Ming Yuan*, the 'Round Bright Garden', the huge and exclusive pleasure garden of China's Emperors.

The Summer Palace, as it came to be known, had been begun in 1709, in the time of the famous Emperor K'ang Hsi and added to by successive Sons of Heaven, notably the Ch'ien Lung Emperor. Its grounds covered at least sixty thousand acres, filled with rare and outlandish creatures from around the Empire, including exotic goldfish, pheasants, raptors and the *ssu-pu-hsiang* 'the four aspects that do not mix', a creature said to possess the tail of a donkey, hooves of a cow, neck of a camel and the antlers of a stag, known today as Père David's deer. Within the Summer Palace lay thirty palaces and lodges, each with its attached village for the Son of Heaven's guards, eunuchs and household staff. The Imperial buildings had been constructed in various styles, including, bizarrely, a European Baroque Palace, built by the Jesuit fathers who

served at Ch'ien Lung's court. For all their architectural symmetry, it was not in the beauty of the buildings themselves
that the true charm and fascination of the Yuan Ming Yuan
lay, but in the location of these structures within the landscape. The whole area had been lovingly designed, meticulously sculptured by thousands of labourers, to resemble
the most beauteous and harmonious scenic views that the
human mind could conceive – art concealing art on an
almost superhuman scale. According to an English visitor in
1793 there was an

> abundance of canals, rivers and large sheets of water,
> whose banks, although artificial, are neither trimmed,
> nor shorn, nor sloped like the glacis of a fortification, but
> have been thrown up with immense labour in an irre-
> gular and, as it were, fortuitous manner, so as to repre-
> sent the free hand of nature ... The views appear to have
> been studied; the trees were not only placed according
> to their magnitude, but the tints of their foliage seem
> also to have been considered in the composition of the
> picture ... .[1]

The Chinese peasantry appeared oblivious to the charms of
this Garden of Wonders. They had already taken advantage of
the lack of guards around the pavilions, and were looting the
buildings of the Summer Palace with quiet intensity. And once
the French troops had seen inside the buildings, and viewed
the priceless treasures the pavilions contained, it proved
impossible to restrain their own Visigothic tendencies. If these
riches were disappearing the French wanted their share, and
the *soldats* plunged in enthusiastically, chasing off the native
looters and systematically picking off the choicest pieces for
themselves. When the British finally caught up with them, they
were assured by their Gallic allies that looting had been strictly
forbidden, despite the fact that, even as they gave these assur-
ances, the French were pocketing everything in sight. As the
English fumed against their own prohibition on looting, 'Gold
objects and watches ... were whipped up by these gentlemen
with amazing velocity, and as speedily disappeared into their

capacious pockets'.[2] But by the following day the British had been given their head too: the order against looting was rescinded, and the whole allied army now fell upon the treasures of the Summer Palace, stripping the buildings of all moveable valuables and, in a frenzy of wanton vandalism, destroying whatever they could not carry off.

Two days later the sweet taste of victory turned sour in the allies' mouths, and their joy to sombre anger. For almost three weeks Lord Elgin had been demanding to know the fate of the allied personnel – British, French, Sikh, and several Chinese coolies – that had been seized, against all diplomatic convention, by the Chinese. On 8th October the first of the prisoners were released, and their comrades could hear at last the full story of their capture and captivity.

The chief interpreter, Harry Parkes, and Henry Loch, Lord Elgin's private secretary, were the first to return. After Seng Guo Lin Sen had ordered them bound and transported to Beijing they had been cast into an unsprung cart with two other captives (a Frenchman and an old Sikh comrade, Nal Sing) and had suffered terribly, thrown about in the back of the cart as it crashed over the rutted road to the capital: 'I believe if it had lasted much longer we would have died' Loch said of this dreadful journey. It was late dusk when they entered the city by the western gate, and black night when eventually they stopped before a large building, shadowed and shapeless in the gloom. Three men came forward with lanterns. Loch felt Parkes stiffen, then shudder as he whispered, 'This is indeed worse than I expected, we are in the worst prison in China; we are in the hands of the torturers; this is the Board of Punishments'. Swiftly they were dragged inside, and foreseeing their imminent torture Loch tried to comfort his friends, telling them not to fear. The old Sikh drew himself up. '"Fear"?' replied he in Hindustani, 'I do not fear; if I do not die today I may tomorrow, and I am past 60 and am I not with you? I do not fear'.

Their rope bonds were exchanged for chains in a fearsome room hung with various implements 'the use of which it was unpleasant too closely to investigate'.[3] The chains were fastened around the neck and across the ankles, with just three inches allowed between the feet, which prevented all but a slow shuffling gait. Another chain was attached between the neck and ankles, and they were half-pushed, half-carried to separate communal cells, pestilential rooms filled to bursting with Chinese prisoners in various states of emaciation. Loch was particularly badly treated by his jailers. They fastened his neck chain to a beam, giving him just enough room to recline awkwardly on his back. The Westerners must have expected the worst from the swarms of condemned men that surrounded them, but the Chinese were surprisingly solicitous. When Loch awoke shivering after a few hours sleep, he found himself squashed between two Chinese convicts. One of them 'feeling me shaking with cold, drew his tattered, vermin-eaten rug over me – and I was thankful'.

This was not the only kindness these unfortunates showed the foreign captives. Each day the Chinese prisoners carefully cleaned the wounds on the Britons' wrists and ankles, wiping them with a cloth to prevent fly larvae entering the cuts and infecting the flesh. As the experiences of the other allied captives rapidly showed, this was more than a simple act of kindness. Keeping the fly maggots at bay quite literally saved their lives.

Harsh though Parkes' and Loch's captivity had been, it was positively gentle compared to the treatment meted out to other members of their party. The Chinese had treated their own countrymen brutally: the captured coolies had been buried to their necks in the ground, and left there for the pye-dogs to eat their heads. The foreigners had been given different torments. One Frenchman reported:

When we had all been tied up, they poured water on the ropes that bound us, to tighten them. Then they carried us off and threw us down in a courtyard, where we lay exposed to the cold by night and to the sun during the day. At the end of the second day they gave us two small pieces of bread and a little water. In the daytime anyone who liked might come and torment us. At night they placed an official by the side of each of us. If we spoke a

word, they stamped on us and gave us blows on the head.
If we asked for food or drink, they filled our mouths with
filth. The rest cannot be told.

Filth and blows could be borne, but the hand-binding was a
death sentence. As practised by the Chinese, it all but cut the
circulation to the fingers, which turned black and swelled to an
obscene size. The bonds cut into the wrist, and eventually the
pressure exerted on the dying cells became too much and the
skin split, exposing the flesh to the attentions of the myriad
flies that were an integral part of every Chinese habitation.
These were the same flies that Chinese captives in Loch's and
Parkes' prison had taken such pains to guard against. With
good reason. The flies laid their eggs on living flesh. Javalla
Sing, a duffadar, 1st troop Fane's Horse, reported the horrifying
consequences:

> ... Lieut. Anderson became delirious, and remained so,
> with a few lucid intervals, until his death, which
> occurred on the ninth day of his imprisonment. Before
> his death his nails and fingers burst from the tightness of
> the cords, and mortification set in, and the bones of the
> wrist were exposed, whilst he was alive, worms were gen-
> erated in his wounds, and ate into and crawled over his
> body ... five days after this a sowar (trooper) named
> Ramden died in the same state – his body was taken
> away immediately [Lieut. Anderson's corpse was left
> lying with the prisoners for three days].

Another Sikh member of Fane's Horse, sowar Bughel Sing,
was taken captive with Thomas Bowlby (*The Times* correspondent), an unnamed French officer and Phipps, a British
dragoon:

> Mr Bowlby died the second day after we arrived; he died
> from maggots forming in his wrists ... His body remained
> there nearly three days, and the next day it was tied to a
> cross beam and thrown over the wall to be eaten by dogs
> and pigs. The next day the Frenchman died; he was
> wounded slightly on the head and hand. Maggots got into

his ears, nose and mouth, and he became insensible. Two days after this the first Sikh died; his hands burst from his rope wounds, maggots got into them, and he died. Four days afterwards, Phipps, King's Dragoon Guards, died; for ten days he encouraged us in every way he could, but one day his hands became swollen like Mr Anderson's, and maggots were generated the next – one maggot increased a thousandfold in a day. Mahomed Bux, duffadar, died ten days ago; maggots formed on him four days before his death, and his hands were completely eaten away. I should have died had not my chains been taken off.

The Chinese jailers were unconcerned by the prisoners' plight. Indeed, they seemed intent on watching the prisoners succumb in this barbaric manner. Javalla Sing reported that 'When Lieut. Anderson and our comrades called on us to help by biting [their] cords the Chinamen kicked us away'.

The Chinese tried to use their prisoners to extract concessions, but Elgin would not negotiate, telling Prince Kung bluntly that if the allied captives were not returned he would destroy Beijing.[4] This brinkmanship had its effect: Prince Kung ordered Parkes and Loch removed from their cells in the Board of Punishments and held in more comfortable conditions under the careful eye of a mandarin, Hang Ki, until he finally agreed to to their release on Monday 8th October. Just fifteen minutes after they had walked free, a vermilion warrant arrived from the Imperial court in Jehol authorising their deaths. Over the next week, under the threat of severe reprisals, the rest of the prisoners were returned, along with those who had succumbed to the torments of their captivity.

The first bodies were brought out at night, four coffins carried on Chinese carts. When the corpses of those tortured and killed were examined, they were so thoroughly burned with quicklime that it proved almost impossible to identify the remains. A body-count revealed that of the thirty-nine allies taken captive, no less than a third had been 'barbarously murdered'.[5] As news of these atrocities spread through the allied camp a murderous mood took hold and the desire for vengeance became almost palpable among the soldiery. Had Elgin or Gros given the word, there is no doubt that the French and British guardsmen would cheerfully have razed Beijing to the ground and happily slaughtered every one of its inhabitants.

Thankfully, both allied commanders realised that simple revenge was not enough – it would serve only to confirm the Chinese elite in their prejudices and turn the common people against the 'barbarian', and might even help unite Chinese and Manchu against a common enemy, bolstering the Dynasty's confidence and prolonging the war. At the same time such a barbarous act could not simply be passed over. The question was: what should the allied response be?

The Russians had already suggested that the Board of Punishments should be razed to the ground and a monument to the dead erected in its place. The French tended to agree, and wanted the torturers, those who had physically tormented the prisoners, handed over for execution. Elgin would have none of it. The monument would simply stand as a provocation to all Chinese, and would undoubtedly be destroyed just as soon as the Westerners had vacated the city. And hanging those who had tortured, but not those who had ordered the atrocities, was not justice in his eyes. Besides, the Manchu elite would in all likelihood rustle up a bevy of condemned prisoners and pass them off as those responsible for the maltreatment and death of the barbarians. No, what was needed was an act that would awaken the Chinese from the dream they had dreamed for more than two thousand years – an act that would strike deep into the age-old pride of the 'Central' Kingdom, that would drag the Emperor from his golden pedestal and forever destroy the myth of his divinity – an act that would reverberate across the Empire and reveal the Son of Heaven to his subjects as simply another ruler of one country among many others.

Elgin believed he knew the answer – he would destroy the Summer Palace.

The French (having pillaged the area like a swarm of locusts) affected to be horrified by the idea. Baron Gros, with one eye on public opinion in Europe, refused to be involved in what he termed an act of 'barbarism'. But Elgin was adamant

– the Summer Palace was the Emperor's sacred place, his personal fairyland. Of all things, people and locations in the Middle Kingdom, nothing so personified the power, the exclusiveness, of the Son of Heaven. And nothing would so effectively proclaim his helplessness against the barbarians than its destruction. Baron Gros was not convinced. 'I fear,' he wrote, 'that this act of useless and savage vengeance will so frighten Prince Kung that he will take flight and disappear into Manchuria'. His refusal to deploy French troops for this operation laid all the responsibility on Elgin's shoulders. It was a doubly heavy burden for him to bear alone – all Europe knew of the 'Elgin marbles', and how his father had pillaged Greece, carrying off to Britain the choicest pieces of Hellenic art. Even in 1860 the affair had the whiff of scandal about it, and the dour Scotsman realised this act of retribution against the Emperor would do great harm to his own reputation – 'like father like son' would be the inevitable conclusion in the drawing-rooms of polite society across Europe. Yet it is a measure of the man that he persisted with his plan, convinced that it was the best and only way both to avenge the allied dead on a prideful Emperor and his underlings, and to drag a reluctant China (for its own good, as he saw it) into the modern world.

On 13th October, Lord Elgin ordered his men to their work. The whole of the Summer Palace was put to the torch, including the Yuan Ming Yuan and the Imperial Hunting Lodge (which led directly to the extermination of the unique *ssu-pu-hsiang* in China).[6] Five palaces and more than two hundred buildings were razed to the ground, the smoke of the conflagration was visible from Beijing, leaving no one in any doubt as to the disaster that had overtaken the Emperor. Captain Charles Gordon, soon to be fighting alongside the Manchu against the Tai Ping as 'Chinese Gordon', was among the incendiaries. He wrote to his mother: 'You can scarcely imagine the beauty and magnificence of the places we burnt. It made one's heart sore to burn them; in fact, these places were so large, and we were so pressed for time, that we could not plunder them carefully. Quantities of gold ornaments were burnt, considered as brass. It was wretchedly demoralising work for an army. Everybody was wild for plunder.'[7]

Despite its undoubted Vandal dimension, Elgin's strategy worked. Contrary to Baron Gros' belief, Prince Kung did not flee Beijing when the Summer Palace was fired. 'On the contrary, it was then, and then only, that he understood the uselessness of further subterfuges. The flames were still mounting upwards when a despatch from the Chinese Plenipotentiary was brought to the French camp; the first despatch that expressed, in clear and unequivocal terms, the formal acceptance of the Allies' proposals. Baron Gros seized the opportunity with enthusiasm. Lord Elgin did so with considerable *hauteur*.'[8]

The ruins of the Summer Palace still smouldered when, on 24th October, Lord Elgin, surrounded by outriders, made his way to the Tribunal of Rites on a scarlet-covered palanquin carried by sixteen Chinese bearers, to sign the Anglo-Chinese treaty with Prince Kung. The atmosphere between the parties was icily formal: no smiles, no small talk or conciliatory speeches; the participants bowed to each other on arrival and on completion of the ceremony. It was hardly to be wondered, for more than timber and stone had been destroyed when the Summer Palace had gone up in smoke. With it had gone the myth that for so long had sustained Chinese pride – the belief that their Emperor was the supreme ruler of All Under Heaven, unique and omnipotent, to whom all barbarians must inevitably bow.

CHAPTER EIGHT

Silent conspiracy

*T*he Manchu nobles who clustered around the ailing Emperor at Jehol Palace in the autumn of 1860 were under no illusions concerning his omnipotence: Hsien Feng was dying, and the new Emperor would be a child, Yehonala's son, Tsai Ch'un. For an ambitious noble this was the opportunity of a lifetime. A boy-Emperor required regents to govern his realm, regents who would 'Sway the Wide World' in his name, and hold the power of life and death over friend and foe alike, until the Emperor reached manhood. But who would the moribund Hsien Feng name as temporary rulers of the Middle Kingdom? This was the unspoken question that hovered over the Imperial sick-bed: who would command after he was gone – Yehonala and her faction, or Minister Su Shun, President of the Board of Revenues, supported by the Princes I and Cheng.

At first sight, Su Shun and his allies held all the cards. Their star had been ascending in direct proportion to Yehonala's fall from grace. Su Shun now applied his formidable powers for decadence and deceit to two vital undertakings: to aiding the Emperor's desire for oblivion by arranging ever-more-perverted drunken debauches; and to pouring poison in the ailing monarch's ear concerning his erstwhile favourite, the Yi Concubine. He succeeded brilliantly in both tasks. During the dark, cold Manchurian winter, Hsien Feng, sunk in debauchery, weakened still further with drugs, drink and sensual pleasures, slid ever-closer to the death that would bring Su Shun and the princes the power they craved. The Minister's black propaganda was no less effective; his claims that Yehonala was acting the coquette with the Emperor's bannermen body-guard, and was conducting an affair with their commander Jung Lu, resulted in the Emperor ordering the heir's removal from his mother's protection. Henceforth, the heir was to be 'cared for' by Su Shun's wife. Hsien Feng would hear no explanations from Yehonala, and refused to allow the Yi Concubine to enter the Imperial presence. The Emperor did, however, see the Empress Consort Sakota, and gave to her a secret edict which, decades thence, would have far-reaching and fatal consequences for the two cousins.

The depth of the breach between Emperor and his former favourite became even more apparent when he refused Yehonala permission to attend the celebratory audience for his thirtieth birthday. She had become, in the Chinese phrase, 'an autumn fan', a reference to a two-thousand-year-old poem by the Lady Pan Chieh Yu, who likened herself to a favourite fan that was put away after the autumn heat, when another fickle Emperor tired of her charms:

> O fair white silk, fresh from the weaver's loom,
>   Clear as the frost, bright as the winter snow,
>   See! Friendship fashions out of thee a fan.
>   At home, abroad, a close companion thou,
>   Stirring at every move the grateful gale;
>   And yet I fear, ah me! that autumn chills
>   Cooling the dying summer's torrid rage,
>   Will see thee laid neglected on the shelf,
> All thought of bygone days, like them, bygone.

The portents were grim indeed. To all intents, Yehonala was powerless before her enemies. And in such a contest, death was inevitably the loser's lot.

There remained, apart from Jung Lu's warriors and her own unshakeable courage, one additional asset – the eunuchs. Yehonala had long been careful to placate and sweeten these castrati, treating them with unaccustomed kindness and being careful not to neglect the occasional donation of gifts and silver taels to the fraternity. And now this far-sighted strategy bore fruit. While she took pains not to precipitate an open conflict with the conspirators planning her demise, she 'hid a dagger behind a smile' and using her favourite eunuch, An Te-hai, as go-between, she secretly sent information on court happenings to Jung Lu, who transmitted the details to her ally, the Emperor's brother Prince Kung, who was simultaneously attempting to negotiate with the impatient and truculent Westerners in Beijing.

Following his thirtieth birthday audience, Hsien Feng never appeared again in public. His health deteriorated alarmingly after this time. He suffered from excruciating cramps and used another of Yehonala's covert allies, a young eunuch masseur named Li Lien-ying to obtain a measure of relief from his agony. But Li's massage could only alleviate, not cure, the Emperor's malady, and he was not expected to survive a return to the capital. Forty days after his birthday celebrations his condition was judged so dire that the conspirators, fearful that the Son of Heaven might die too soon, summoned to the Emperor's bedchamber all the Grand Councillors and Ministers of the Presence who had accompanied the royal party to Jehol. All were of Su Shun and the Princes' faction. Yehonala, the Empress Consort Sakota, and anyone who might thwart their plans was specifically excluded from this deathbed council. What was said has not been recorded, but the conspirators so worked upon the dying monarch's enfeebled mind that, when the conference concluded, Su Shun left the death chamber with an edict that named himself, the two Princes, I and Cheng, and several others as Regents for the duration of the heir's minority, and which explicitly excluded Yehonala from responsibility in the boy-Emperor's upbringing. The next day (and with convenient timing, it was pointed out by those of suspicious temperament) Emperor Hsien Feng was dead. The Son of Heaven's 'deathbed wishes' were published, and the newly appointed Regents quickly made much show of raising the late Emperor's Consort to the title of Empress Dowager, as custom demanded. Curiously, they also conferred this same title upon Yehonala. It was a charade; both sides knew that these were empty honours. The long silent battle for power between the Su Shun and Yehonala factions

appeared to be finally, definitively, over. The game had been
played; Su Shun had emerged as *victor ludorum*. And 'woe to
the vanquished'.

However, all was not as it seemed. The conspirator's coup,
apparently a fait accompli, contained a vital weakness. The
edicts they brandished so confidently were, in reality, a
gigantic bluff. Over long ages, it had been acknowledged that
for an Emperor's valedictory decree to be recognised as licit,
the Son of Heaven's signature was not enough. The edict must
be finalised with a unique seal, or 'chop' (which the Emperor
himself held), bearing the ideograms 'Lawfully Transmitted
Authority'. Without this stamp of legality, the proclamations
were worthless. Strangely, the seal had gone missing a few days
before the Emperor's death, and despite frantic efforts by the
conspirators to discover its hiding place in the Emperor's bedchamber, its whereabouts remained a mystery. Lacking the
seal's imprint, the edicts upon which Su Shun and his allies
pinned their hopes were legally meaningless, if only an effective challenge could be mounted.

When the contents of the Emperor's deathbed edict became
public, there was a stream of memorials sent from Beijing to
Jehol, rejecting the Su Shun Regency, and calling upon the
boy-Emperor to command the two Empresses Dowager to take
up the task of governing the Empire, to 'administer the Government with suspended curtain'. This was a refence to the
custom that female regents should be shielded by a silken curtain, from which they whispered their administrative decisions
to the boy-Emperor, who then voiced them as if they were
his own considered answers to the problem in hand. Such
demands seem to have unsettled the conspirators, for they
quickly published a decree conferring the title 'Chien Kuo' on
the Chief Regent, giving him virtually dictatorial powers. This
was a mark of their desperation: to take on such powers was a
clear breach of protocol for which there was no precedent; previously, the title Chien Kuo had been used only by brothers or
uncles of the Emperor.

But by now the plotters were riding a tiger. Given the humiliation heaped on Yehonala during the last weeks of Hsien

Feng's life, the affronts and loss of face that were due almost entirely to the malign influence of the conspirators with the Emperor, it was now impossible for them to throw in their hand and to pass over the reins of power to the two Empresses Dowager. Such a retreat could lead only one way – to the execution ground and the headsman's sword. Su Shun was the boldest of the plotters – he advised assassinating Yehonala there and then, in Jehol, and taking their chances with the reaction of Jung Lu and the Yeho-Nala bannermen. But the two Princes were averse to such risk-taking. They had their bodyguard of picked troops, but it was far outnumbered by the enemy force led by the Yi Concubine's rumoured paramour. They too desired Yehonala's death, but faced with the prospect of imminent physical violence and death, persuaded themselves that this expedient could wait. Their formidable opponent could be done away with at a more appropriate time, on the road from Jehol to Beijing. And so, while the incense floated around the body of the dead Emperor and the bonzes droned his praises to heaven, they let the moment pass. It was a fatal mistake. The Princes were to find their adversary a reverse-image of their own vacillating timidity. They had backed away from the one deed that would have assured their success and at the same time offered Yehonala the breathing space she so vitally needed.

Ironically, it was the Regents' assumption of supreme power that gave Yehonala, with the threat of immediate assassination behind her, the opportunity she sought to finesse her enemies. The funeral rites of Chinese Emperors laid an obligation upon the Regents to be in constant, close attendance on the corpse during its carriage from Jehol to Beijing, a journey of some hundred and fifty miles. And the passage was likely to be a slow one. Following the preliminary ceremonies at the Jehol Palace, the rites demanded that Hsien Feng's earthly remains should be placed on an enormous catafalque, a

> domed pavilion, curtained with yellow satin, embroidered in gold. It was borne shoulder high, on a network of poles, lacquered in crimson and gold. The secondary

poles crossed and recrossed each other as the weight was divided up among the [one hundred and sixty] bearers. Unless the transport was effected with infinite precautions, the oscillations might have tossed the coffin in the air. The bearers, keeping time under orders from their chief, had to advance three steps, then stop during three beats (struck on a musical wooden gong), then advance three steps, and again stop during three beats without moving – and so on, for a hundred and fifty miles. At each halt the bearers were changed, and at each resting place (every fifteen miles) temporary pavilions had been erected, to shelter the dead Emperor and his suite. These pavilions were made of poles and matting, and were called the 'mat-shed palaces'.[1]

No deviation from these rites could be countenanced, and the Regents were required to be in attendance every step of the way. Even assuming good weather, the cortège could not hope to reach Beijing for ten days.

Such an obligation of attendance was not incumbent upon the wives and concubines of the dead Emperor. The two Empresses Dowager, Yehonala and Sakota, were free to return to Beijing as soon as they might. Indeed, it was their specific obligation to be in Beijing before the cortège arrived, so as to organise its proper reception according to the rites. But both sides knew that this was not all that would be set in motion when the Empresses reached the capital. Yehonala had powerful allies in Beijing and would undoubtedly organise resistance to the conspirators, whose only protection lay in the edicts they had wrung from the dying Emperor, seal-less and legally suspect. In the space of just a few short days the prospects of the protagonists had reversed. The omens for Su Shun and his party were decidedly unpropitious. Their only hope of success lay in effecting Yehonala's death before she reached the Great Within.

It was decided that the Empresses should be accompanied to Beijing by an escort of Su Shun's men, and that they would both be assassinated at Kou Pei K'ou, at a pass leading down from the mountains into the Chinese plains. That the two Empresses were aware of the fatal nature of their journey is certain – the brooding presence of Su Shun's escort was too obvious a threat for them to ignore. But again, nothing was said. When they left for the capital, both sides acted their part, exchanging formal wishes for a safe journey. Su Shun and his colleagues must have believed that this was the last time they would see the troublesome Yi Concubine alive, but as ever they underestimated Yehonala's courage and resourcefulness. Behind the careful phrases, the mock acquiescence and the dance of etiquette, her precise and calculating mind worked unceasingly for the downfall of her enemies. She was to prove herself a master in this deadly game of plot and counterplot. For the conspirators were in more danger than they realised: unknown to them (though they may, perhaps, have suspected the truth) Yehonala carried with her the 'missing' seal of the Emperor, without whose imprint all edicts and proclamations concerning the succession were rendered null and void.

Once again Yehonala's alliance with the eunuchs of the Imperial Presence had saved her. Li Lien Ying, the eunuch masseur who had attended to Hsien Feng in the last days of his life, was secretly of the Yehonala faction. Allowed almost unfettered access to the royal bedchamber during his long periods of treating the Emperor, he had been able to discover the hiding place of the Imperial Seal, and to somehow smuggle it from the Imperial quarters undetected, before carrying it to his mistress.[2] This one act undoubtedly saved Yehonala's life, and that of her ally and cousin, Sakota. Possession of the 'chop' by the Regents would have been disastrous for the two women and would quite literally have sealed their fate. But with the seal safe in her possession, the possibilities were infinite. For while decrees without the vital imprint were worthless, the converse was also true (and absolutely vital in this context): any document carrying the seal must, perforce, be regarded as legitimate.

The Regents were anxious to reduce to a minimum the time Yehonala's Beijing allies might have to regroup once the assassination of the Empresses became known, and orders were given for the main party to quit Jehol immediately the two women and their entourage had left the Palace. But fate was against them. The heavens opened almost as soon as the cortège began its long march from Jehol to the capital. The highway quickly turned to mud and made transport of the catafalque impossible. Yehonala and Sakota, by now some ten miles ahead of the main procession, were likewise travel-bound, though they were sure to make more progress in the coming days than the lumbering juggernaut that followed them. Despite the cramped quarters she was forced to occupy and the tremendous strain of travelling with men who might at any time put her and her companion to the sword, Yehonala maintained an outward show of *sang froid*, and sent messengers and letters to the Regents enquiring as to the disposition of her late Lord's coffin.

Her courage may have had less to do with oriental fatalism than careful planning with her supporters. One story relates that Jung Lu and his Yeho-Nala bannermen had been ordered by the Regents to accompany the cortège to Beijing, a ruse to keep Yehonala's clansmen occupied until the fatal blow had been struck against their mistress. They appeared to comply, but as the catafalque neared its first mat-shed palace, Jung Lu barked a command and he and his men took horse and sped off into the night. Riding hard, they quickly caught up with Yehonala's caravan, taking Su Shun's men completely by surprise and swiftly drawing a protective screen of swords and armour around the palanquins of the two Empresses.[3]

With their assassination plot thwarted and Yehonala safely surrounded by a bodyguard of loyal troops, the Regents must have known that they were 'fey' men, doomed to death. But it does not seem to have occurred to any of them either to flee to foreign lands or perhaps to turn their coats and attempt to come to some accommodation with the Tai Ping rebels who still held Nanking and most of South China. They kept their places in the cortège and answered Yehonala's formal letters praising their care of the Emperor's body with equally polite missives of their own. Shackled by custom, they continued to escort the coffin of Hsien Feng to the capital, and the cortège they commanded became their own funeral procession. In many ways there is no better symbol of the difference between Yehonala and those ranged against her. Like her enemies, Yehonala was punctilious in the performance of the rites, assiduous in the exercise of etiquette and proper form. In this they and she were no different from the mass of scholars and nobles for whom *Li* (the conventions governing Chinese social life) was all. But while most Chinese unthinkingly allowed tradition to order their lives, Yehonala used these same traditions to order others. She was adept at putting forward the relevant precedent that sanctioned whatever action she wished accomplished. And, perhaps her greatest strength, where this could not be achieved she was quite prepared – almost invariably with exquisite timing – to set the hallowed traditions to one side and to act in whatever way appeared to her the most expedient to achieve her aims. Once these were achieved, she would then take up the rites once more and unblushingly enforce them with religious zeal – until circumstances once again demanded she discard them.

The cortège was to arrive at the North-West Gate of Beijing, and here a large marquee was erected to greet the Regents and receive from them the catafalque bearing the dead Emperor's remains. Once the golden-domed litter had been safely lowered to the ground within the city precincts, the Regents, led by a sullen-faced Prince I, made their way to their appointed stations. Their feelings as they entered the tented reception area, facing almost certain death, can only be guessed at. Yet even at this late stage, the same grim courtliness prevailed. As custom demanded, they prostrated themselves before the boy-Emperor to report the successful completion of their task. Behind the new Son of Heaven stood his aunt Sakota, the brothers of the dead sovereign, and Yehonala, savouring her moment of victory.

It was characteristic of Yehonala that she seized the initiative, and took command of the situation from the start. Calmly assuming her primacy over all the assembled nobles, she stood forward and with grave formality thanked Prince I and the other Regents for their efforts, before summarily relieving them of their offices. Prince I would have none of it. He and the other Regents were the legally appointed custodians of the Empire, he blustered, and he reminded Yehonala that no one, including herself, would be allowed to see the new Emperor during his minority without the Regents' permission. It was a bold, but ultimately futile move. All knew that the Regents' edicts lacked the vital Seal of Legally Transmitted Authority. By contrast, Yehonala had in her hand a conflicting edict, giving herself and Sakota the self-same powers that Prince I and his fellow Regents had arrogated to themselves. And, thanks to the wiles of the eunuch Li Lien-ying, this document possessed the requisite imprint of the Seal of Legally Transmitted Authority. Just as important, perhaps more so, the Regents' military resources were few, while ranged around Yehonala and her allies, and scattered in large numbers about the city, were a large force of highly trained, well-equipped and well-motivated men, the Beijing Field Force. And as is true everywhere, and at all times, 'God is on the side of the big battalions'.

According to one account, Su Shun had not accompanied the rest of the Regents, and was surprised in his quarters, in bed with his favourite concubine in direct violation of the funeral rites. Another version places him at the audience with the young Emperor and Yehonala, claiming that it was at this critical moment that the swaggering braggart, the least self-controlled of the conspirators, finally let the mask of formality slip. Fury overwhelmed him and he turned on his fellow Regents hissing, 'Had you listened to me when I first proposed to do away with this woman, we should not have come to such a pass!' The others heard him in stoical, Confucian silence. There was nothing to say. He was right.

The conspirators were arrested, and conveniently blamed (though not without reason) for the debacle with the red barbarians, for the capture and torture of the allied emissaries, the burning of the Summer Palace, and much else besides. In time-honoured fashion, Yehonala had found a scapegoat, upon which the sins of the past could be heaped, allowing her son a propitious accession to the throne, blame-free and guiltless. Su Shun, Prince I, and the rest of their faction, flanked by guards, were conveyed to the 'Empty Chamber', the place of confinement for members of the Imperial clan. Yehonala issued a

decree in her own name and that of her cousin, Sakota, stripping the three principal conspirators Prince I, Prince Cheng
and Su Shun of all their titles and ranks, and appointing her
ally, Prince Kung, to preside over the Imperial Clan Court that
would try the Regents. The result was a foregone conclusion.
Everyone knew that Yehonala would never allow these men to
threaten her or her son again. The edict concluded: 'Their
audacity ... shows a degree of wickedness inconceivable, and
convicts them of the darkest designs. The punishment so far
meted out to them is totally inadequate to the depth of their
guilt.'[4] It was the young girl from Anhui's first experience of
absolute power, and she found it tasted sweet – and addictive.

Yehonala had conceived a particular hatred for Su Shun,
because of his arrogant behaviour towards her and the insults
she had received at the hands of Su Shun's wife while she had
been out of favour in Jehol. The morning after the arrests she
issued another decree, singling out Su Shun for especial
obloquy, and – before Prince Kung's commission had delivered
a verdict – confiscating the whole of his property, both at
Beijing and Jehol. Su Shun's wealth was legendary, the fruit of
years of corruption and graft, an immense fortune amounting
to many millions of taels. With this one stroke, Yehonala had
become a wealthy woman, influential and powerful in her
own right.

Several days later, after a perfunctory enquiry, the Clan
Court duly announced its judgement, finding Prince I, Prince
Cheng and the arch-villain Su Shun, guilty of treason and sub-
version of the state – capital crimes carrying the severest of
penalties: execution by the lingering death, slow dismemberment. However, with her enemies at her feet, and Su Shun's
enormous wealth safely in her pocket, Yehonala could afford
to be magnanimous. She commuted the sentences: in deference to Prince I's and Prince Cheng's high rank, they each
received a silken cord, the time-honoured invitation to hang
themselves, which they duly did, from a beam in the Empty
Chamber. Su Shun too, was granted clemency, but of a different
kind. 'As to Su Shun ... he fully deserves the punishment of
dismemberment and the slicing process, if only that the law

may be vindicated and public indignation satisfied. But we cannot make up our mind to impose this extreme penalty and therefore ... we sentence him to immediate decapitation ... .'[5] Su Shun, once the most powerful minister in the Middle Kingdom, was dragged to the public execution ground and beheaded. But even here Yehonala's vengeance followed the ex-Minister. It was customary for the headsman to sew the victim's head back onto the corpse immediately, so that the dead person's spirit might travel to next world complete. This was expressly forbidden by Yehonala. Su Shun's head was displayed in a cage, and the town dogs were left to lap up the blood from his headless trunk.

CHAPTER NINE

An auspicious beginning

'There is nothing so sweet in life as to vanquish your enemy', and with Su Shun and the Princes I and Cheng all safely consigned to the Nine Springs (a Chinese euphemism for death), Yehonala could begin to enjoy the fruits of her triumph. Her first task was to blot out all memory of the usurping Regents, and for this it was necessary to change the young Emperor's reign-title. The conspirators had given her son the characters Chi Hsiang (Well-Omened Happiness), a singularly unapt title as far as their own personal fortunes were concerned. Yehonala chose T'ung Chih (All-Pervading Tranquillity), no doubt a reference to the hoped-for suppression of the Tai Ping revolt. Two edicts were issued, one proclaiming the formal beginning of the Emperor's reign, the other a disingenuous statement of Yehonala's (and Sakota's) reluctance to assume the Regency, which in its cynical hypocrisy set the pattern for numerous similar decrees throughout Yehonala's long years of power:

> Our assumption of the Regency was utterly contrary to our wishes, but we have complied with the urgent request of our Princes and Ministers ... So soon as ever the Emperor shall have completed his education, we shall take no further part in the Government, which will then naturally revert to the system prescribed by all Dynastic tradition. Our sincere reluctance in assuming the direction of affairs must be manifest to all ... .[1]

Once secure, Yehonala was magnanimous in victory and there was no general proscription of the conspirators' allies and cronies. She satisfied herself with simply removing from their official positions many who were strongly implicated in the conspiracy and, had matters gone differently, would certainly have gloried in her own humiliation and death. The Chinese are ever-mindful of obligation, and such merciful treatment undoubtedly gained her a host of supporters from among her erstwhile enemies. She was, moreover, at the height of her physical beauty: dark almond eyes, long blue-black hair, a tiny nose, and a winning smile. She knew her power and it was a strong man who could not be swayed by her charms:

> she was so kindly in manner and so suave of disposition that she won every heart, persuaded every hearer, disarmed envy and hatred ... Her language abounded with witty sallies, quaint notions clothed in racy words, embellished with poetic images, bright with bursts of musical laughter. People loved to listen to her, were proud of her notice, and captivated by her smile. While she spoke, an intense force lighted her eyes, kindled her mobile tongue, and as one of her own countrymen puts it 'made her lips drip honey' ... clever statesmen were swayed by her, despite their intelligence. A magnetic force seemed to go out of her, hypnotising her environment and making instruments of all who came within the radius of its operation.[2]

But not everyone was captivated by Yehonala's undoubted charms. While she garnered allies among her former foes, Yehonala's relationship with her staunchest allies soon began to unravel. Her collaboration with Prince Kung had been very much a matter of necessity on both sides. One of the Empresses' first official actions was to bestow upon their ally the title 'I Cheng Wang', Prince Adviser, and to issue a special decree which granted hereditary status to one of his more important titles 'Ch'in Wang', Prince of the Blood. Surprisingly, Prince Kung declined the latter honour – for he was interested in far more than titles. As the younger brother of the Celestial Prince, he no doubt deemed himself Emperor-material, and it is possible that his acquiescence to the elevation of Yehonala and

Sakota to the Regency owed more to his belief that they could be easily manipulated to his own ends, than in any conviction of the intrinsic worth of the two Empresses Dowager. The Prince saw himself as a father-figure to both Yehonala and Sakota, an elder statesman before whose vast experience the two women should gratefully bow. The Empress of the Eastern Palace, Sakota, was quite happy to oblige. For her, submission was easy: she was not a political animal, and her lack of education (she could not speak or write Chinese, and her written Manchu was weak) was an additional handicap. Sakota was the icon of Confucian femininity: wanting pleasure and prestige without responsibility and posing no threat to male supremacy. By contrast, the Western Empress's life priorities were diametrically opposed to those of her cousin. Alert, nimble-witted and sufficiently skilled in calligraphy, poetry and painting to hold her own with any man, she could see no reason to adopt the supine, tractable demeanour that Prince Kung seemed to expect of her. Her aspirations blossomed with the successful campaign against Su Shun's machinations, and grew in line with her expanding political awareness. Her ambition fed upon each successful intrigue. She flowered under the constant flattery of the eunuch attendants and the sycophantic admiration of her subordinates until nothing would suffice but total and absolute control of the Empire: *aut Caesar aut nullus.*

Such an attitude could not but jar with Prince Kung's own dreams of greatness. At first, aware that she was a tiro in governing, and still feeling her way towards ultimate power, she was grateful enough for his advice, but maturing rapidly, as the months went by she increasingly listened to his guidance attentively and then failed to act upon it. The Prince was as proud and as jealous of his position as Yehonala (in many ways the two characters were remarkably similar), and he increasingly saw this behaviour as insulting. Friction escalated rapidly, and in response to Yehonala's increasingly autocratic tone, the Prince began a deliberate policy of cultivating Sakota's friendship, and persuading her to take his part whenever disagreements arose in council. Given Yehonala's temperament, this could only inflame an already tense situation, and lead to a deterioration in relations between the two Empresses. Time and again in Chinese history, real or imagined slights have resulted in acts of revenge which twisted the course of the nation and bred unimaginable suffering and horror for the general populace. The consequences of conflict between the two Empress cousins would, within a few years, provide the motive for a fatal clash.

But all this was in the future. For the present, there were far more pressing demands to attend to. In 1861 the Tai Ping rebellion still raged below the Yangtse, with Hung Hsiu-chuan's followers in command of four provinces, Chejiang, Kiangsi, Jiangsu and Anhui, while the rebel Heavenly King continued to hold state in Imperial splendour at Nanking, the traditional southern capital of the Emperor. During the previous year a remarkable general, Li Hsiu-cheng had revived the fortunes of the Tai Ping cause with a series of well-fought victories. A former charcoal-maker, he had risen through the ranks and reached the upper echelons of the Tai Ping hierarchy on merit alone. Unlike the rest of the elite, success did not appear to corrupt him or inflame his ambition (he was dubbed the Chung Wang, or Loyal Prince). General Li was intelligent, a master strategist, and humane, at least by the standards of the day. He remained convinced of the importance of the Tai Ping mission to bring a Christian society (as he envisaged it) of equality and justice to China. Many authorities believe that had he, and not the visionary Hung Hsiu-chuan, enjoyed supreme command of the Tai Ping forces, their success would have been assured. Li himself eventually blamed the Heavenly King for Tai Ping reverses, writing in his 'confession' that 'If one tried to petition about affairs of the Kingdom for the sake of preserving the state, whatever one said, the Heavenly King would only talk of Heaven and Earth'.[3] But in 1861 such criticisms were far from the mind of the Loyal Prince. Li had driven westward and produced panic in both the Western Powers and the Chinese merchants by advancing on Shanghai. It was a bold move. The Tai Ping movement was landlocked, hamstrung by the lack of a major international port, through which it could treat and trade with the world. The taking of Shanghai would, at a stroke, have given the rebellion a tremendous, and perhaps vital, advantage.

That Li did not succeed in his plan was due in no small part to a wiry young American adventurer, with long dark hair that hung 'like an Indian' to his shoulders. Born in Salem, Massachusetts, in 1831, Frederick Townsend Ward took to the sea early in life, and by the age of sixteen was already a mate on a merchant ship, a considerable achievement which prefigured his great ability to command men and gain their respect. Before arriving in China, Ward had seen active service in Mexico and Central America and had fought with the French during the Crimean War. When he first came to China he had apparently conceived a great sympathy for the Tai Ping cause, but later he took ship as mate on a Manchu gunboat. Ward was a small man, but made up in personality what he lacked in inches. He had piercing brown eyes and was one of those rare people who combined an intensity of motivation with an extremely genial nature. It was a mixture that for some reason worked magic on the band of drunks and gutter-dregs who made up the first mercenary army he recruited in 1861.

The Chinese Shanghai merchants, fearful of the Tai Ping advance and despairing of any real defence being mounted by the Western nations, entrusted Ward with the task of repelling the rebels. With Chinese backing, Ward put together a small band of desperadoes, whom he led in an attack on Sungkiang. Unfortunately, by the time his little army arrived at their objective, the putative 'wild geese' had consumed so much liquor that the Tai Ping defenders had no trouble repelling their intoxicated foe and chasing them back to Shanghai. It says much for the force of Ward's personality that he was able to weather this military fiasco and to quickly persuade more men to join his mercenary force. His next sortie was more successful and the young American soon gained a reputation for both luck and personal bravery. He always led from the front, and insisted on carrying nothing more lethal than a rattan cane into the fight.[4] This 'gimmick' was carried on by Ward's British successor, the far more famous 'Chinese' Charles Gordon, who was to achieve immortality in 1885 on his death while fighting against the Mahdi's forces at Khartoum. It was one of the stronger ironies of Chinese history that, at the very moment

Ward was defending Imperial interests in Shanghai, his successor Gordon was taking part in the destruction of the Emperor's most prized possession, burning and looting the Summer Palace with the rest of the allied expeditionary force to Beijing.

The Chinese found Ward easy to deal with and he was the most well-liked of the Westerners. So pleased was Yehonala with the results of Ward's force (now numbering over four thousand men[5] dressed in green uniforms with turbans of the same colour) she issued a decree renaming the force the 'Ever-Victorious Army'.

Tseng Guo-feng, the untidy martinet 'with a black straggling beard and moustache' (who was Yehonala's appointee as commander-in-chief against the rebels), had been the most successful Imperial officer to take the field. But Tseng was getting on in years, and he appointed two younger men, neither of them Manchu, as his immediate subordinates: Tso Tsung-t'ang, from his native Hunan, and the tall and imposing Li Hung-chang, who would later become Yehonala's right-hand man in several crises.[6] Li was conscious of China's weakness in military affairs and he was extremely impressed by skills of the foreign troops he saw: 'Their formations are orderly, their cannon accurate in hitting targets and most powerful against buildings; the brigands [Tai Ping rebels] are quite frightened by them. However … the foreign soldiers often insult us and arbitrarily order movements of our troops.' To the proud Chinese, with their culture of barbarian inferiority, such behaviour was quite unacceptable. Ward, however, seems to have worked his charm on the Manchu officials as well as his own troops. An old China-hand, he knew how important face was to the Chinese: he suggested rather than demanded, and was happy to share the glory with those above him (or at least he affected to be, which for a mandarin amounted to the same thing). Ward became 'ban Chunguo ren' (half-Chinese) wooing and marrying a Chinese woman, the daughter of one of the most prominent Shanghai merchants, Yang 'Takee' Fang. Most important of all, he did what the Chinese required of him: in a series of brilliant small campaigns the Tai Ping were gradually pushed back from Shanghai. Li Hung-chang was impressed and inclined to wink at the American 'colonel's' lack of Chinese etiquette: 'Ward, who valiantly defends Sung and Ching, is indeed the most vigorous of all. Although he has not yet shaved his hair or called at my humble residence, I have no time to quarrel over such a little ceremonial matter.' After Ward's spectacular capture of the important city of Ch'ing-p'u on 10th August, the mercenary leader's stock rose even higher in Li Hung-chang's eyes: 'Ward commands enough authority to control the foreigners in Shanghai and he is quite friendly with me ... Ward is indeed brave in action. I have devoted all my attention to making friends with him, in order to get the friendship of various nations through that one individual.'

Alas, all Li Hung-chang's efforts proved vain. On 19th September, Ward led the Ever-Victorious Army on the small town of Tz'u-ch'i, south of Shanghai and close to the port of Ningpo. He rested his men at the Pan-ch'iao temple just outside Tz'u-ch'i and, at dawn the next day, contrary to his normal practice, he inexplicably remained in the rear and allowed his officers to lead the men in storming the walls. While he was 'directing his troops from the rear and watching the brigands through his telescope, they suddenly fired from the walls and shot him through the breast and back. He instantly fell down unconscious; he was attended to and carried back to the vessel by his aides.'[7] Ward lingered on in agony until the next day, dying on 21st September 1862, just thirty-one years old. The hero who had rushed so often into the heat of action armed only with a swagger stick and an invincible sense of his own invulnerability had been struck down, far from the battle, by a one-in-a-million shot.

Ward's second-in-command, Henry Burgevine, now took control of the Ever-Victorious Army. A native of the American deep south, Burgevine was an eccentric, prone to violent rages and with none of Ward's warmth and understanding of Chinese ways. When *tao-tai* Yang Fang delayed the disbursement of the Ever-Victorious Army's pay, Burgevine marched into his house with several dozen musketeers, beat him mercilessly 'until he vomited a great deal of blood' and then broke open the treasury, making off with over forty thousand silver dollars (still less than one month's costs for the mercenary force). But this action against a Chinese official was too much for Li Hung-chang's mandarin sensibilities. Throughout their relations with the West, the Chinese elite steadfastly held to the principle that a mandarin's person was inviolate. Burgevine's attack was therefore intolerable, and besides, Li was concerned that under such leadership the whole of the Ever-Victorious Army might go over to the rebels.[8] He sought the help of the British General Stavely, who agreed to a reduction in the EVA's numbers from four thousand five hundred to three thousand men, and to allow a British officer to command the troops. The officer chosen was Charles George Gordon.

At thirty-one, Gordon was the same age as Ward, but in all other respects the two men could not have been more different. Where Ward had been active and impulsive, given to acts of bravado, Gordon was thoughtful, quiet, almost introverted. Ward had not cared about the morals of his men as long as they fought well; Gordon, brought up in the strict Christianity of Victorian England, could brook no loose living. On taking command he made it plain that discipline would return to the Ever-Victorious Army, and wine, women and loot were forbidden. In response, almost half of his force deserted. Nothing daunted, and following a tradition that was accepted practice in both Britain and China, Gordon enlisted his defeated foes, taking on around two thousand Tai Ping prisoners and incorporating them into the Ever-Victorious Army.

Like Ward, Gordon was nominally under the command of Li Hung-chang. At first, Li was doubtful of Gordon's reputation for honesty and bravery, but the Englishman's behaviour and success in battle soon persuaded him otherwise. 'Since taking over the command, Gordon seems more reasonable [than the others]. His readiness to fight the enemy is also greater.'[9] Later, in a memorial dated 12th April, Li admitted, 'When the British General Stavely formerly stated ... that Gordon was brave, clear-minded and foremost among the British officers in Shanghai, your official dared not believe it. Yet since he took up command of the Ever-Victorious Army, their exceedingly bad habits gradually have come under control. His will and zeal are really praiseworthy.' A further memorial dated 2nd June repeats the refrain: 'As the foreign officer and others did not use their heavy guns ... when they succeeded in capturing the ringleaders and exterminating the dens, their feats exceeded your official's [i.e., Li Hung-chang's] expectations.' But these victories came at a terrible human cost. On the same day Li wrote poignantly of the terrible conditions in the countryside over which the war was being fought:

> ... the province of Jiangsu used to have a densely populated countryside, a village every half li (one-sixth of a mile), a town every three li (one mile), smoking chimneys ... and chickens and dogs to be heard everywhere. Now we see nothing but weeds, briars and hazels obstructing the roads. There may be no inhabitants for twenty or thirty li. At times, among the broken walls and ruined buildings, one or two orphan children or widows survive out of a hundred inhabitants. Their faces have no colour and they groan while waiting for death. When asked about their livelihood, they answer 'as it is impossible to beg or walk afar, grass and roots have to be plucked to make cakes to stay our hunger'. As I, your official, am holding the post of governor, my heart grows sick when I see these terrible conditions with my own eyes.

Li was sincerely affected by what he saw and he pushed his forces mercilessly, hoping that, with Gordon's help, the twelve-year rebellion might be crushed and normality restored quickly

Over the next few months his dreams seemed to be realised. Gordon's skill at arms, plus the bravery of the Chinese soldiery, provided more victories for the Imperial armies than Yehonala and her court at Beijing had seen in many a year. And Li Hung-chang, the mandarin so confident of Chinese superiority, began to see in the young Englishman behaviour that unsettled his preconceptions concerning the Western barbarians. He was 'brave, industrious and especially well-versed in strategy and the use of firearms. It is requested that an edict may be issued in acknowledgement of his work so that he may carry himself with pride after returning to his country.'[10]

Just one incident marred this burgeoning understanding between East and West. As the Imperial armies increasingly gained ground – taking several major cities and eventually surrounding Nanking and laying siege to the Heavenly King himself – some of the less committed of the Tai Ping leaders began to reassess their options. At Suzhou, the lovely canal city known as the Venice of the East, several of the lesser Tai Ping 'Wangs' entered into secret negotiations with the Imperial commander, colonel Cheng Kuo-k'uei, on how best they might surrender. They were informed that no submission would be possible unless they first captured or killed Tan Shao-kuang, known as the Mu Wang, a rebel chief of formidable reputation who was also in the city with a 'suicide squad' of over one thousand men, all prepared to defend it to the death. With Tan removed, the rebels were promised a hearty welcome, and that they would be given high positions in the Manchu army. The Tai Ping turncoats jumped at the chance of escaping a rebel's death and a secret plan was agreed with the Imperial commanders.[11]

Also in Suzhou at that time was the most successful of all the Tai Ping generals, Li Chung-wang, the Loyal Prince Li. The Imperial forces would no doubt have wished his capture too but, whether through his spies or through instinct, the Loyal Prince suddenly deserted Suzhou with ten thousand followers and fought his way west towards the besieged Tai Ping capital of Nanking.

On 4th December, as the Imperial forces prepared to attack Suzhou, the Mu Wang gave orders to defend the walls. As he turned to direct his own men, the trap was sprung: Tai Ping general Wang Yu-wei stabbed Tan Shao-kuang from behind with his dagger, and immediately a great mob of men fell upon Tan's thousand-strong 'suicide squad' and hacked them to pieces. Then they hauled down their flags, opened the gates, and surrendered the city.

Some of the former *Chang Mao*, the long-haired bandits of the Tai Ping, shaved their heads in token of submission. But many did not. The six main Tai Ping leaders, afraid of treachery and conscious of the fact that, at that moment, they still commanded some one hundred thousand men, attempted to negotiate their safety from a position of strength. They demanded from Li Hung-chang documents guaranteeing their positions as brigadier-generals and colonels in the Imperial army. Seeing their belligerent attitude, Li worried that in Suzhou the Tai Ping tail might soon wag the Manchu dog. And so, 'to avoid the predicament of having a big tail or incurring other mishaps', Li abruptly reneged on his promises to the rebels, and summarily ordered the Tai Ping chiefs executed. They were beheaded immediately.

Gordon was shocked to the very core of his moralistic heart. These men had surrendered according to the Articles of War and had been promised safe conduct. And now they had been treacherously slain. Armed with two pistols and breathing fire, he went in search of Li, intending his death. Fortunately, Li made himself unavailable to the irate Englishman, knowing that 'Gordon has a violent temper'.[12] His murderous intentions thwarted, Gordon threatened to go over with the Ever-Victorious Army to the Tai Ping, but eventually as Li had foreseen, the Englishman's anger cooled, and he allowed himself to be reconciled, though he was never to completely forgive the treacherous treatment (as he saw it) meted out to the Tai Ping commanders. Li took a far more practical approach to the killings, an attitude that revealed the gulf that still remained between European and Chinese perceptions. He had already explained his reasons for ordering the executions – the rebels still had a formidable number of men under arms and their allegiance to the Manchus was unproven – 'a man who sells one Lord will sell another'. Promises made to such men were of little account. Li believed that the action taken had been justifiable in the circumstances, and he felt that this should be the end of the matter. But with typical mandarin *sang froid*, he was also willing to submit to the exigencies of the moment and offer himself up as a scapegoat. Should the British government rally to Gordon's cause '... and dispute about this with any heat,' he wrote to Yehonala, 'then it would be only fair to deal with Your official severely, according to the situation, in order to appease their mind'.

Li Hung-chang avoided contact with Gordon for over two months, at the same time meticulously sending all pay and

equipment the mercenary force required. Gordon was molli-
fied, and via the good offices of the slight, dapper Irishman
Robert Hart (who was then in charge of Imperial Customs,
and well-thought-of by both Chinese and foreign diplomats)
a reconciliation was effected. But Li was still wary; the Ever-
Victorious Army could be a thorn in the flesh of the Manchus
were they to change sides, and Gordon's 'bad temper suddenly
comes and goes, I do not know whether there will be any
change later on'. Li was adamant that, as soon as the rebellion
posed no threat, Gordon would be relieved of command and the
mercenary force disbanded.

He did not have long to wait. By 1863, the Tai Ping had
been split into three main groups, centred on Hangzhou,
Changchou and Nanking, where the Heavenly King had been
besieged along with two hundred thousand defenders for several years. The Imperial strategy was to pick off each area
separately. Hangzhou was the first to fall, and as the
area around the city succumbed to the Imperial advance,
Gordon was wounded in the leg during mopping up operations against the insurgents at the town of Chin-t'an. Echoes
of the death of Ward must have tormented Li Hung-chang
when the news was first reported, but fortunately the wound
was slight.

The defence of the Tai Ping western territories now hinged
upon Changchou, and the battle for the city was desperate. Li
recorded that while the rebels were initially awed by the European artillery used against them, they now understood that
'although the artillery is able to blow up strong defences, the
troops climbing over the walls can be obstinately resisted
... there are approximately one hundred thousand brigands in
Changchou ... the violent bands of Guangdong [Canton] and
Guangxi are suicide troops of long experience ...'. Li doubted
that the fight for Changchou would be costly, and at first, on
26th April, he wrote of his hopes to starve the rebels out rather
than mount a frontal assault. But less than two weeks later, he
agreed to an attack and surprisingly the city fell after just
five hours of ferocious street-fighting. The Canton and
Guangxi die-hards were exterminated to a man, with the

approval of Gordon, who asked quarter only for those Tai Ping conscripts who were willing to surrender. Li agreed.

The fall of Changchou was effectively the end of the Tai Ping revolt. Although Nanking still held out, the rebels there were in no position to mount offensive actions. They could do no more than repulse the incessant attacks on the city and bay their defiance at the encircling Imperial troops. Li judged it time to disband the Ever-Victorious Army, and Gordon, his mission to suppress the rebellion achieved (and perhaps weary of the enormous blood-letting that was a characteristic of Chinese warfare) agreed. Demobilisation was effected quickly, with the Chinese giving generous bonuses (up to four thousand dollars) to the one hundred and four foreign officers who had commanded the force, several of whom had been severely wounded. A few foreigners were retained to drill Chinese recruits, but within a few short weeks the Ever-Victorious Army, one of the greatest and romantic 'free companies' the world has seen, had simply ceased to be.[13]

Gordon's reward was commensurate with his status. The year before, Yehonala decreed that he be rewarded for his services with ten thousand ounces of silver, but with characteristic distaste for lucre, Gordon had declined. This had left a great impression on all the Chinese, from the Empress Dowager down. Via the trusted intermediary, Robert Hart, Gordon let it be known that he served China not for money, but 'only to win a good name'. Yehonala was much taken with the Englishman's heroic attitude and, on Li Hung-chang's personal recommendation, she granted Gordon his wish and bestowed upon the foreigner the coveted Yellow Jacket, the highest of military distinctions. Gordon was immensely proud of the award, which placed him in the highest echelons of Chinese society. He wrote to his mother in England that the 'country is clear of rebels, and the Imperialists are quite able to be left to themselves. I may say the Chinese government have conferred upon me the highest military rank and the yellow jacket, a distinction conferred on not more than twenty other mandarins [Gordon obviously considered himself one of China's scholar-gentlemen] in the empire and which constitutes the recipient as one of the emperor's bodyguard.' With the good name he had craved, Gordon left the Middle Kingdom to be lionised in English and European society as 'Chinese Gordon' until his heroic death at Khartoum in 1885 eclipsed the memory of his Chinese adventures in Europe – though not in China, where even today his memory is honoured.

This left only Nanking, the old, high-walled southern capital of the Empire, held by the Tai Ping Heavenly King since 1853, which, for reasons of national pride, Yehonala and the Manchu elite were insistent should be taken only by Chinese troops.

The situation inside the Tai Ping capital was desperate. The city had been under siege for over two years, the food supply was almost exhausted, and the defenders were reduced to one meagre meal a day. Despite this, Hung Hsui-chuan, the 'Heavenly King' and the root and origin of this huge conflict that had destroyed so many millions of lives, continued to act as if victory for his forces was assured and imminent. According to one account, when informed of the lack of food in the city, the Heavenly King 'caused roots and leaves to be kneaded and rolled into pellets, which he had served out to his immediate followers, the rebel chiefs, saying, 'This is manna from heaven; for a long time we in the Palace have eaten nothing else'. He gave orders that every household should collect ten loads of this stuff for storage in the palace granaries; some of the more ignorant people obeyed the order, but most of the rebels ignored it. Apparently immune to reality, on one tour of the defences the Heavenly King distributed pearls to his starving men. They wept in hopeless frustration. Pearls could not be eaten.

The account of the Loyal Prince Li Hsiu-cheng (who had successfully fought his way to the Tai Ping capital from Suzhou) reveals the atmosphere within the Heavenly King's palace as utterly delusional. When he first arrived in Nanking, Li requested a conference with his leader to discuss the danger they faced. But the 'Younger Brother of Jesus' would not listen to talk of strategy, preferring to retreat into his visions which, he was adamant, had guaranteed him victory. He boasted that 'The Most High Father has issued to me his sacred decree. God the father, and my Divine elder brother [i.e. Christ] have commanded me ... to become the one true lord of all nations. What cause have I then to fear? Remain with me, or leave me, as you choose ... I have at my command an angelic host of a million strong: how then could a hundred thousand or so of these unholy Imperialists enter the city?'[14] Hearing this nonsense, the Loyal Prince, the most faithful of the Heavenly King's supporters, finally realised his folly. He burst into tears and fled the council chamber.

Despite his vain boasting, as the Manchu battalions pressed ever more strongly upon the city defences, bombarding the walls and mining beneath them, even the Heavenly King came to realise that there could be only one outcome to the siege. On the 27th day of the 5th Moon (12th May 1864), he mixed poison with his wine. How his thoughts must have raced as he reviewed the last thirteen eventful years: from failed scholar to the Emperor of the southern half of the Middle Kingdom! And now it was ending. Holding the poisoned chalice aloft, he cried, 'It is not God the Father that has deceived me, but it is I who have disobeyed God the Father'. Given the great fall from his early ideals of justice and equality in a Kingdom of Heavenly Peace to a gold- and jewel-bedecked 'Emperor' who presided over inequalities as great as anything in Manchu China, Hung Hsui-chuan's final words are not without merit. He quaffed the cup in a single draught, but if Hung sought a speedy exit from this world he was to be disappointed. The poison was slow-acting and he lingered in agony until midnight. His immediate followers, fearful of a total collapse of morale among the defenders, buried his body in the palace grounds and tried to suppress any knowledge of his death. As the Heavenly King held himself in Emperor-like seclusion, this ruse was successful for some sixteen days. When the news did finally leak out, far from depressing the fighting spirit of the surviving Tai Ping troops it seems if anything to have strengthened their resolve to defend Nanking to the death.

At dawn on the 22nd July 1864 the final assault on Nanking was made. A huge mine was detonated, creating a sixty-yard breach in the walls, through which the Imperial army surged, sweeping away all opposition. The rebels exploded a magazine, killing many Imperialists and beginning a panic-stricken retreat which was only contained when the Manchu officers shot or cut down those leading the rout. By late afternoon it was obvious that the city had been won. Even so, not a single rebel surrendered voluntarily – all were either slain, or 'buried themselves alive rather than be taken', a fate chosen by the Heavenly King's own son. Some few were overpowered after hard fighting, among them the wounded Loyal Prince, and two elder brothers of the rebel King. The latter pair seemed completely disorientated 'and could only repeat incessantly "God the Father, God the Father". As I could get no information from them, and as they were sick unto death, I had them both beheaded ...'.[15]

The grave of the Heavenly King was discovered by Tseng Guo-feng and the body exhumed: 'Even the feet of the corpse were wrapped in dragon embroideries,' he reported to Yehonala, 'he had a bald head and a beard streaked with grey.' Tseng had the head of the decaying corpse removed and the trunk and limbs burned on a large bonfire. The Heavenly King's severed head was fastened to a long pole and carried around the provinces he had conquered during the rebellion, officially 'to assuage public indignation' but also, it seems, to prove to the populace that Hung was truly dead, and to prevent any Tai Ping propaganda that he had escaped and would return to wreak vengeance on the Manchu.

Yehonala had ordered Tseng Guo-feng to bring the Loyal Prince, Li Hsiu-cheng, in an open cage to Beijing, where she had intended to display him publicly before his execution. However, Tseng had had several conversations with the rebel leader, and seems to have been favourably impressed with his prisoner. Tseng asked the Loyal Prince to write an account of the rebellion in his own words (an account which still survives, and gives a unique perspective on a popular rising – the losing side are rarely allowed a voice).[16] In a memorial to Yehonala, Tseng Guo-feng mentions that the Loyal Prince had advised the Manchu not to be too hard on the rebellious soldiery of Canton and Guangxi, the provinces at the heart of the insurrection. Such action would only produce even greater animosity towards the Dynasty, and foment further rebellions.

Tseng concluded: 'It seems to me there is much sense in his advice.' He also noted the high prestige that the Loyal Prince was held in by the rank and file of the rebellion, and more worryingly by the ordinary peasants. 'I feel that there would be some risk of Li starving himself to death on the journey, or that a rescue might even be attempted, for Li was extraordinarily popular with the common people.' So worried was Tseng that, as soon as the prisoner had completed his history of the revolt, and directly against Yehonala's orders, he immediately had the Loyal Prince beheaded.

The fall of the Tai Ping did much to enhance Yehonala's status. In the mind of the ordinary people, the beginning of her reign (for no one in China was under any illusion who held the whip hand within the Forbidden City) was forever associated with the return of peace and good governance. Moreover, it had been Yehonala who had supported the promotion of Tseng Guo-feng, the generalissimo who had finally put paid to the thirteen year rebellion. With such an auspicious beginning, many were willing to turn a blind eye to the manner in which she had come to power.

One person now stood between Yehonala and the total, absolute power she craved – her erstwhile ally and would-be mentor, Prince Kung. While the Tai Ping rebellion still raged, strategy demanded the maintenance of at least the appearance of amity between these two rival personalities. But with the end of the rebellion, Yehonala's hands were no longer tied. Prince Kung was about to discover that his position and privileges were entirely dependent upon the goodwill of the young concubine he had helped make the most powerful female in the realm.

Just nine months after the fall of Nanking, and while mopping up operations against the rump of the Tai Ping still continued, Yehonala struck. During one of his regular discussions with the Emperor and the two Empresses Dowager, Prince Kung rose from his knees before the audience had ended. This was forbidden by long custom, as a precaution to prevent assassination of the sovereign. Prince Kung was therefore, *sensu strictu*, in the wrong. It may have been absent-mindedness, or a belief that his undoubted loyalty allowed him privileges denied to others, but Yehonala saw her chance and took it. She yelled wildly for aid, screaming treachery and ordering the palace guards to remove the Prince. Shocked and angry, he was hustled from the audience chamber. Retribution was swift; an Imperial decree in the name of the Empresses Regent stripped the Prince of all his titles and positions, accusing him of attempting to usurp the authority of the throne. However, it was the genius of Yehonala that, a month later, Prince Kung had been rehabilitated and all but one of his honours restored. This was done by way of a 'Decree of Explanation' in which Yehonala – and nominally Sakota – restated her reasons for punishing the Prince, but explained the measure as a device simply to chastise him for his arrogance, and to save him from himself! As this laudable end had now been accomplished, and following a deluge of memorials requesting that the Prince be pardoned for his errors, the decree stated that the Emperor (for which read his mother) was not averse to reconciliation.

The message was clear. Just as medieval European Popes claimed the right to make and unmake kings, Yehonala now considered herself the source and origin of all titles and honours within the Middle Kingdom. And the price demanded from both Pope and Empress was the same – unquestioning loyalty. If Yehonala could destroy Prince Kung in a moment, what might she do to lesser men?

Just to emphasise the point, a second decree (again in the name of the two Empresses) gave an account of the Prince's first Imperial audience following his reinstatement, which is probably mostly fiction and stands as a fine example of hypocritical self-aggrandisement, a pattern which was to be repeated throughout Yehonala's long reign:

He prostrated himself humbly and wept bitterly, in token of his boundless self-abasement ... and the Prince seemed full of remorse for misconduct which he freely acknowledged. Sincere feelings of this kind could not fail to elicit our compassion ... For our part we had no prejudice in this matter and were animated only by strict impartiality; it was inconceivable that we should desire to treat harshly a Councillor of such tried ability or to deprive ourselves of the the valuable assistance of the Prince. We now therefore restore him to the Grand Council, but in order that his authority may be reduced, we do not propose to reinstate him in his position as 'Adviser to the Government'.

Prince Kung, see to it now that you forget not the shame and remorse that have overtaken you! Strive to requite our kindness and display greater self-control in the performance of your duties![17]

There could be no mistake. In the race for absolute power, it was Yehonala first and the rest of the field nowhere. The Empress of the Western Palace was now firmly in control of the Celestial Empire.

CHAPTER TEN

Death of a favourite

*D*espite his claimed bitter remorse, there is no doubt that Prince Kung harboured great resentment for the humiliation he had suffered. By this time, Yehonala was beyond his vengeance, untouchable, and in his anger the Prince redirected his aggression at softer targets – the palace eunuchs. He especially directed his spleen upon Yehonala's favourite eunuch, An Te-hai. If indeed he was a eunuch. The gossipmongers of Beijing had it that An Te-hai was *Homo intactus*, one of a small number of men throughout history who (or so it was claimed) had lived a double life within the Forbidden City, with all the dangers and advantages that accrued from such an ambiguous position. There were more than three thousand wives, concubines and maidservants of the Emperor, the majority neglected and frustrated and no doubt grateful for any male companionship. The same was true of the ladies of a deceased Emperor, Yehonala included, whom custom required to spend the rest of their lives in chaste widowhood. A mockeunuch might live in close proximity to such a lady without exciting comment. And the rumours implicated An Te-hai as a lover of the Western Empress.

It seems Prince Kung believed that An Te-hai had been the eunuch responsible for informing Yehonala that the Prince had risen from his knees before the due time at the fateful audience that had stripped the Manchu noble of most of his power and titles. Seated behind a yellow silk screen the Western Empress would not have known of the Prince's breach of etiquette. Prince Kung may have had other reasons for singling out this particular individual. It was standard Chinese politics to hurt a more powerful opponent by striking at his friends and those he held dear, and Yehonala's attachment to An Te-hai was common knowledge. Besides, the eunuch had arrogated to himself honours and titles far beyond those allowed by the Manchu house-laws: he had a huge personal retinue, dressed in the most sumptuous silks, and was known as Lord of Nine Thousand Years, regarded by many as a calculated insult towards the person of the Emperor, the Lord of Ten Thousand Years. Such arrogance can only have rankled with the newly demoted, but equally imperious, nobleman. And so, just as Yehonala had bided her time, waiting to strike at Prince Kung, he stoically held his peace, patiently seeking an opportunity to wound her through her favourite.

It was almost four years before the chance came. In 1869, increasingly confident in her hold over the Empire (although she still issued issued all decrees jointly with her co-Regent, the Empress Sakota) Yehonala became careless. She found herself short of funds, and ordered her favourite on an unofficial mission south to Shandong Province to collect tribute. In doing so she broke one of the cardinal rules of Manchu house-law, that no eunuch might leave the capital, under pain of death. True to his flamboyant character, and confident of his mistress's protection, An Te-hai made the journey in ostentatious style, sailing down the Grand Canal

> ... in two dragon barges, with much display of pomp and pageantry ... His barges flew a black banner, bearing in its centre the triple Imperial emblems of the sun, and there were also Dragon, and Phoenix flags [signifying the Empress] flying on both sides of his vessel. A goodly company of both sexes were in attendance; there were female musicians, skilled in the use of string and wind instruments. The banks of the Canal were lined with crowds of spectators, who witnessed his progress with amazement and admiration. The 21st of last month happened to be this eunuch's birthday, so he arrayed himself in Dragon robes, and stood on the foredeck of his barge, to receive the homage of his suite.[1]

An Te-hai was obviously enjoying his excursion beyond the walls of the Great Within. But unknown to him, or to Yehonala, word of the eunuch's extravagant progress had been sent secretly by the Governor of Shandong to Prince Kung. Here was the ideal opportunity for the Prince to revenge himself upon the Western Empress, and he seized it with both hands. Shrewd statesman that he was, the Prince also saw an opportunity to drive a wedge between the two Empresses Dowager. He sought out Sakota, and persuaded the slow, malleable Empress to sign a decree condemning the eunuch to death, without the customary trial in Beijing. Biddable as she undoubtedly was, she clearly understood the storm that would break about her head when Yehonala discovered, too late, the fate of her minion: 'The Western Empress will assuredly kill me for this,' she reportedly said as she handed over the decree to Prince Kung. Why Sakota agreed to this is a mystery: it may be she believed the fateful and mysterious document given her by the dying Emperor Hsien Feng in 1860 at Jehol (and whose contents she had revealed to no one) would save her from the worst of Yehonala's wrath.

Prince Kung sped the decree to Shandong, where the Governor, Ting Pao-chen, acted immediately. The edict specifically commanded the governor that 'no attention is to be paid to any crafty explanations which the eunuch may attempt to make'. An Te-hai was arrested near his gorgeous barge in Tai'an Prefecture, and vainly protesting his high position and his authority from the Western Empress, was summarily beheaded in front of his gaily bedecked entourage. And, as was normal in Chinese society, An's whole family fell with him – they were arrested and sent off as slaves to the frontier guards in the north-west, China's most dangerous border region. Not content with this, several eunuchs travelling with An Te-hai were also given their quietus at the same time by strangling. Six more managed to escape and to evade capture for a while. Five were eventually taken and executed, but the sixth eunuch successfully eluded his pursuers and made his way back to the capital. Here, in great secrecy, he recounted the tale of An Te-hai's fall to An's deputy, Li Lien-ying, the same Li who had acted as masseur to the dying Emperor in Jehol, and had stolen the Imperial Seal, by which, indirectly, Yehonala had been able to ascend to the Dragon Throne.

Li can hardly have been heartbroken by the news. His own promotion to Chief Eunuch was only possible via An Te-hai's disgrace or death and, while he must often have longed to hear the news the surviving eunuch now brought to him, he could never have expected to achieve his ambition quite so soon. No doubt hiding his satisfaction, Li immediately informed his mistress. When she first heard of An's execution, Yehonala refused to accept it. She had long since discounted Sakota as a force within the Forbidden City, and could not believe that the Eastern Empress would have dared so openly to flout her own authority. When she finally accepted the accuracy of the report, true to her temperament, she acted immediately. Striding in rage to the ironically named 'Palace of Benevolent Peace', she confronted her cousin and demanded an explanation. Sakota tried to place all the blame on Prince Kung, but it was a hopeless defence – her own seal was on the decree ordering An Te-hai's death. Some accounts claim that the Palace of Benevolent Peace rang to the fearsome sound of Yehonala's full-throated anger as she openly vowed to answer An Te-hai's 'murder' with the death of her cousin. This is unlikely: correct form, perfect etiquette, were de rigueur within the Forbidden City, at least between social equals. No matter how bitter the enmity, the time-honoured rules of *Li* were punctiliously observed. But while Yehonala almost certainly refrained from direct threats, both Empresses knew that the death of An Te-hai had produced a sea-change in their relationship: the close companionship of their youth, the intimate alliance forged in the furnace of palace intrigue and their fight against Su Shun, had been irrevocably severed. And Yehonala, at some time and in some way, would have her vengeance.

Prince Kung received similar treatment. The following morning she received him at audience and coldly threatened him with a second dismissal and loss of honours. But Yehonala never followed through on her threats: the howls of protest from Censors and memorialists that followed her first chastising of the Prince had convinced her that, for the present, he was far too popular to remove. Even had she wished to act, she had no reasonable motive: An Te-hai's mission had been utterly illegal. Yehonala had relied on her prestige and power to cow all protest, but (and it was so unlike her) she had no suitable historical precedent or pressing state emergency to excuse the eunuch's journey outside the Forbidden City. It was specifically against the Dynasty's house-laws, and the punishment for the miscreant was death. That she was in the wrong was more an irritation than a source of shame. She continued to nurse her grievance carefully, and for decades thereafter she wounded the Prince at every opportunity, most notably by ignoring all precedent and refusing to acknowledge his son as heir to the throne, and carefully arranging that all descendants of the Prince be excluded from the Imperial succession. All protests were ignored – this able and astute nobleman was marginalised, and the history of China changed irrevocably – because of the death of a eunuch.

Figure 1 Yehonala and her eunuchs. Li Lien-ying, the Grand Eunuch, stands in the right foreground.
Reproduced with permission of the Freer Gallery of Art/Arthur M. Sackler Gallery. Smithsonian Institute.

Figure 2 Prince Kung at the signing of the Sino-British Agreement, Beijing 1860.
Courtesy of Santa Barbara Museum of Art, from the Michael and Jane Wilson Collection. Photography by Scott McClaine, 1998.

Figure 3 Despite her ruthless nature, Yehonala loved to portray herself as Kuan Yin, Goddess of Mercy; Grand Eunuch Li Lien-ying, and a lady-in-waiting act the part of attendant deities.
Reproduced with permission of the Freer Gallery of Art/Arthur M. Sackler Gallery. Smithsonian Institute. Photography by Xunling, Court Photographer.

Figure 4 The reality of beheading: four Boxer rebels executed during the Boxer uprising, c.1900. Reproduced with permission from the Mary Evans Picture Library. Photographer unknown.

Figure 5 The cangue. The victims could neither eat nor drink while wearing the cangue. Unless released, a slow death was certain.
Source: Worswick, C. and Spence, J., *Imperial China in Photographs 1850–1912*, Scolar Press, London, 1979. Photographer unknown.

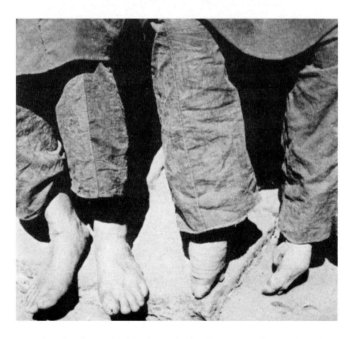

Figure 6 Foot-binding. The 'lily-feet' which Chinese gentlemen found so erotic.
Source: Beers, B. F., *China in Old Photographs 1860–1910*, Charles Scribner's Sons, New York, 1978. Photographer unknown.

Figure 7 Yehonala at thirty-five, probably the earliest photographic image of Emperor Hsien Feng's former concubine and undisputed ruler of the Middle Kingdom.
Reproduced with permission of Hulton Archive.

Figure 8   Lord Elgin, British Envoy to China, 1860.
Courtesy of Santa Barbara Museum of Art, from the Michael and Jane Wilson Collection. Photography by Scott McClaine, 1998.

Figure 9 The Forbidden City, facing south from Coal Hill towards the Gate of Spiritual Valour. Source: Worswick, C. and Spence, J., *Imperial China in Photographs 1850–1912*. Scolar Press, London, 1979. Photographer unknown.

CHAPTER ELEVEN

The Emperor's 'good fortune'

*A*s expected, Li Lien-ying was raised to the position of Chief Eunuch to replace the late An Te-hai, and he very soon enjoyed as close a relationship with the Empress of the Western Palace as his unfortunate predecessor. Yehonala's affinity for eunuchs was obvious and well known, but Li Lien-ying, handsome and with impeccable manners, was allowed unusual liberties. Uniquely for a servant, he was allowed to initiate discussions with Yehonala on subjects of his own choosing, and to remain seated in her presence, sometimes even using the Imperial throne to relax upon while he conversed. As their friendship matured he began to use the word *tsa-men* 'we two' when speaking of his dealings with the Western Empress, a term normally used between family members or intimate social equals. As she aged, it was Li who coined the soubriquet 'Lao fu-yeh' (Venerable Buddha) for Yehonala, an affectionate title she greatly enjoyed.

In stark contrast to her eunuch favourite, Yehonala appeared incapable of forming and maintaining normal family ties, especially with her son, the Tung Chih Emperor. From an early age, he preferred the company of his more easy-going and less demanding aunt Sakota, the now-hated Empress of the Eastern Palace. By 1870, at the age of fourteen, the young Emperor saw his mother less and less and, like the adolescent he was, delighted in his ability to shock. Palace gossip already implicated him in an illicit affair with a maidservant, behaviour guaranteed to add tension to an already strained relationship. This growing estrangement between mother and son was a great cause for concern – and the anguish was not purely, or even primarily, maternal. It was first and foremost a threat to Yehonala's continued authority.

When she had first taken power, ten years before, the span of her regency must have seemed almost limitless. But the years had passed, and in two more years, Tung Chih would reach the age of maturity, and Yehonala would be expected to step down and to gradually relinquish her control of the Empire to her son. No doubt she had expected Tung Chih to remain compliant, allowing her to exert her influence from behind the scenes. But his rebellious attitude put her continued ascendancy at risk. As he matured Tung Chih could only come to rely less and less on Yehonala's 'advice'. With his liking for his aunt, there was even a danger that he might go over to the 'enemy's camp', and to make common cause with Sakota and Prince Kung, leaving his mother isolated and vulnerable. Her lack of influence over her son and the danger this posed to her continued rule became the single most important factor in Yehonala's policy, and led to the most terrible consequences.

There was more. In the longer term, an even greater difficulty presented itself. Once he had reached the age of maturity, the Emperor Tung Chih must marry. Apart from good stewardship of the Empire, the Celestial Prince's prime duty was to sire a son to secure the succession. For without an undisputed heir, dissension was sure to arise, and with it the risk of civil war. A son for the Emperor was the *sine qua non* of stability. Everyone in the Middle Kingdom, from the lowliest peasant to the most exalted nobility, desired such an outcome.

Everyone except Yehonala. Until her own pregnancy, she had been merely a concubine of the second rank, a relatively minor place in the hierarchy of the Great Within. After winning the Emperor's affection, Yehonala had achieved her pre-eminent status among the Emperor's ladies solely by being the mother of the heir. Her authority was, and remained, entirely dependent upon her position as the mother of Tung Chih. But when, in the fullness of time, Tung Chih's future wife in turn gave birth to a son, everything would change. The Emperor's wife would now be entitled to the honorific 'Empress Mother'. A single act of parturition would sweep away much of Yehonala's status and power.

Worse might follow. For if the Emperor himself was to predecease his wife, Yehonala would lose even the title Empress Dowager in favour of the late Emperor's spouse and with it the remainder of her influence. She would remain an Empress Dowager of a senior generation, theoretically of higher status, but she would not be *the* Empress Dowager. Obscurity beckoned. She would be relegated to some backwater, far from the wellsprings of power, and forgotten. And, quite as hard to stomach, her now-hated cousin Sakota, the Empress of the Eastern Palace, would retain all her ranks and distinctions, as these honours were based on Sakota's position as wife of the late Emperor, Hsien Feng.

This was more than a simple question of status, of Yehonala's desire to continue to enjoy the fruits of supreme authority. Her period of autocratic rule had offended many of the Imperial clan. Once stripped of rank, powerless, she knew she could expect no mercy from her foes. The coming danger was redolent with echoes of the Su Shun crisis – but this time she had no Prince Kung, no cousin Sakota, with whom to make common cause. Except for her eunuch allies, Yehonala was alone.

The solution was simple – Tung Chih must have no sons.

Yehonala must have been aware of the implications. A grandchild could threaten not only her power but her existence. She could not allow a grandchild to be born. But Tung Chih's illicit liaison at the tender age of fourteen was potent evidence that, once married to a fertile female, children were a virtual certainty. This led to a further conclusion, one that seems to fly in the face of all maternal instinct. Tung Chih must die intestate. And so he must die young.

In the normal course of events, such an eventuality was remote – Tung Chih was in his teens, Yehonala was thirty-five. In the normal course of events, it was likely that the Celestial Prince would outlive his mother, and sire a family. But Yehonala had seen to it that the life of the young Emperor had been far from normal. From a very early age, his mother had allowed his eunuch companions to introduce him to a whole series of decadent 'pastimes'. Members of the Imperial Household, notably Wen Hai and Kuei Pao, aided him in 'secretly' leaving the Great Within and disporting himself in brothels and dancing houses in the worst parts of the capital. His licentious habits brought their own reward – reading between the lines of contemporary reports, it is obvious that the Emperor contracted a venereal disease, perhaps even syphilis. And the diarists and commentators are unanimous that, when this occurred, his mother '... allowed it to wreak havoc with his delicate constitution, without providing him with such medical assistance as might have been available'.[1] Yehonala seemed intent on orchestrating the early death of her son – despite his youth, everyone at court knew that Tung Chih would not live to see old age.

There are some who say that Yehonala dearly loved her son and that she was not aware of the debauches and perversions in which he indulged. But this is disingenuous, a refusal to admit the depth to which the Western Empress was prepared to descend in order to maintain her autocratic rule. Yehonala's intelligence network was the most efficient in the Middle Kingdom. It is inconceivable that she did not know of the shameful exploits of her son, and the fatal consequences of such adventures. It was within her power to forbid these revels, yet she did nothing to prevent them. When a member of the Imperial Household, Kuei Ching, denounced the malefic influence of the eunuchs on the Solitary Prince, and had several of the worst offenders beheaded, Yehonala had this true friend of the Emperor removed from his post. Sadly, Tung Chih, too blind to see the bleak future that awaited him, approved the dismissal. To many, it appeared that the Western Empress wished only to hasten the demise of her son. Can this be true? Did she really plot the death of her own son? Even though it means their own demise, most parents have no wish to outlive their offspring, and will happily lay down their lives to ensure the survival of the next generation. Did such a selfish, implacable nature dwell within the beautiful, petite figure of Yehonala that she would sacrifice her own child on the altar of her ambition? Or was the motive a mix of personal ambition and the vindictive deep-rooted vendetta between the Aisin Gioro and her own clan that produced such a reversal of maternal affection? That there was nothing she would not do to deny the Imperial clan direct succession to the Dragon Throne? There appears to be no other explanation for her actions.

Unless one of the wilder stories concerning her pregnancy is true. Several rumours were widespread before and after the birth of Tung Chih in April 1856. One claimed that the child was the result of the union between Yehonala and her former love, Jung Lu. This can be safely discounted. Jung Lu exercised considerable influence over Yehonala throughout her life, and for him to have allowed her to do away with their child requires a degree of pitiless, unnatural behaviour in the Manchu warrior that is quite contrary to everything we know of him. However, one tale may fully explain Yehonala's incomprehensible actions, without our having recourse to branding her a heartless filicide. This story claims that Yehonala's son was not her son at all. The child had been purchased secretly from Chinese peasants and smuggled into the Forbidden City at the time of Yehonala's confinement. She subsequently passed the infant off as her own, and the offspring of the Emperor. Fanciful though the story appears to be, it does fit with Yehonala's temperament. We know that she would prefer death to obscurity and the life of an nonentity within the Forbidden City. The risks were undoubtedly enormous, she was gambling with her life and facing a certain, hideous death were she to be discovered. But if Yehonala did pass off another couple's child as the Emperor's son she knew that the doors to power and wealth would fly open. Perhaps she was prepared to chance it.

If so, it would explain her indifference to Tung Chih's fate and her active connivance in an early death for the Emperor. Given the Manchu disdain for their Chinese subjects, especially the 'stupid people', she may have regarded Tung Chih (were he the child of Chinese peasants) as little better than an animal, as simply a tool to achieve power, one that could be discarded at any time should it prove expedient.

Whatever the truth of this, despite his illness and lack of proper medical care, the Emperor survived until his sixteenth year. This was the age of majority according to the Manchu house-laws, the time when he should assume the reins of government, and the Empresses Regent should stand down.

He was also eligible to marry, and marriage meant that a new heir to the throne might well be born within a year. Certainly, for Yehonala, time was running out.

Worse was to follow. Unlike his father, Hsien Feng, Tung Chih insisted on being allowed to select his own wife from among the Manchu maidens summoned to the Great Within. His choice fell on A-lu-te, the eighteen-year-old daughter of Ch'ung-chi, the assistant Imperial tutor, and member of a prestigious Mongol clan. Many at court approved his choice: not only was A-lu-te possessed of surpassing beauty, such a union would help to cement the unequal alliance between the Mongol and Manchu nations, strengthening the Dynasty's increasingly shaky hold on the Middle Kingdom. Yehonala was less pleased. With a perhaps unconscious acknowledgement of her own 'strategic' marriage (which ostensibly strengthened the ties between the Yeho-Nala and the Aisin Gioro clans) Yehonala mistrusted her daughter-in-law: 'How could we tell that her beauty was false? She was so very beautiful, but she hated us.'[2] She might have been speaking about herself.

The young couple seem to have been genuinely happy together, and to have possessed that naive belief in the infinite continuation of their own good fortune that true love often imparts. The Emperor began to assert himself, refusing to submit official papers to Yehonala for her comments, and gradually but inexorably reducing his mother's participation in government. By himself, the Emperor might never have dared so much, but A-lu-te applauded and encouraged his increasing confidence and autonomy, and eager to please his new wife, the slow paring away of his mother's authority continued. Tung Chih's moon was waxing as Yehonala's waned.

Then suddenly, disaster struck. In December 1874 a decree was issued in Tung Chih's name announcing that he had had the 'good fortune to contract smallpox', the Chinese of the time believing that the disease augured well for the future. 'Their Majesties the Empresses Dowager,' the decree continued, 'have shown the greatest possible tenderness in the care of our person. They have also consented to peruse all Memorials and State papers, on our behalf, and to carry on the business of the

State, for which we are deeply grateful. We feel bound to confer upon their Majesties additional titles of honour, so as to make some return, however small, for their infinite goodness.'[3]

It is hard not to see the hand of Yehonala in the composition of this decree. It granted her all she required: the official papers that Tung Chih had proscribed were now hers to 'peruse' at will; she was the recipient of new honorifics – and the additional yearly stipend that accompanied them; and the decree even documents the gratitude of her son the Emperor for compassionate ministrations during his illness. Until the Emperor recovered, a forlorn hope given his weakened constitution and the consequences of his licentious past, Yehonala was again the supreme power in the land (for no one believed that the co-Regent, Sakota, could oppose her cousin's implacable will).

By 23rd December, the Emperor appeared to have weathered the worst of the pox and to be on the mend. However, just a few days later, the Emperor suffered a relapse from which he never recovered. One official, Yun Tu-ting, later wrote that the Emperor's mother had crept into his sick-room while he conversed with his wife. Hearing A-lu-te daring to voice criticisms of her mother-in-law, Yehonala flew into one of her well-documented rages, 'her cheekbones were sharp and the veins on her forehead projected; she showed her teeth as if she were suffering from lockjaw'.[4] She dragged the hapless A-lu-te around the room by the hair, slapping her face repeatedly and, calling on the eunuch attendants, ordered them to take her from the room and beat her. This domestic quarrel, said Yun Tu-ting, had produced the Emperor's relapse. Tung Chih lingered on until 13th January 1875, dying at eight in the evening, at the age of nineteen. Yehonala was at his deathbed, along with Sakota, Jung Lu, Prince Kung and around twenty of the more important princes and ministers. A-lu-te was refused permission to enter the room. Tung Chih's short span of authority had been snuffed out, and his mother's brief eclipse at court was over. From facing certain ruin she was again in command of the Empire. Once more, Heaven had chosen Yehonala to rule.

But many believed that Heaven had been a very small player in the drama of Tung Chih's death. The timing of the Emperor's

demise was just too convenient for the Empress of the Western
Palace, and it stimulated suspicion in many minds. Rumours
abounded: it was claimed that she had not only allowed her
son to ruin his health in the lowest brothels in Beijing, she
had been the source of his fatal smallpox infection.

Except among the peasants and the poor, Chinese meals are
sumptuous affairs, with table manners sometimes diametrically opposed to those of the West. Rather than leaving an
empty plate, it was considered an insult to the host if all the
meal was eaten – the idea being that more than enough
courses had been provided to satisfy the guests' hunger. The
meal always consists of many dishes (never less than one hundred at the Imperial table) and between courses, and especially
at the end of a meal, hot towels are given to each diner, with
which they can refresh themselves by wiping their face, and
then their hands. This civilised custom had, on several occasions in Chinese history, been put to foul and infamous ends.
Saturated with poison, the towel would be rubbed over the skin
and the unsuspecting victim would be the agent of his or her
own demise. In the case of Tung Chih, it was alleged that the
towel marked for the Emperor had first been rubbed over the
open, active pustules of a smallpox victim, and then proffered
to the Celestial Prince. As the Son of Heaven would never
perform such a menial task himself, it was left to one of the
eunuch attendants, under the supervision of Yehonala's confidant the Grand Eunuch, Li Lien-ying, to diligently wipe the
Emperor's face with the virus-permeated cloth, so ensuring
his infection.

The sudden and, from Yehonala's view, convenient 'relapse' of
the Emperor following his apparent triumph over the disease
also raises questions. Yun Tu-ting's story of Yehonala's assault
on A-lu-te and the Emperor's nervous collapse may well be
true. But as later events proved, Yehonala was no tiro in the
use of subtle poisons. The Emperor's 'relapse' may have had
more to do with an induced physiological collapse than any
emotional crisis.

Some time after, Yehonala is quoted as saying of Tung Chih's
passing, 'Since that time I have been a changed woman, as all

happiness was over as far as I was concerned when he died'. But if the Western Empress was crushed by the death of her only son, she managed to hide it well. Within the day she had ordered a solemn conclave of ministers to select a new Emperor. There was good reason for speed: Yehonala knew that she must act quickly to give her enemies the shortest time possible to organise against her. With the Emperor dead, her power base was gone: 'It was to motherhood she owed her first claims to power; now she had nothing but her own boundless ambition, courage and intelligence to take the place of lawful claims and natural ties.'[5]

There was another reason, perhaps *the* reason for the Emperor's illness and death. Yehonala's worst nightmare had come true. A-lu-te was said to be pregnant with the dead Emperor's child. If Tung Chih was indeed Yehonala's natural son, the foetus was destined to be Yehonala's own grandchild. But if it was a son, it would be Emperor, A-lu-te would become Empress Mother, and Yehonala's enemies would pounce. Something had to be done.

The speed with which matters moved forward indicates a preconceived and well-executed plan. Even before the meeting to choose the new Emperor took place, Jung Lu with his predominantly Yeho-Nala bannermen had been placed on special duty within the Forbidden City. Li Hung-chang, the Chinese commander who had distinguished himself during the Tai Ping rebellion and who owed his command to Yehonala, had also sent trusted troops from Anhui to Beijing at the Empress's express command. And her loyal and trusted confidant the Grand Eunuch Li Lien-ying, had placed his eunuchs at strategic points throughout the palace. The stage had been skilfully set for a silent *coup d'état*. Nothing was said, but it was obvious to the twenty-seven officials attending this historic meeting that defying the will of the Western Empress would result in the most dire consequences.

The meeting was held at dusk, among the blue- and gold-painted columns of the Palace of Mind Nurture, the braziers of the Forbidden City alternately flaring and dying away in the wind that presaged one of the periodic dust-storms that assailed Beijing at this season. The assembled Imperial clansmen and high officials kowtowed as the two Empresses Dowager entered the palace, each sumptuously dressed, Yehonala wearing a ceremonial dragon-robe of Imperial yellow. As soon as they were seated, Yehonala took command of the council. She had already chosen the new Emperor, but she knew that there were two rivals for the Dragon Throne whose challenges must be met and quashed, the son of her erstwhile ally Prince Kung, and Pu Lun, who could trace his lineage back to the august Emperor Tao Kwang, the same ruler of China who had attempted to suppress the opium trade in 1838. And then there was A-lu-te. Yehonala had pre-empted any crisis here by ordering A-lu-te excluded from the council. The problem (as she saw it) of A-lu-te's pregnancy would be resolved at another time. The astute and ruthless female who had ruled China for over fourteen years years had no intention of allowing a newly widowed girl the chance of spoiling her carefully laid plans with an emotional plea to the assembled members.

Characteristically, Yehonala seized the intiative, arrogating to herself the position of 'chairman' and launching into a prepared statement which brushed aside the claims of A-lu-te's unborn child, on the basis that the Dragon Throne should not be held empty on the assumption that a boy-child would be born. Prince Kung begged to disagree. He argued that as the Emperor's widow was very near full term, the news of the Emperor's demise could be suppressed until the child was born. If a boy was born, all was well; if a girl, then there was still time to decide the best successor to Tung Chih. Many of the Imperial clansmen supported this view. But with instinctive political savvy, Yehonala immediately took a new tack, bringing to mind the recent Tai Ping rebellion and revolts that still threatened in the south. 'When the nest is destroyed, how many eggs will remain unbroken?' she asked pointedly. Fearful that news of the Emperor's death would fan the flames of rebellion anew, several Grand Councillors, including three representatives from the south, indicated their support for her arguments.

Sakota, in a rare show of intitiative (or perhaps as part of a prearranged plan with her old ally), suggested that Prince Kung's son be chosen as heir. As custom demanded, Prince

Kung kowtowed and declared his son unworthy of such a high honour (which he of course coveted) and suggested instead that Pu Lun, a child of just two months, would be the better candidate. He was, as all present knew, the grandson of the esteemed Emperor Tao Kwang's eldest son. Continuing the age-old dance, Pu Lun's father (seething with repressed ambition) made obeisance and in turn declared his son unequal to the task.

Yehonala took them both at their word. She was dismissive of Pu Lun's claim, stating (rightly) that his father was an adoptive son, and not a blood relative, and asking for a historical precedent to support such a move. Prince Kung, after some hesitation, suggested one from the fifteeenth century. Yehonala shot back immediately that this was a bad precedent, saying tartly that the Emperor in question 'was not really the son of his predecessor, but was palmed off on the Emperor by one of the Imperial Concubines. His reign was a period of disaster ...'. It was a masterful demolition of the opposition (and a bold one considering the rumours concerning the legitimacy of her own son), but it revealed something far more telling: that this 'sudden crisis' had been thought through some time ahead. It is inconceivable that the Western Empress could have simply brought to mind such a fitting rebuttal to Prince Kung's statement. China has an almost inexhaustible mine of historical events on which to draw. It would have taken much toil to research which historical precedents might be used to support the various claimants, and more time again to prepare a fitting riposte. The speed and appositeness of the response within a day of Tung Chih's death shows the depth of planning that had gone into this quiet coup. Whatever else she might be guilty of, Yehonala had prepared the ground well.

Prince Kung's own son was dismissed in a similar peremptory manner, and again by manipulating Chinese tradition to her own ends. In Confucian society a child should always kowtow to family members of an older generation, and especially to its own father. But equally, tradition demanded that all should make obeisance to the Emperor. If a man were chosen as Son of Heaven, a terribly embarrassing situation arose, for the Emperor as the son of his father should kowtow, but as the Son of Heaven he could never abase himself to anyone. The Chinese circumvented this problem by having the father retire from all duties and confine himself to public areas where there was no possibility that he should meet his son. Yehonala claimed that the worthy Prince Kung was so valuable a resource for his country that he simply could not be allowed to retire, as must perforce occur if his son became Emperor. His son, therefore (despite having perhaps the best claim to the throne of all those present), simply could not be Emperor. It was not the strongest argument, but it was backed up with the presence of Jung Lu's troops – and violence has its own, unique form of logic. As she stared truculently from face to face, no one, not even Prince Kung, could find the courage to gainsay the Western Empress.

Yehonala's light, silvery voice spoke out into the heavy silence that had descended on the audience chamber. 'As for me, I propose as heir to the Throne, Tsai Tien, the son of Yi Huan,' adding ominously, 'and I advise you all that we lose no time.' The autocrat had spoken. She had given her adversaries face by listening to their arguments, and now proposed to do exactly what she had planned to do from the start. An open vote was taken and the princes and ministers, aided no doubt by the proximity of Jung Lu's troops, voted fifteen to ten in favour of the Western Empress's 'suggestion'.[6] Tsai Tien was Emperor, and was given the reign-title Kuang Hsu, 'Glorious Succession'. Maintaining the initiative, she immediately, despatched Jung Lu and a detachment of mounted bannermen to accompany the Imperial palanquin as it battled in a torchlit procession against the whirling dust-storm towards the house of Prince Ch'un. There, the sleeping three-year-old Tsai Tien was pulled from his warm, quilted bed, and deposited, mewling his resentment, in the royal litter, draped with yellow satin and embroidered with Imperial dragons. Silently (the bearers' feet and the horses' hooves had all been muffled with sackcloth), the new Emperor was carried back through the narrow streets of the capital to the Forbidden City, dressed in dragon-robes as befitted his new status, and forced, all-unknowing, to kowtow before the shadowed bier of his dead cousin. It was a mournful beginning, and many viewed the Emperor's arrival through the swirling sand-blizzard as an ill omen of his coming reign.

Yehonala was safe. Her successful nominee was an infant, which meant that her position as Regent (once the empty formalities of being asked, and giving her reluctant assent, to taking up the Regency had been gone through) was secure for another thirteen years. Moreover, the new Emperor was the son of Prince Ch'un, who had married Yehonala's younger sister. So the accession of Tsai Tien to the Dragon Throne was not merely a personal victory for Yehonala. It greatly stength-ened the power base of her own clan.

But the coup was not without its loose ends. It is difficult to convey to Western ears the enormity of the sacrilege Yehonala had forced upon the Middle Kingdom. The clan-loyalty and nepotism of the choice were obvious to all, but it was the over-weening disregard for tradition that rankled most with the conservative element that formed the bedrock of Chinese society. According to the Confucian rites, Tung Chih's spirit required the performance of regular prescribed prayers and time-honoured rituals for the comfort and security of his departed soul. Unfortunately for Yehonala, not everyone could perform such ceremonies for the dead. Only a direct male des-cendant (a natural or an adoptive son) could make the neces-sary obeisance and intercede with the gods on behalf of the departed. Here was the nub of the problem, for Tung Chih had neither sired, nor adopted a son. Of the three possible candi-dates for the new Emperor only the two-month-old Pu Lun was eligible to care for the shade of the departed Tung Chih. As members of Tung Chih's own generation, neither Prince Kung's son, nor Yehonala's choice, Tsai Tien, were acceptable. Once again, the ostensibly tradition-bound Yehonala had picked her moment and flouted all time-honoured custom to achieve her own ends.

With her usual cunning, Yehonala came up with a solution, which was issued as a decree in the names of the Empresses Dowager. With breathtaking mendacity, the proclamation stated that the Regents had been 'absolutely compelled to select

Tsai Tien for the throne, and that he should become Heir by adoption to his uncle Hsien Feng [Tung Chih's father], but that, so soon as he should have begotten a son, the Emperor Tung Chih would at once be provided with an heir'. No mention of A-lu-te and Tung Chih's unborn child. The dead Emperor's wife had already become a non-person.

The whole thing was a charade from start to finish. But it was even more of a sham than appeared on the surface. There was a further problem arising from Yehonala's selection of Tsai Tien as Emperor, a physical dysfunction far more fundamental than the intricacies of Confucian rites and more far-reaching in its consequences. It was a problem of which Yehonala was perfectly aware, and which increases the suspicion that she was indeed following a secret agenda of tribal vendetta against the ruling Aisin Gioro clan, and fully intended that the Dynasty's demise should coincide with her own. Tsai Tien was not a normal infant – his testicles were abnormal and he would be infertile as an adult. As Yehonala knew full well, the young Emperor would never be blessed with children and Tung Chih would never 'be provided with a heir'.

History would show that the Western Empress never intended that the new Emperor should outlive her. And without Yehonala's strong hand and mind controlling the competing factions for the throne, when Tsai Tien eventually 'Mounted the Dragon' the question of the succession would likely descend into bloodshed and civil war. That Tsai Tien's physiological problems were known to the councillors long before they agreed to the young boy's accession only serves to reveal the phenomenal power of personality and strength of will that dwelt within the tiny frame of the Empress of the Western Palace.

That left only A-lu-te and her unborn child. On the 27th March it was announced that the late Emperor's wife had 'died of grief'. She had committed suicide, and followed Tung Chih to the Nine Springs.

Perhaps she had. Perhaps, as some commentators have suggested, A-lu-te immolated herself and her unborn child as an act of protest against the 'grievous wrongs done to her, to the memory of her husband, and to the claims of his posthumous heir'.[7] Female suicide-as-protest has a long and honoured tradition within China,[8] and the insults done to Tung Chih's shade by denying him an heir was later to produce another suicide that was even better remembered than that of the late Emperor's widow. But there is another explanation, one that marries well with Yehonala's implacable nature and which was current at the time in the taverns and tea-houses of Beijing. A-lu-te was the greatest living impediment to Yehonala's continued rule. The gossipmongers had it that the Western Empress had ordered A-lu-te's murder, and that of her unborn child.

But was the child unborn?

A granddaughter would have been no threat to Yehonala. Once she had established A-lu-te as a non-person and successfully arranged for the accession of Tsai Tien, she may have felt it expedient to show mercy to Tung Chih's widow and so appease the Mongol clans – but only if A-lu-te did not bear a son. In that case, did her ruthless temperament and her implacable desire to rule assert itself? Did she order both lives snuffed out?

This proposition becomes more likely when the time interval between the deaths of the Emperor and his wife are considered. Tung Chih died on 13th January, A-lu-te on 27th March, a span of some sixty-three days, just over two months. We know from the Chinese records that at the time of Kuang Hsu's accession (14th January) Prince Kung suggested that, as A-lu-te was close to term, they should await the outcome of the birth before making any firm decision on the succession. But if A-lu-te had not given birth by the time she 'committed suicide', she must have been less than seven months pregnant when her husband died and the council was held. For Prince Kung's plan to work, news of the death of Tung Chih would therefore have had be suppressed for more than two months – an almost impossible task in the hothouse atmosphere of the court, where gossip and innuendo was a way of life. Given that Prince Kung is on record as believing this impossible task easy, it seems likely that A-lu-te was actually much closer to term than the official record of her death would have us believe. If this is true, then the late Emperor's child would have been born prior to its mother's death on 27th March.

The possibility therefore exists that Yehonala confined A-lu-te until she had given birth, and that once the sex of the infant was confirmed as male, she knew that the continued existence of her grandson and his mother would jeopardise her power. Her son, her daughter-in-law, and her own grandchild – Yehonala is potentially implicated in all their deaths. If true, we can see how complete was her estrangement from her son (if, of course, Tung Chih was indeed her son), and how total her lust for power. For the former Yi Concubine, the young girl from Anhui Province, no price was too high to maintain her despotic grip on the Celestial Empire.

CHAPTER TWELVE

Slicing the melon

Since the ending of the Tai Ping rebellion in 1864, relations with the foreign devils, if not entirely amicable, had at least settled down to a state of mutual toleration. In the main, this was due to a slow, reluctant acquiescence on the part of the Chinese. More Western traders were working within the Middle Kingdom, and (a slowly increasing source of friction that was later to explode into xenophobic violence) more and more missionaries practised their proselytising vocation. among the 'heathen', even in the most remote provinces of the Empire.

In 1873, after the accession of the Tung Chih Emperor, the Chinese had finally acquiesced to the combined vociferous and insistent demands of the Westerners for an audience with the new Emperor, and had even dropped their centuries-old insistence that foreign ambassadors kowtow before the Son of Heaven. The historic meeting was choreographed down to the last detail by the etiquette-obsessed Manchu (who were greatly put out by the jokes and sniggers of the assembled dignitaries during the numerous rehearsals). They got their own back by staging the audience at the Tzu Kuang Ko, the Pavilion of Violet Light, which, unknown to the Westerners, was a building normally used for the reception of tribute bearers from Chinese satellite states such as Tibet or Korea. The pretence of superiority was continued at the meeting itself. The ambassadors convened at the Tzu Kuang Ko just before dawn on 19th June, and were kept waiting for several hours, imbibing endless bowls of tea with Prince Kung, until they were finally conveyed to the Presence around 9 a.m. The epoch-making audience, over which so much effort, prevarication and mendacity, and so much blood and suffering, had been squandered, lasted a bare thirty minutes. The representatives of France, the Netherlands, Russia, the United States of America and Great Britain, each in turn made obeisance to the Celestial Prince, not the normal kowtow required of every Chinese, but by a simple bow of the head. The Emperor spoke quietly in Manchu and Prince Kung translated into Chinese. Very little of moment was said, but then, that was not the reason for the audience. The Western ambassadors, the emissaries of the Western barbarians, had finally been received by the Emperor, and they had not kowtowed. For the representatives of the West the principle of parity between all sovereign states had at last been formally acknowledged.

The Chinese, of course, saw it differently. Or pretended to. While acknowledging that the ministers had not kowtowed before their Emperor, the *Peking Gazette* nevertheless informed its readers that the foreigners had been cowed into quivering silence by the majestic aura of the Celestial Prince. They had '... admitted that divine virtue certainly emanated from the Emperor, hence the fear and trembling they felt even when they did not look upon his Majesty'.[1] With the near-complete separation of Occident and Orient, the two competing versions of reality were never in any serious danger of meeting or being compared, and so honour was satisfied on both sides.

With the the Tung Chih Emperor's death in 1875, and the beginning of Yehonala's second Regency with her cousin Sakota, this state of relatively peaceful coexistence, this hard-won, precarious equilibrium, was once again disturbed. In their imperialist greed, the Western nations sought either to conquer Chinese territory or to divide the Empire into 'spheres of influence', a de facto conquest where Chinese interests in a particular region would be subordinate to whichever colonialist power happened to hold sway. The Chinese called this process of carving up their nation 'slicing the melon'.

Under the pretext of friendship, in 1871 Russia invaded the Ili region in the predominantly Muslim province of Xinjiang. An Islamic rebellion was then in full flower with the majority

Muslims threatening to set up an independent Islamic state, and the Russian bear's incursion was portrayed by the Westerners as help for the Dragon Throne until the revolt was suppressed. Eight years later, Russian troops still guarded all of Ili's strategic points and refused to be dislodged. The danger from the Czar's Empire was great – it was the only Western nation with lands bordering the Middle Kingdom. To the north of their sacred soil, the Russian bear ambled ever eastwards, annexing territory and casting hungry glances on China's frontier provinces.

From their position in India, the British were more interested in trade and influence than in the physical acquisition of territory. They saw south-west China as the natural entry point to the Middle Kingdom, and sent parties on exploratory trips through Burma towards the Chinese provinces of Sichuan and Yunnan to survey possible trade routes between the two countries. Unfortunately, a surveyor named Margary was murdered in Yunnan in 1875, and, following the sad precedents of the previous decade, the British immediately used his death as an excuse to squeeze China anew. The negotiations were conducted by the brusque Sir Thomas Wade, who as plain Thomas Wade had made his name in China during the 1860 Franco-British march on Beijing. Sir Thomas forced China to the Convention of Chefoo, which opened even more Chinese cities to the foreign trader. The Chinese representative was Li Hung-chang, hero of the Tai Ping rebellion and now, as Viceroy of the important province of Chihli, fast becoming a power in the land. Li's greed was legendary; over a long career, through 'squeeze', and fraud, and bribery, he amassed a fortune that made him certainly the richest man in China, if not the world.[2] But running in parallel with Li's boundless cupidity was an equally prodigious intelligence. He was far-sighted enough to realise China's present weakness before its foes, and he was a near-constant advocate of appeasement (at least until the Empire should strengthen itself sufficiently to throw off the hated foreigner), much to the anger of the literati and the more hot-headed members of Yehonala's council. Although she hated his advice, more often than not the

Western Empress was sufficiently discriminating to realise its worth.

It was Li Hung-chang who again controlled the final negotiations with the French in their attempt to annex the Kingdom of Annam, a Chinese tributary state. Having supplanted Spain in 1862 as rulers of Cochin China (roughly the southern half of Vietnam), they, like the British, were seeking trade routes into China's soft underbelly via 'South of the Clouds', the province of Yunnan. Under sustained pressure, the King of Annam accepted French overlordship in 1874, but tried to appease his former Manchu masters by continuing to send the customary tribute to Beijing. For years Annam remained a battleground, with French *condottieri* and the Black Flags (led by a former Tai Ping rebel, Liu Yung-fu, who had fled China when the rebellion collapsed) fighting proxy battles for the two great powers. Each side accused the other of duplicity and aggression, while not at any time declaring war upon the other. Li Hung-chang realised the hopelessness of the Chinese position, and agreed to cede Annam. But Yehonala and other anti-foreign elements delayed compliance. When French troops, trusting to Li Hung-chang's concessions, moved to occupy the area, they were unexpectedly attacked and cut to pieces. In retaliation, the French navy occupied the port of Foochow, and on 22nd August 1864, suddenly fired on Chinese shipping and land bases, sinking numerous junks and destroying the Foochow arsenal, symbol of China's resurgence. Incensed, but outgunned, the Chinese fought on for seven months, suffering numerous reverses. It was an unequal struggle: not only were China's troops handicapped with outmoded weapons, the Middle Kingdom was fighting on two fronts, for at the opposite end of the country the Japanese had begun to stir. Li Hung-chang was sufficiently perspicacious to identify the main threat to the Dynasty, and he summarised the position succinctly in a memorial to Yehonala: 'Although the various powers are strong, they are still seventy thousand li away from us, whereas Japan is as near as in the courtyard ...'. In Li's opinion, the Empire could not fight two enemies at once – circumstance dictated that the 'lesser evil' should be appeased.

Fuming with suppressed indignation, Yehonala let go her southern tributary the better to fight the eastern barbarians. In March 1885, China ceded Annam to France on the basis of Li Hung-chang's original agreement made more than six months before.

But despite the concentration of Chinese forces against the 'eastern dwarf men', the Japanese easily succeeded in humiliating the still-slumbering Chinese giant. Unlike the disdainful Middle Kingdom, by the 1860s Japan had consciously acknowledged the technical superiority of the European states, and had come to understand the power inherent in the new technology – and the desirability of acquiring this foreign expertise. Under the leadership of the Meiji Emperor, Mutsohito, who ascended the throne in February 1867, the tradition-bound state undertook a metamorphosis unparalleled in history, casting off many of its ancient customs and transforming itself almost overnight into a modern industrial society.[3] Feudalism was abolished; universal education was made mandatory; newspapers were published; and the Western Gregorian calendar was introduced. Not all Japanese agreed with the opening of the country. In 1877 the Satsuma rebellion set an army of samurai against the government. They were protesting at the formation of a modern military corps composed of commoners, which threatened their privileged positions as purveyors of the Bushido code. The revolt was swiftly suppressed, the traditional sword-wielding samurai cut to pieces by the same army of commoners (wielding modern firearms) they affected to despise. Industrialisation continued apace – the first railroad was opened in the early 1870s – and within a very short space of time Japan had mastered the intricacies of Western science and technology and had marked out for itself a prominent place among the world's 'powers'.

Japan's astounding transmutation should have served as a beacon to Yehonala and China's ruling elite, lighting the way to the Middle Kingdom's own revival. But Yehonala, aided and supported by China's corrupt, hidebound bureaucracy, ignored the lesson and hid their collective heads ever more deeply in the sands of tradition. Soon, a more forceful instruction was given: over the 1870s, Japan began to flex its newly acquired muscles, and Yehonala could only sit back helplessly and watch as the despised 'dwarf men', by now far too powerful to confront militarily, took control of the Okinawan archipelago and eclipsed Chinese influence on the strategically important island of Taiwan. Worse was to follow. Flushed with their own success, in 1876 the Japanese sent a naval force to Korea, China's most important tributary state, and extracted a treaty which opened the Hermit Kingdom to Japanese trade. The Chinese did not even issue a diplomatic protest. Other countries took advantage of the obvious weakness of the Middle Kingdom: the United States concluded a similar treaty in 1882 which took no cognisance of China's claims on the Kingdom and which implicitly recognised Korea as a sovereign and independent nation. Inside the country, pro-China and pro-Japanese factions emerged, each bent on seizing control.

Grudgingly, Yehonala and her advisers came to understand that at least some degree of Westernisation was inevitable, if they wished to prevent further slices being taken from the Chinese melon. 'Self-strengthening' measures were instituted, culminating in 1885 with the setting up of a Board of Admiralty, with responsibility for constructing a modern navy to face down the foreign gunboats and the ships of Japan's rapidly expanding sea forces. Slowly, it appeared that the Middle Kingdom was shedding its ancient isolated persona and preparing to enter the modern world.

But in China nothing was ever as it seemed. Within the Forbidden City, surrounded by fawning sycophants and flattering eunuchs, it was easy for the nobility to believe the ancient ingrained fiction of Imperial omnipotence, that nothing would, or needed, to change. In the face of this modernising threat to age-old privilege, reactionary forces had begun to stir.

CHAPTER THIRTEEN

When a bird is dying

In 1879, at the time of Tung Chih's funeral, Yehonala's decision to further her own interests at the expense of her son's departed soul came back to haunt her. The Manchu Emperors had built two tomb complexes to contain their earthly remains, one to the east and the other to the west of Beijing. These were used alternately by the Dynasty. Each necropolis nestled in the mountains, surrounded by pine trees (symbols of longevity) and approached by a wide marble-paved ceremonial highway flanked by enormous carved stone figures of griffin, camels, elephant, horse and fighting men. Every tomb was fronted by an elaborate wooden-built pavilion, in which the Imperial regalia, gold-satin thrones and Imperial yellow dragon-robes of the departed Lord were kept. These were displayed for the edification of the deceased's soul on the yearly day of sacrifice. Each mausoleum had its attendants, and its troop of guardian warriors, and the necropolis as a whole was under the authority of a governor, who took great care to restrict access and maintain the holy seclusion of the site.

The burial rites of a Celestial Prince were long and intricate, but a full forty-eight months after Tung Chih's death his body was ready to be laid in its final resting-place. What scandalised the literati was that, after all this time, Yehonala still had not fulfilled her vow to provide Tung Chih's spirit with an heir, who alone could perform the rites to placate his unquiet soul. But, although this blasphemous omission was one of the main topics of gossip among the scholar-gentlemen who governed the Empire, all knew that to formally complain about this lack was to incur the wrath of the Empress of the Western Palace and risk instant decapitation.

Some few chanced their lives and penned memorials to the 'Venerable Mother'. Thankfully, none were executed, but all complaints were treated with contempt, and a petulant anger that betrays that Yehonala's own conscience in this matter was perhaps secretly eating away at her accustomed confidence. It was probably not remorse that consumed her, but fear for her own future. She was painfully superstitious, and leaving her son's soul untended after death could not help but invite the ill-fortune she dreaded, and she hated to be reminded of her misconduct. 'We have already issued an absolutely clear Decree ... providing for an heir to the late Emperor,' she told one memorialist, 'and the Decree has been published all over the Empire. The memorialist's present request gives evidence of unspeakable audacity, and an inveterate habit of fault-finding, which has greatly enraged us, so that we hereby convey to him a stern rebuke'. No doubt the memorialist was thankful that it was a 'stern rebuke', and not a silken cord, that was conveyed to him. Like all the rest of the court Censors, he let the matter lie, perhaps contenting himself that, at the risk of his own life, he had done his duty by drawing Her Majesty's attention to the situation.

But one man found he could live the lie no longer. Wu K'o-tu, a scholar noted chiefly for his self-righteous, intolerant, xenophobic memorials to the throne, now revealed an altogether more admirable aspect of his personality. He had waited four years, hoping against hope that the slow but steady flow of memorials demanding 'an unbreakable and unchangeable pledge as to the succession to the Throne',[1] but saw only pious platitudes and vague bromides issuing from 'behind the curtain'. With the calm objectivity that was one of the treasures of the Confucian philosophy, Wu K'o-tu decided that only his own death would suffice to draw attention to the gravity of the situation, that suicide was the correct, the only, course open to him to impeach Yehonala for her failures and to indict her for usurpation of the Dragon Throne.

Wu K'o-tu left nothing to chance. He chose the minor Daoist temple of Ma-shen ch'iao for his death, as close to the mausoleum of Tung Chih as a man of his rank could venture. Instructions were left, apologising to the priest of the temple for the inconvenience his suicide would cause him, and of astonishing mundane detail considering that they were written by a man about to end his own life:

> Priest Chou, be not afraid. I have no desire to bring evil upon you. I was compelled to borrow the use of your hallowed ground, as a spot appropriate for the death of an honest man. Inform now the Magistrate at once, and see to it that the memorial enclosed in my despatch box is forwarded without delay.
>
> Buy for me a cheap coffin and have it painted black inside. My clothes are all in order, only the leather soles of my boots require to be cut off [having touched the soil, they were regarded as impure] before you lay me in your coffin. I should not think that the Magistrate will need to hold an inquest. Please have a coating of lacquer put on the coffin, to fill up any cracks in the joints, and have it nailed down, pending the Empresses' decision as to my remains. Then, buy a few feet of ground ... and have me buried quickly. There is no need for me to be buried in my ancestral cemetery; any spot is a good enough resting place for a loyal and honest man.
>
> ... You can cut my body down tomorrow morning, and then have it placed in some cool and shady spot. Fearing that possibly you might come in by accident and find me hanging, I have taken a dose of opium, so as to make certain of death ... All I ask of you is that you notify the Magistrate and that you do not allow women and children to come in and gaze upon my remains. There is nothing strange or abnormal here; death had become an unavoidable duty. Those who understand will pity. That is all.
>
> The last earnest instructions of Wu K'o-tu.[2]

With these instructions written, and a letter composed to his eldest son, this worthy successor of Confucius calmly and resolutely hanged himself from a temple beam. Close by him was his swan song, his memorial to Yehonala, a document that was to shake the soul of that fierce and indomitable personality to its foundation. Considering the depths of circumlocution normal in court circles, the memorial is shockingly blunt. Wu K'o-tu informs the Empresses that

the Empresses Dowager have doubly erred in appointing an heir to the Emperor Hsien Feng and not to his late Majesty. The new Emperor [i.e. Kuang Hsu] being heir to his Majesty Hsien Feng, the future succession must revert to the heir of the new Emperor ... this Decree [of Yehonala] expressly ordains that this shall be so; it follows that a precedent will be established, whereby the Great Inheritance may pass by adoption ... But for more than two centuries, the ancestral tradition of our House-law has been observed that the Throne shall pass from father to son ...

We should therefore seek if perchance we may find some way out of this double error, whereby we may return to the right way. I therefore beg that the Empresses may be pleased to issue a second decree explicitly stating that the Great Inheritance shall hereafter revert to the adopted son of his late Majesty Tung Chih, even though the new Emperor be blessed with a hundred sons. Thus, to the late Emperor, now childless, an heir will be provided ... And, for all time the orderly maintenance of the succession will be ascribed to the Empresses, whose fame will be changeless and unending ...

Humbly, I offer up these years of life ... humbly I lay them down in propitiation of the Empresses Dowager, to implore from them a brief Decree on behalf of the late Emperor ... 'When a bird is dying its song is sad. When a man is dying his words are good' ... These are my last words, my last prayer, the end and crown of my life.

The death sent shock waves through the Empire (as Wu K'o-tu had intended it should). Wu K'o-tu's sacrifice was headline news, and it put the subject for which he had died back at the top of everyone's agenda. Yehonala could no longer rely on vague promises and the hope that, once the Tung Chih Emperor was buried, his memory would fade and with it concerns over the succession. Both sides of her nature counselled submission: the consummate politician in her realised the strength of public support and approval for the Censor's protest; and her superstitious psyche, knowing his protest was justifiable, was afraid of the ill-luck that his angry spirit might bring upon her, should he (and the spirit of Tung Chih) remain unplacated. She acted at once, promulgating a decree (in the name of herself and Sakota) which acceded to the demands of the dead scholar. But despite her capitulation, the ghost of Wu K'o-tu continued to haunt her. To the end of her life, Yehonala was wont to divine in every future misfortune the unseen hand of the hanged man.

But we should not lose sight of fact that, without the suicide of Wu K'o-tu, Yehonala would have continued to have given vague promises on obtaining an adopted heir for her son, and to have in fact carried out the central thrust of her first decree, which would have made Kuang Hsu's posterity holders of the Great Inheritance. But as Kuang Hsu was incapable of siring children, upon his death, and without any clear precedents to follow for a successor, civil strife was almost certain – and with it the possibility that the Aisin Gioro, the Imperial clan, would be entirely swept from power, if not eliminated. There seems to be no other reason for Yehonala's insistence on Kuang Hsu as new Emperor, and her attempt to establish a new precedent on succession to the Dragon Throne. The dying command, two hundred years before, of the head of the Yeho-Nala clan to destroy their conquerors was still potent. Yehonala's every action reveals that she was intent on wreaking vengeance on the Aisin Gioro. The ancient prophecy of the Ming Emperor had been made flesh in the small implacable figure of the Western Empress.

If Yehonala's capitulation to Wu K'o-tu's ghost had served to placate the mass of literati, relations with her 'co-Regent' Sakota, continued to deteriorate. The temperaments of the two cousins were as different as the opposing halves of the Daoist Tai Chi: Yehonala all a-bustle, soaking up information like a sponge, ever-watchful, always planning; Sakota placid, conciliatory, unconcerned with world affairs, ready always to compromise. As the Kuang Hsu Emperor grew, it was this quiet charm that attracted him to Sakota, and away from his more demanding aunt. The Empress of the Eastern Palace let him play, and sympathised with his aversion to schoolwork. Yehonala demanded excellence in everything. This can only have been a further source of friction between the two cousins, for the cultivation of Kuang Hsu's favour was no light thing. Despite half-hearted reforms, China remained an oriental despotism. And when the Emperor grew to manhood and took over responsibility for the Empire, his word would be law. Those he held in high esteem would prosper. The fate of those he despised did not bear contemplation.

Just as worrying for Yehonala was the fact that, despite her apparent easy-going attitude, Sakota could rule. When Yehonala fell seriously ill of a liver complaint in 1880, she was surprised to discover that her cousin was more than competent in overseeing the workings of the Empire. The Islamic rebellion that had erupted in China's north-west nine years before (prompting the Russians to 'help' China by taking over the Ili region) had finally been suppressed in 1878. But when the mandarin Ch'ung-hou was sent to arrange Ili's return to the Middle Kingdom, the Russians stubbornly refused to remove their troops. Ch'ung's negotiations in St Petersburg were a disaster: under intense pressure he granted Russia half the Ili region, allowed them control of several important lines of communication, and even agreed to pay their 'expenses' of five million roubles. Yehonala ordered his immediate beheading, and Ch'ung-hou escaped the headsman's sword only when several foreign dignitaries (including Queen Victoria) implored the Throne to spare his life. Renegotiations on the 'Ili problem' were conducted by Tseng Chi-tse (son of the Tai Ping hero Tseng Guo-feng) while Sakota was at the helm and resulted in the Russians vacating the whole of Ili, but only for a payment nearly double the original expenses, nine million roubles. As none of the sacred soil of the Middle Kingdom had been lost, the court's all-important 'face' had been saved, and Tseng's mission was counted a great success. Sakota, of course, gained great prestige from this 'victory' and was accounted an able administrator in her own right.

It must have been galling for Yehonala to discover that she was not indispensable; and worse, that everyone at court and throughout the country knew it. It was perhaps at this time that she began to see in her quiet cousin a serious rival to her authority.

An incident in 1880 can only have confirmed her worst fears. Since ancient times, the court had made an annual progress to the Eastern and Western Tombs, where obeisance was made and sacrifices offered up to the departed shades of Emperors long dead. At state ceremonies in the Forbidden City, Yehonala invariably took the lead, despite the fact that, strictly speaking, Sakota actually ranked higher in the complicated scaffold of status that made up the court. The Empress of the Eastern Palace never forced the issue, but on this occasion, apparently prompted by her ally Prince Kung and others of the Imperial clan, she demanded precedence in all the proceedings, in the ancestral sacrifices and the obeisances that are made to each of the 'Jewelled Cities', the tumuli covering the royal tombs. Yehonala refused, and a heated argument took place in front of the assembled court, Sakota reminding Yehonala that her original rank had been concubine and that she, Sakota, had been Hsien Feng's consort and therefore indisputably of higher rank. She endeavoured to embarrass her cousin further by demanding that she stand slightly behind her during the ceremonies, and on her right side, the place of honour on Sakota's left being held vacant for the departed spirit of Hsien Feng's first wife, whose early death had brought Sakota to prominence. True to form, Yehonala brushed all these arguments and demands aside and assumed the central position for the remainder of the rites. But she knew that the incident had been designed to embarrass her, and to diminish her authority. That Sakota had acted in conjunction with members of the Imperial clan was doubly worrying: was this the beginning of a conspiracy against her? One that would sweep away the power of the Yeho-Nala clan and perhaps co-opt Sakota as puppet-Regent?

Worse, in personal terms, was to follow. Jung Lu, her cousin and former fiancé (and if the rumours were true, her long-time lover) had been given the right to enter the Forbidden City at any time of the day or night. He had used this privilege to begin a liaison with a certain lady of the Great Within, a former concubine of Yehonala's dead husband, the Emperor Hsien Feng. As Jung Lu should have known, the affair soon became common knowledge, and the young Emperor's tutor, Weng Tung-ho, carried the story to Yehonala. One account relates that Yehonala refused to believe the tale until she had seen evidence of Jung Lu's guilt with her own eyes. Informed that he was visiting the lady, she discovered him, if not *in flagrante delicto*, at least within the woman's quarters, a grave offence punishable by death. Faced with the indisputable fact of Jung Lu's betrayal, Yehonala must have felt horribly isolated and alone. Jung Lu had been her strong support, probably the only person she could rely on in the shifting alliances and duplicities of the Forbidden City. It was perhaps naive of her to expect chaste abstinence from a virile man in his forties, especially if she herself had begun to hold him at arm's length. Possibly she was merely angered that his chosen paramour lived within her own personal domain, and that public knowledge of the affair had caused her intense embarrassment and loss of face. Whatever the reason, Jung Lu was lucky to escape with his life. He was summarily stripped of his official posts at court, and given a military appointment in Xian, where he was to languish, in de facto exile, for seven years. The eunuchs whispered to Yehonala that the Empress of the Eastern Palace had known of the liaison, and had turned a blind eye, or even helped to ease the passage of the affair. It must have occurred to Yehonala that there could well have been a deeper, more deadly motive behind Sakota's involvement. By helping the illicit love affair, knowing it would come to light, Sakota (and her Imperial clan allies) would have counted on a violent, angry counterblast from Yehonala, that she would respond either with the death or banishment of her only true friend at court. And Yehonala had not disappointed them. Jung Lu was now in Xian; and her pride prevented his recall. Yehonala was thus more isolated and friendless than she had ever been since arriving at the Great Within. Only the eunuchs remained as trusted associates.

at he 'seems to think that his duties are satisfact-
ed by adherence to a routine of procrastination,
g devoid of the first elements of knowledge'. Weng
ho earlier had informed Yehonala of Jung Lu's
one of her husband's former concubines) was also
t as a mark of Imperial favour was permitted to
s on the Board of Works and as tutor to the young
ang Hsu.

s reproductive shortcomings, in all other respects
ephew, the Emperor Kuang Hsu, continued to
mally. By 1887 he had grown into a short, slim
ung man of seventeen, and had attained the right
n his own. Nevertheless, thanks to his quisling
ce Ch'un, Yehonala was able to retain the sceptre
r two years. Prince Ch'un 'spontaneously' pleaded
la to continue her rule, not once, but many times,
n etiquette demanded that the Dowager Empress
fuse his entreaties the required number of times
tantly' accepting. Which eventually she did.
perial edict (undoubtedly dictated at Yehonala's
ang Hsu declared that when he heard the decree
his assumption of power 'I trembled as though I
ocean, not knowing where the land might be. But
l Majesty will continue to advise me for a few years
t matters of state … .'[2]
f respite gave Yehonala two additional years of the
craved. But by 1889, even for so brazen and auda-
it, it was simply too embarrassing to continue to
y the Emperor his legitimate right to rule and Yeho-
nced that she would pass on the reins of power to
, and retire. The impression was given, especially to
servers, that Yehonala's day was done, that the
mpress Dowager, now fifty-five, would withdraw
rld and take no more interest in affairs of state. This
tically not the case. Her position as elder represen-
e Imperial family gave her, in Confucian society, an
le dominance: 'She would have taken precedence
eror Kuang-hsu, not merely because she was the

Given the court milieu, and her own suspicious nature, she
must have sensed the wolf-pack circling.

Whether the danger was imagined or real is hard to determine. But Sakota seems to have had a change of heart and to
have attempted a genuine reconciliation with her cousin. She
still possessed her trump card, the secret document which
Hsien Feng had entrusted to her in 1860 as he lay dying in
Jehol. It was this document she now showed to Yehonala at a
private meeting. Its contents must have sent shards of ice
shafting through Yehonala's stomach. The document was an
Imperial decree, a command from the dead sovereign which
still, twenty years after his death, carried the force of law. It
ordered that, should the Concubine Yi presume to meddle in
the rule of the country, the Grand Council was to be convened,
the decree shown to them, and by its authority she was to be
'assisted to commit suicide'. The document Sakota held before
Yehonala's eyes was her death warrant. For a woman of Yehonala's undoubted arrogance, whose desire for total power was
limitless, it must have been galling in the extreme to realise
that throughout all her days of victory and triumph she had
been in fact been at the mercy of someone whose abilities and
political skills she disdained. Sakota could have had her put to
death at any point since the dangerous days at Jehol when they
had triumphed over Su Shun and his co-conspirators. The
damage to Yehonala's self-image, the internal humiliation this
disclosure engendered must have been intolerable to such a
proud spirit.

Sakota believed that her suppression of the edict proved that
she was motivated only by feelings of love and amity for the
Empress of the Western Palace. And as a pledge of her good
faith and friendship, she burned the fatal document to ashes
in Yehonala's presence.

If she expected gratitude she was soon to be disappointed.
Hiding her true feelings, Yehonala left her cousin with all the
normal expressions of courtesy and goodwill. A few days later,
it is said, a eunuch arrived at Sakota's quarters with a present of
cakes from her loving cousin, the Western Empress. Sakota
sampled the cakes, and suddenly fell sick. The mysterious illness

proved impervious to all medical arts, and realising her end was near, Sakota drafted the traditional 'last words', in which she speaks of how her expectation 'to attain a good old age' had been thwarted by a 'slight illness' which had been followed 'most unexpectedly' by 'a most dangerous relapse ... and now all hope of recovery appears to be in vain'. Along with the traditional platitudes, the valedictory decree contains oblique criticism of her more audacious cousin. Sakota claimed that she had 'set a good example of thrift and sobriety in the Palace, and to have steadily discountenanced all pomp and vain display ...'. The implication that Yehonala was guilty of all these vices (she had been accused of many more by her Censors) was plain, and would not have been lost on the literati, well-versed in the subtle phraseology of the court.

Yehonala's childhood playmate, ally of her youth and co-Regent of China for so many years, lingered for a few more hours. Before the day was out Sakota was dead. For Yehonala it may have been a wonderful release from the charade she had lived so long. There need be no more pretence of sharing power with anyone – she was, finally, the undisputed ruler of the Middle Kingdom.

CHAPTER F

'Retire

For six years after the death unfettered freedom as sole position in 1884 with what can o any official of influence, leaving anchored to the pinnacle of power her long-term strategy of clan v contrive the final eclipse of the Ai

Prince Kung was the first to go. Y long hatred for him since, with Sa death of her favourite, the eu suspected him of intriguing with t own removal. He was removed Imperial decree of being 'unduly inf displaying nepotism and slothful i given the corrupt milieu of the cou stick to anyone. 'As a mark of our Im continued, 'we have decided to perm hereditary Princedom, together with but he is hereby deprived of all his of which he has hitherto enjoyed is wit retire into private life and to attend to

At the same time, other grandees Prince were removed from the Gra Grand Secretary, Pao Yun, was re Hung-tsao (who in 1861 had draft valedictory decree at Su Shun's beh but not, as he must have feared, his Board of War, Ching Lien, was ren

comment t
orily perfor
the man be
T'ung-ho (
liaison wit
removed, b
keep his po
Emperor K
Despite
Yehonala's
develop n
energetic
to govern
father, Pr
for a furth
with Yeho
for Confu
modestly
before 're
In an
request),
confirmi
was in n
her Impe
in impor
This
power s
cious a
openly
nala an
Kuang
Wester
veneral
from th
was en
tative
unassa
of the

mother of his predecessor, but also because she belonged to the senior generation.'[3]

Kuang Hsu was required to visit the Empress Mother at least once every five days, and to perform the customary kowtow at each meeting. Often, because of the malice of the eunuch Li Lien-ying (whom Kuang Hsu had ordered beaten years before), the Emperor was kept waiting on his knees for over an hour, at the threshold of his aunt's palace. But it was not simply symbolical obeisance that was demanded of Kuang Hsu. Yehonala insisted on retaining a controlling interest in most of the important facets of government. She remained privy to all key state documents and memorials, and with characteristic thoroughness she read them all. She may have ceased to concern herself with the day-to-day minutiae of administrative affairs, but no major appointment or decision was ever made without her express approval. With one notable exception, whenever Kuang Hsu eventually decided to dispense with the 'advice' of his august aunt, Yehonala was swiftly aware of his plans through her network of spies and eunuchs.

What she did lose by her retirement was some of the outward trappings of power. During her sole Regency, Yehonala had come as close as any woman in Chinese history to ascending to the Dragon Throne. Despite her sex, she had been, in all but name, the Celestial Prince. It was this ceremonial position, rather than any real reduction in power, that she reluctantly relinquished.

But she would not go empty-handed. The Empress Dowager exacted from the nation a fitting retirement present, a reward commensurate with her own opinion of her worth. She required nothing less than the reconstruction of a new Summer Palace where, like the Empress Mother of the renowned Emperor K'ang Hsi, she could pass her leisure hours amid a fairyland of pavilions and verdure. In 1888 a decree, promulgated in the name of the Emperor but in fact authored by Yehonala, had Kuang Hsu apparently stating that he had:

> remembered that in the neighbourhood of the Western
> Park there was a palace ... that ... only required some

restoration to make them fit for use as a place of solace
and delight ... We conceived the idea of restoring the
Ch'ing I Yuan, and conferring upon it the new name of I
Ho Yuan (from a sentence in the book of rites meaning 'to
give rest and peace to Heaven-sent old age').

After the traditional refusals, Yehonala continued the farcical
correspondence with herself, finally giving her reluctant
acquiescence to the suggestion. Her decree was classical
Yehonala, saccharine sincerity, the Western Empress at her
most cynical. She knew, she wrote, that:

... the Emperor's desire to restore the palace in the west
springs from a laudable concern for my welfare, and for
that reason I cannot bear to meet his well-meaning petition with a blunt refusal. Moreover, the costs of the construction have been provided for out of surplus funds
accumulated as a result of rigid economies in the past.
The funds under the control of the board of revenue will
not be touched, and no harm will be done the national
finances.[4]

It was all pure eyewash. There was no money available to fund
the reconstruction of Yehonala's pleasure garden. Undismayed,
with the help of the Grand Eunuch Li Lien-ying, and the
acquiescence of the poodle-like Prince Ch'un, Yehonala proceeded to defraud the nation. She mulcted the national purse
of around thirty thousand taels, taken principally from the
Board of Admiralty, where Prince Ch'un ruled as president.
Funds that ought to have been spent on arms and ammunition,
on renovating China's run-down navy, were diverted to
refurbish the I Ho Yuan. Marble boats preceded real boats in
Yehonala's priorities.

None of this was particularly unusual in the looking-glass
world of the Forbidden City where bribery and peculation constituted normality. All would have gone well had China been,
as the Chinese elite still endeavoured to persuade themselves,
the centre of the world, secure in its Heaven-bestowed superiority. This was, unfortunately, far from true. To many Chinese,

and especially the younger generation, the humiliation of China before the Western Powers was obvious and intolerable. It was whispered that the Emperor, Kuang Hsu was very much enamoured of Western science and institutions, a fact calculated to fill the arch-conservative in Yehonala with both anger and angst.

Her last major act before relinquishing power to her nephew was to organise Kuang Hsu's marriage. In 1889 a decree announcing the wedding was promulgated. The bride chosen for Kuang Hsu, known at court as Lung Yu (Honorific Abundance), was a twenty-two-year old homely maiden not renowned for her beauty. Kuang Hsu had preferred another, but his choice had been overruled by his imperious aunt. The marriage took place on 26th February 1889, a date deemed auspicious by the court astrologers. It was a sumptuous affair, paid for by 'voluntary' donations from the provinces, a goodly proportion of which found its way into the coffers of the Chief Eunuch, Li Lien-ying. The bride was carried from her family home to the Forbidden City in a cunningly wrought litter, carried by sixteen bearers and hung with Imperial yellow silk, on which was embroidered the *fu* ideogram, signifying happiness. The *fu* character was joined and doubled, symbolising to the Chinese 'conjugal fidelity'. A gaggle of yellow-robed eunuchs surrounded the palanquin, flanked on each side by mounted troops of the Imperial Guard. Those responsible for negotiating the marriage (with the exception of Yehonala herself) walked at the head of the gorgeous procession, the route of which had been strewn with yellow sand. They were followed by musicians and scores of attendants dressed in magnificent blood-red robes, the huge Chinese lanterns or magnificent embroidered umbrellas they carried swaying like multi-coloured clouds above the procession. The Book and the Seal of the bride-Empress followed, carried with all due pomp and ceremony, then line upon line of attendants bearing costly gifts. More attendants brought up the rear, each holding aloft multi-coloured standards and pennants, many showing the Dragon and the Phoenix (symbols of Emperor and Empress) entwined in a loving embrace. This gorgeous procession was seen by none of the inhabitants of Beijing. Troops of the eight Manchu banner regiments lined the processional course; they had enforced the closure of all houses, the shuttering of all windows, and the entire route had been screened with blue cloth to prevent the procession's violation by the gaze of the 'stupid people'. Despite dire penalties, many ordinary folk peered through cracks, or poked holes through the screens, and counted themselves blessed to catch a glimpse of this fabled event – which was, of course, a major reason for staging the ceremony. The Manchu were experts in public relations, pastmasters at maintaining and enhancing the fragile mystique of royalty.

As with most things contrived by his aunt during Kuang Hsu's sombre existence, this magnificent ceremony, and the marriage itself, had less to do with the Emperor's happiness than with keeping a close watch on his activities and ensuring his aunt's continued survival at the pinnacle of power. His bride had been chosen years before by Kuang Hsu's shrewd and calculating aunt; she was the daughter of Yehonala's brother, the Duke of Chow (brother also to the mother of Kuang Hsu), and this union of first cousins served to consolidate the power of the Yeho-Nala clan at court. It also answered another purpose. Yehonala knew that the 'happy couple' had nothing in common. They grew to dislike each other intensely; they had frequent quarrels after their marriage, in which Kuang Hsu was often bested by his wife, who evidently inherited some of Yehonala's iron will and would never give way even when arguing with the Son of Heaven himself. This sorted well with Yehonala's plans. She remembered how formidable had been the alliance of Tung Chih and his bride A-lu-te, and wanted at all costs to avoid history repeating itself. With Kuang Hsu and Lung Yu at daggers drawn, it was easy to persuade the Emperor's wife to keep a close watch on the Emperor.

It was an astute move. The young Emperor was becoming more and more convinced that China's only hope of salvation lay in learning from and emulating the science and technology of those same Western Powers that were squeezing the Middle Kingdom from all sides. This, he knew, meant overturning the old order within the Middle Kingdom, meant sweeping away reactionary forces who could not bring themselves to acknowledge 'barbarian' superiority in any field. If these anti-progressive elements included his redoubtable aunt, then Kuang Hsu had determined that she too would have to go. The disastrous events of the coming decade would serve only to confirm Kuang Hsu in this judgement and to set him on a course that was ultimately to prove disastrous both for himself and for China.

CHAPTER FIFTEEN

Rebel Emperor

*K*uang Hsu's estrangement from his aunt and most of his class began in a seemingly innocuous boyhood interest in toys. As a god on earth, the young Kuang Hsu was mollycoddled and pampered unmercifully – the response to the boy-Emperor's frequent overeating was not to curtail his diet, but to fall before him and kowtow incessantly, at the same time pleading for better behaviour.[1] Nothing was too good for the Son of Heaven, nothing in the Chinese world was denied him, with the inevitable result that the spoilt mini-Emperor was soon unconscionably bored with everything and everyone. As he was the future ruler of the Middle Kingdom his eunuch attendants counted the infant worth humouring, and would spend hours trawling through the streets of Beijing in an effort to find some object that might bring a fleeting smile to the already-jaded lips of the Celestial Prince. It was on one of these expeditions that, hidden away close to the German Legation buildings, the eunuchs came upon a 'foreign devil' shop, a general store owned by a Dane named Kierulf and containing among its myriad articles for sale some German clockwork toys. Hoping that these might amuse, the eunuchs bought several and carried them back to the Great Within.

Kuang Hsu was entranced by these foreign wonders and soon regular orders were being placed for anything that Mr Kierulf could obtain from Europe and America. As he grew, Kuang Hsu procured more and more barbarian playthings of ever-increasing sophistication. Soon, toys were left behind and adult technological wonders demanded: a telephone was installed, and a small-gauge railway built in the grounds of

Given the court milieu, and her own suspicious nature, she must have sensed the wolf-pack circling.

Whether the danger was imagined or real is hard to determine. But Sakota seems to have had a change of heart and to have attempted a genuine reconciliation with her cousin. She still possessed her trump card, the secret document which Hsien Feng had entrusted to her in 1860 as he lay dying in Jehol. It was this document she now showed to Yehonala at a private meeting. Its contents must have sent shards of ice shafting through Yehonala's stomach. The document was an Imperial decree, a command from the dead sovereign which still, twenty years after his death, carried the force of law. It ordered that, should the Concubine Yi presume to meddle in the rule of the country, the Grand Council was to be convened, the decree shown to them, and by its authority she was to be 'assisted to commit suicide'. The document Sakota held before Yehonala's eyes was her death warrant. For a woman of Yehonala's undoubted arrogance, whose desire for total power was limitless, it must have been galling in the extreme to realise that throughout all her days of victory and triumph she had been in fact been at the mercy of someone whose abilities and political skills she disdained. Sakota could have had her put to death at any point since the dangerous days at Jehol when they had triumphed over Su Shun and his co-conspirators. The damage to Yehonala's self-image, the internal humiliation this disclosure engendered must have been intolerable to such a proud spirit.

Sakota believed that her suppression of the edict proved that she was motivated only by feelings of love and amity for the Empress of the Western Palace. And as a pledge of her good faith and friendship, she burned the fatal document to ashes in Yehonala's presence.

If she expected gratitude she was soon to be disappointed. Hiding her true feelings, Yehonala left her cousin with all the normal expressions of courtesy and goodwill. A few days later, it is said, a eunuch arrived at Sakota's quarters with a present of cakes from her loving cousin, the Western Empress. Sakota sampled the cakes, and suddenly fell sick. The mysterious illness proved impervious to all medical arts, and realising her end was near, Sakota drafted the traditional 'last words', in which she speaks of how her expectation 'to attain a good old age' had been thwarted by a 'slight illness' which had been followed 'most unexpectedly' by 'a most dangerous relapse ... and now all hope of recovery appears to be in vain'. Along with the traditional platitudes, the valedictory decree contains oblique criticism of her more audacious cousin. Sakota claimed that she had 'set a good example of thrift and sobriety in the Palace, and to have steadily discountenanced all pomp and vain display ...'. The implication that Yehonala was guilty of all these vices (she had been accused of many more by her Censors) was plain, and would not have been lost on the literati, well-versed in the subtle phraseology of the court.

Yehonala's childhood playmate, ally of her youth and co-Regent of China for so many years, lingered for a few more hours. Before the day was out Sakota was dead. For Yehonala it may have been a wonderful release from the charade she had lived so long. There need be no more pretence of sharing power with anyone – she was, finally, the undisputed ruler of the Middle Kingdom.

CHAPTER FOURTEEN

'Retirement'

For six years after the death of Sakota, Yehonala enjoyed unfettered freedom as sole Regent. She consolidated her position in 1884 with what can only be described as a purge of any official of influence, leaving herself even more securely anchored to the pinnacle of power. In addition, and in line with her long-term strategy of clan vengeance, she attempted to contrive the final eclipse of the Aisin Gioro.

Prince Kung was the first to go. Yehonala had conceived a life-long hatred for him since, with Sakota, he had engineered the death of her favourite, the eunuch An Te-hai. She also suspected him of intriguing with the Emperor to engineer her own removal. He was removed from office, accused in an Imperial decree of being 'unduly inflated with his pride of place, displaying nepotism and slothful inefficiency', charges which, given the corrupt milieu of the court, could have been made to stick to anyone. 'As a mark of our Imperial clemency,' the decree continued, 'we have decided to permit Prince Kung to retain his hereditary Princedom, together with all the emoluments thereof, but he is hereby deprived of all his offices, and the double salary which he has hitherto enjoyed is withdrawn. He is permitted to retire into private life and to attend to the care of his health.'[1]

At the same time, other grandees, all suspected allies of the Prince were removed from the Grand Council: the venerable Grand Secretary, Pao Yun, was retired from public life; Li Hung-tsao (who in 1861 had drafted Emperor Hsien Feng's valedictory decree at Su Shun's behest) likewise lost his post but not, as he must have feared, his life; the President of the Board of War, Ching Lien, was removed with the insulting

comment that he 'seems to think that his duties are satisfactorily performed by adherence to a routine of procrastination,
the man being devoid of the first elements of knowledge'. Weng
T'ung-ho (who earlier had informed Yehonala of Jung Lu's
liaison with one of her husband's former concubines) was also
removed, but as a mark of Imperial favour was permitted to
keep his posts on the Board of Works and as tutor to the young
Emperor Kuang Hsu.

Despite his reproductive shortcomings, in all other respects
Yehonala's nephew, the Emperor Kuang Hsu, continued to
develop normally. By 1887 he had grown into a short, slim
energetic young man of seventeen, and had attained the right
to govern on his own. Nevertheless, thanks to his quisling
father, Prince Ch'un, Yehonala was able to retain the sceptre
for a further two years. Prince Ch'un 'spontaneously' pleaded
with Yehonala to continue her rule, not once, but many times,
for Confucian etiquette demanded that the Dowager Empress
modestly refuse his entreaties the required number of times
before 'reluctantly' accepting. Which eventually she did.

In an Imperial edict (undoubtedly dictated at Yehonala's
request), Kuang Hsu declared that when he heard the decree
confirming his assumption of power 'I trembled as though I
was in mid-ocean, not knowing where the land might be. But
her Imperial Majesty will continue to advise me for a few years
in important matters of state ... .'[2]

This brief respite gave Yehonala two additional years of the
power she craved. But by 1889, even for so brazen and audacious a spirit, it was simply too embarrassing to continue to
openly deny the Emperor his legitimate right to rule and Yehonala announced that she would pass on the reins of power to
Kuang Hsu, and retire. The impression was given, especially to
Western observers, that Yehonala's day was done, that the
venerable Empress Dowager, now fifty-five, would withdraw
from the world and take no more interest in affairs of state. This
was emphatically not the case. Her position as elder representative of the Imperial family gave her, in Confucian society, an
unassailable dominance: 'She would have taken precedence
of the emperor Kuang-hsu, not merely because she was the

mother of his predecessor, but also because she belonged to the senior generation.'[3]

Kuang Hsu was required to visit the Empress Mother at least once every five days, and to perform the customary kowtow at each meeting. Often, because of the malice of the eunuch Li Lien-ying (whom Kuang Hsu had ordered beaten years before), the Emperor was kept waiting on his knees for over an hour, at the threshold of his aunt's palace. But it was not simply symbolical obeisance that was demanded of Kuang Hsu. Yehonala insisted on retaining a controlling interest in most of the important facets of government. She remained privy to all key state documents and memorials, and with characteristic thoroughness she read them all. She may have ceased to concern herself with the day-to-day minutiae of administrative affairs, but no major appointment or decision was ever made without her express approval. With one notable exception, whenever Kuang Hsu eventually decided to dispense with the 'advice' of his august aunt, Yehonala was swiftly aware of his plans through her network of spies and eunuchs.

What she did lose by her retirement was some of the outward trappings of power. During her sole Regency, Yehonala had come as close as any woman in Chinese history to ascending to the Dragon Throne. Despite her sex, she had been, in all but name, the Celestial Prince. It was this ceremonial position, rather than any real reduction in power, that she reluctantly relinquished.

But she would not go empty-handed. The Empress Dowager exacted from the nation a fitting retirement present, a reward commensurate with her own opinion of her worth. She required nothing less than the reconstruction of a new Summer Palace where, like the Empress Mother of the renowned Emperor K'ang Hsi, she could pass her leisure hours amid a fairyland of pavilions and verdure. In 1888 a decree, promulgated in the name of the Emperor but in fact authored by Yehonala, had Kuang Hsu apparently stating that he had:

> remembered that in the neighbourhood of the Western Park there was a palace ... that ... only required some

restoration to make them fit for use as a place of solace and delight ... We conceived the idea of restoring the Ch'ing I Yuan, and conferring upon it the new name of I Ho Yuan (from a sentence in the book of rites meaning 'to give rest and peace to Heaven-sent old age').

After the traditional refusals, Yehonala continued the farcical correspondence with herself, finally giving her reluctant acquiescence to the suggestion. Her decree was classical Yehonala, saccharine sincerity, the Western Empress at her most cynical. She knew, she wrote, that:

... the Emperor's desire to restore the palace in the west springs from a laudable concern for my welfare, and for that reason I cannot bear to meet his well-meaning petition with a blunt refusal. Moreover, the costs of the construction have been provided for out of surplus funds accumulated as a result of rigid economies in the past. The funds under the control of the board of revenue will not be touched, and no harm will be done the national finances.[4]

It was all pure eyewash. There was no money available to fund the reconstruction of Yehonala's pleasure garden. Undismayed, with the help of the Grand Eunuch Li Lien-ying, and the acquiescence of the poodle-like Prince Ch'un, Yehonala proceeded to defraud the nation. She mulcted the national purse of around thirty thousand taels, taken principally from the Board of Admiralty, where Prince Ch'un ruled as president. Funds that ought to have been spent on arms and ammunition, on renovating China's run-down navy, were diverted to refurbish the I Ho Yuan. Marble boats preceded real boats in Yehonala's priorities.

None of this was particularly unusual in the looking-glass world of the Forbidden City where bribery and peculation constituted normality. All would have gone well had China been, as the Chinese elite still endeavoured to persuade themselves, the centre of the world, secure in its Heaven-bestowed superiority. This was, unfortunately, far from true. To many Chinese, and especially the younger generation, the humiliation of China before the Western Powers was obvious and intolerable. It was whispered that the Emperor, Kuang Hsu was very much enamoured of Western science and institutions, a fact calculated to fill the arch-conservative in Yehonala with both anger and angst.

Her last major act before relinquishing power to her nephew was to organise Kuang Hsu's marriage. In 1889 a decree announcing the wedding was promulgated. The bride chosen for Kuang Hsu, known at court as Lung Yu (Honorific Abundance), was a twenty-two-year old homely maiden not renowned for her beauty. Kuang Hsu had preferred another, but his choice had been overruled by his imperious aunt. The marriage took place on 26th February 1889, a date deemed auspicious by the court astrologers. It was a sumptuous affair, paid for by 'voluntary' donations from the provinces, a goodly proportion of which found its way into the coffers of the Chief Eunuch, Li Lien-ying. The bride was carried from her family home to the Forbidden City in a cunningly wrought litter, carried by sixteen bearers and hung with Imperial yellow silk, on which was embroidered the *fu* ideogram, signifying happiness. The *fu* character was joined and doubled, symbolising to the Chinese 'conjugal fidelity'. A gaggle of yellow-robed eunuchs surrounded the palanquin, flanked on each side by mounted troops of the Imperial Guard. Those responsible for negotiating the marriage (with the exception of Yehonala herself) walked at the head of the gorgeous procession, the route of which had been strewn with yellow sand. They were followed by musicians and scores of attendants dressed in magnificent blood-red robes, the huge Chinese lanterns or magnificent embroidered umbrellas they carried swaying like multi-coloured clouds above the procession. The Book and the Seal of the bride-Empress followed, carried with all due pomp and ceremony, then line upon line of attendants bearing costly gifts. More attendants brought up the rear, each holding aloft multi-coloured standards and pennants, many showing the Dragon and the Phoenix (symbols of Emperor and Empress) entwined in a loving embrace. This gorgeous procession was seen by none of the inhabitants of Beijing. Troops of the eight Manchu banner regiments lined the processional course; they had enforced the closure of all houses, the shuttering of all windows, and the entire route had been screened with blue cloth to prevent the procession's violation by the gaze of the 'stupid people'. Despite dire penalties, many ordinary folk peered through cracks, or poked holes through the screens, and counted themselves blessed to catch a glimpse of this fabled event – which was, of course, a major reason for staging the ceremony. The Manchu were experts in public relations, pastmasters at maintaining and enhancing the fragile mystique of royalty.

As with most things contrived by his aunt during Kuang Hsu's sombre existence, this magnificent ceremony, and the marriage itself, had less to do with the Emperor's happiness than with keeping a close watch on his activities and ensuring his aunt's continued survival at the pinnacle of power. His bride had been chosen years before by Kuang Hsu's shrewd and calculating aunt; she was the daughter of Yehonala's brother, the Duke of Chow (brother also to the mother of Kuang Hsu), and this union of first cousins served to consolidate the power of the Yeho-Nala clan at court. It also answered another purpose. Yehonala knew that the 'happy couple' had nothing in common. They grew to dislike each other intensely; they had frequent quarrels after their marriage, in which Kuang Hsu was often bested by his wife, who evidently inherited some of Yehonala's iron will and would never give way even when arguing with the Son of Heaven himself. This sorted well with Yehonala's plans. She remembered how formidable had been the alliance of Tung Chih and his bride A-lu-te, and wanted at all costs to avoid history repeating itself. With Kuang Hsu and Lung Yu at daggers drawn, it was easy to persuade the Emperor's wife to keep a close watch on the Emperor.

It was an astute move. The young Emperor was becoming more and more convinced that China's only hope of salvation lay in learning from and emulating the science and technology of those same Western Powers that were squeezing the Middle Kingdom from all sides. This, he knew, meant overturning the Summer Palace, on which, when not engaged in his increasingly time-consuming duties as ruler of the Middle Kingdom, the Emperor liked to travel with the ladies of the court.

For her part, Yehonala seems to have genuinely enjoyed her (semi-) retirement. Now long past the bloom of youth, and unable to rely on the power of her womanly charms, she seems consciously to have taken upon herself a more venerable persona, exacting compliance by virtue of the Chinese deep-seated reverence for the elder generation. She was now, as one of her titles proclaimed, the August Mother, sombre and digni-fied. But despite her age and new-found leisure, Yehonala kept to her lifelong routine, rising early, at six in the morning, to breakfast on millet porridge and milk. It was said, perhaps maliciously, that this first drink of the day was human milk, extracted from a Manchu woman Yehonala kept at the Great Within[2]. She was a great believer in potions and simples (every ten days she would take a potion of crushed pearls, which she believed would enhance her longevity) so the story may well be true. After her meal she was dressed by her ladies, her toilette taking over an hour to complete. Then she might be carried in her palanquin, surrounded by maids and eunuchs, and with a troupe of a dozen musicians leading the way, to the three arti-ficial lakes lying to the west of the Forbidden City, where she would wander for hours in the ersatz wilderness, eating sweet-meats, and admiring the view from the many halls and pavi-lions that dotted the landscape. This was her favourite part of the day, and she lavished much time and thought on the main-tenance of her gardens, especially after 1880, when she had managed to inveigle funds from the submissive Prince Ch'un for the construction of her pet project, the Summer Palace.

At any time during these walks, Yehonala might call for lunch and her entourage would fall to swiftly to provide the hundred or so dishes that the Empress Dowager demanded at each meal, though she herself rarely partook of more than six or seven. In the afternoon, after an hour's siesta, she might paint, or practise her calligraphy (of which she was justly proud). Sometimes she would play dice with her ladies, or the

Chinese obsession, 'mah jong', or 'Eight Fairies Travel across the Sea', a board game of her own devising. Or she might wish to go boating on one of the lakes. Often, she would take a second walk in her beloved gardens, especially if there was a downpour. Punctuating the pleasant monotony of these times, and giving a certain rhythm to the days, were the ceremonial duties still required of the Empress Dowager, and her own favourite pastime, the theatre. At least once a fortnight, on the first and fifteenth of each month, plays were performed in the Forbidden City, or later (when the Summer Palace was completed) at a newly appointed theatre by the shores of the Kun Ming Lake. Yehonala delighted in the old classics, though she was not averse to previewing the work of modern Chinese playwrights. In between the visits of the players, she passed many happy hours performing herself, accompanied by her eunuch attendants. When, in 1903, she allowed herself to be photographed, she insisted on a picture of one of these masques, with herself dressed as the Chinese Goddess of Mercy, Kuan Yin (a favourite character), with the Grand Eunuch and others posed as attendant deities.

Her relations with her nephew also appear to have been cordial during this time. She was content to let him perform such duties as she had left to him, and seemed pleased with his progress in ruling the nation. As he moved into his middle twenties, she allowed him more and more leeway in decision-making, her unsurpassed intelligence network, and reports from her niece, Kuang Hsu's wife, ensuring that she would be instantly aware were the Emperor to overstep the bounds she herself had set. As the year 1894 drew near, Yehonala was engrossed in the pleasant prospect of the splendid pomp and ceremony that was to attend her sixtieth birthday. The celebration was to be of unsurpassed majesty, out-topping the jubilees of previous Emperors, a high point of Yehonala's long reign, conferring dignity and legitimacy upon her usurpation of power.

It was not to be. Japan's modernisation along Western lines had left it economically and militarily resurgent and this, together with the imperialist adventures of its Western exemplars in

China, and its own endogenous warrior culture, persuaded the Japanese that the road to greatness was via the conquest of its gigantic neighbour. Three centuries earlier the Japanese had attempted their first subjugation of the Middle Kingdom. In 1592, the dictator Toyotomi Hideyoshi had set his samurai legions against Korea, intending to use that country as a bridge-head from which to launch his attempt on China's Dragon Throne. The Japanese army of the 1890s, better equipped but still imbued with the same Bushido fighting spirit, planned to use the same strategy. The United States had played, unwittingly, an important role in the drama that now unfolded. In 1882, the *Mei-guo Ren* (Americans) had first prised open the Hermit Kingdom to Western trade, all but ignoring China's claims to suzerainty and concluding a treaty which effectively recognised Korea as an independent state.[3] Japan claimed similar rights and, in order to avoid hostilities, as far back as 1885 China and Japan had agreed that neither should send troops into the area without the agreement of the other. Nine years later, following year-long disturbances and serious rioting, the King of Korea requested Chinese help in quelling an incipient rebellion. China sent in her troops, and informed Japan, whose own forces were soon heading across the Korea strait to the Hermit Kingdom. The stage was set for a serious confrontation, which flared into life when the Japanese took captive the King of Korea's wife and their chil-dren. The King's eighty-year-old father was installed as ruler. The Chinese now sent in more troops, carried on the *Kowshing*, a British-registered ship. This was stopped by a Japanese gun-boat, torpedoed and quickly sunk. Foreshadowing the infamous atrocities they were to commit in eastern Asia during the first half of the twentieth century, the Japanese forces shot most of the survivors as they floundered in the sea. Forty-eight hours later (at the behest of the Japanese) Korea's octogenarian puppet-monarch unilaterally declared war on China and begged his allies in Japan for help, which was punctually supplied. The Sino-Japanese War had begun.

Japan should have had the worst of it. An island nation, it had no option but to transport all its men and munitions to continental Asia by boat. Control of sea routes was therefore vital to victory, and here the Middle Kingdom apparently held the whip hand. In naval matters at least, China seemed to have learned from the West and had bought the best and most modern ships available. Li Hung-chang, hero of the Tai Ping rebellion, saviour of Yehonala during the crisis of Kuang Hsu's succession and now the powerful Viceroy of Chihli Province, had been given responsibility for the northern fleet and, in addition to his modern procurement programme, had also engaged Captain Lang, an English naval officer, to train 'his' navy. On paper, their forces were vastly superior to the Japanese, in terms of both tonnage and numbers of ships: the Chinese fleet possessed armoured cruisers, light cruisers, torpedo boats and, their crowning glory, two 7,000-ton modern battleships with 10-inch guns. By contrast, the best the Japanese fleet could muster was a 4,000-ton cruiser. Any naval battle should have been an easy victory for China. And with the seas won, a blockade of Japan would have ensured a peace on favourable terms to the Middle Kingdom.

It did not work out that way. From the start matters went badly awry for the Chinese. Time and again the Imperial fleet shied away from contact with the enemy. When it was finally brought to battle by Japan's smaller flotillas, the result was a disaster. In two separate engagements in the Yellow Sea separating Korea and China, on 17th September 1894 and again on 12th February 1895, the much-vaunted northern fleet was utterly destroyed.[4] The problem lay not with Chinese courage, but with appalling organisation and the endemic corruption that had sucked the heart out of its forces leaving only an impressive shell. Some time before the confrontation, Captain Lang had resigned following a typical Chinese argument over 'face'. The Admiral of the Fleet was Ting Ju-chang, a cavalry officer who 'made no pretence of knowing anything about a ship';[5] Lang had been given a similar rank, but using a different ideogram that was open to a number of interpretations. Matters came to a head when Admiral Ting was commanded to appear in Beijing. In his absence, 'Admiral' Lang tried to assume command. But the senior Commodore of the Fleet, Liu Poo-chin, claimed Lang was merely an 'adviser' with the rank of admiral, and insisted on taking control of the armada. A violent argument arose and the upshot was that Lang resigned. A new co-Admiral was appointed, the German von Henniken, who was not a sailor, but a soldier-engineer. According to one eyewitness, who seemed to view the whole tragic episode as a scene from a comic opera, this did not really matter; the barbarian 'admiral' was needed primarily as a scapegoat to save the Chinese Admiral from a death sentence should victory elude him.[6]

During the sea battles the Chinese battleships hardly fired a shot, for the very good reason that they had few shells to throw at the enemy ships. Without ammunition, the much-vaunted battle fleet was a toothless tiger, and quite unable to stem the advance of the Japanese. 'A schoolboy would at once have thought of ammunition; yet that elementary need was unattended to' – perhaps not unattended to, but certainly considered unimportant against the possibility of self-aggrandisement. Both Li Hung-chang and Yehonala played their part in this tragic fiasco, for both had siphoned off the funds earmarked to buy shells for the warships. Yehonala's 'cut' was used to finance the renovation of her Summer Palace, where she continued to amuse herself with amateur theatricals and boat-trips, even as her country's warships were sunk and her sailors destroyed. The disaster hardly caused a ripple in the turbid lake that was the Manchu court. A short time afterwards a court eunuch, asked about the embezzlement, replied brazenly, 'Even if the money had been spent on the navy, the Japanese would have beaten us all the same. As it is, at least we have the Summer Palace.'

Their sea passage unopposed, the Japanese reinforced their battalions in Korea and pushed north, crossing the border to the west of the Changbai Mountains. They swung southwards to invest Port Arthur, the model fortress (built with Western help) at the tip of the strategic Liaotung Peninsula, which hung like a defending arm deep into the Yellow Sea. Together with its sister fortress at Weihaiwei on the northern shore of the Shandong peninsula, Port Arthur protected the approaches to the port of Tientsin, the eastern gateway to

Beijing. By 21st November 1894, Port Arthur had fallen. Three months later, on 12th February 1895, the cavalry officer-turned-Admiral, Ting Ju-chang, surrendered Weihaiwei and then committed suicide, along with several of his officers. The Japanese victory was total: their forces now stood poised to take Tientsin and advance upon the Chinese capital itself.

In Beijing, the Manchu elite finally awoke to the danger. Yehonala hurriedly recalled the disgraced Prince Kung to advise her in the crisis, and finally allowed her old love, Jung Lu, to return to the capital. Unwilling to bear her share of responsibility for the debacle in Korea, Yehonala threw her faithful retainer Li Hung-chang to the wolves. The Viceroy of Chihli and 'Warden of the Northern Seas' was stripped of his rank and honours, though the silken cord was withheld and Li kept his life (and his immense fortune).[7] This helped to mollify public indignation. There were many, from noble to peasant, who rejoiced to see so great a fall: stories abounded of Li's peculation, how his massive investments in Japan had subverted him to the enemy's cause. And of course, Li's very public disgrace served to keep Yehonala's own sins firmly in the background.

Envoys were now dispatched to Japan to negotiate a peace, but made little headway against Japanese intransigence. The victors had scores to settle. For centuries the Chinese had derided the 'dwarf men' as ignorant savages, brain-pickers of Chinese culture, content only to ape the more advanced manners and customs of the Middle Kingdom. Determined to humble its giant neighbour before the world, Japan sent the Chinese representatives home, demanding a more prestigious ambassador for the negotiations. There were few volunteers among the Manchu nobility for this humiliating role, but as ever, Yehonala had an answer. The disgraced Li Hung-chang was reinstated as Ambassador and commanded by Imperial edict to complete the negotiations with the Japanese (who the Chinese, in their overweening pride, still referred to as 'dwarf men'). Yehonala knew that Li was already universally loathed for his part in the Chinese defeat – if he managed to placate the Japanese without bankrupting the Middle Kingdom, well and good; if he failed, his stock could not fall much further, and the silken cord was still an option.

But while Yehonala may have been pleased at the subtlety of her diplomacy, she remained absolutely infuriated by the Japanese incursion. What really galled was the timing of the Japanese attack. Yehonala had been born in 1834, and, not content with the illicit refurbishment of her Summer Palace, the tenth moon of 1894 had been marked down as a time for the most extravagant celebrations to honour her birthday. The Empress Mother bemoaned this untimely coincidence in an edict replete with the melancholy disappointment of a thwarted egotist:

> The auspicious occasion of my sixtieth birthday ... was to have been a joyful event, in which the whole nation would unite in paying to me loyal and dutiful homage. It had been intended that His Majesty the Emperor, accompanied by the whole Court, should proceed to offer congratulations to me, and make obeisance at the I Ho Yuan, and officials and people have subscribed funds wherewith to raise triumphal arches [all officials had 'spontaneously' offered a birthday gift of twenty-five per cent of their yearly income] and to decorate the Imperial Highway throughout its entire length from Beijing to the Summer Palace; high altars have been erected where Buddhist sutras were to have been recited in my honour. I was not disposed to be unduly obstinate and to insist on refusing these honours ...
>
> Who would ever have anticipated that the Dwarf-men would have dared to force us into hostilities, and that since the beginning of the summer they have invaded our tributary state and destroyed our fleet? ... Although the date of my birthday is drawing close, how could I have the heart, at such a time, to delight my senses with revelries ...? I therefore decree that the ceremonies to be observed on my birthday shall be performed at the Palace in Beijing, and all preparations at the Summer Palace shall be abandoned forthwith.[8]

It was a bitter blow to Yehonala's pride. But an even greater pounding to the Empress's, and China's, prestige followed hard upon the heels of this humiliation. Li Hung-chang's negotiations in Japan resulted in the Treaty of Shimonoseki, signed on 17th April 1895. In it China agreed to the ceding of Formosa and the coastal Penghu Islands, and handed over the fortress of Port Arthur, effectively allowing the Japanese an unopposed passage to Tientsin and Beijing whenever they next chose to move against the Middle Kingdom. The southern fortress of Weihaiwei was also yielded to Japanese forces, to remain occupied until payment in full of a two hundred million tael 'indemnity'.

Li Hung-chang had been shot in the face on his arrival in Japan by a fanatic of the Soshi class, the bullet lodging just below his left eye. But for this, the terms would certainly have been harsher – the Japanese originally had demanded additional land to the north of Port Arthur, and a 'fine' of three hundred million taels. Given the constraints he was forced to work under, the bargain Li made with the victorious Japanese was worthy of praise, but the old veteran (he was now seventy-two years old) returned to China in 1896 to find every man's hand against him. Censors demanded his execution and most of the rest of the country agreed. But Yehonala had come to realise just how invaluable were Li Hung-chang's experience and knowledge to her purposes. He might be humiliated, shorn of his honours and titles, exiled from court, but his advice on world affairs (about which Yehonala, like the rest of her administration, remained loftily ignorant) was now simply too precious for her ever to exact the ultimate penalty. Lesser men might have been banished to the post roads in Turkestan; Yehonala sent Li to St Petersburg as Chinese representative at the coronation of Czar Nicholas II (a journey on which he was accompanied, bizarrely, by his own magnificently appointed coffin). One result of this was a secret agreement between the two nations, finalised in 1896, in which each agreed to defend the other against any possible aggression from Japan. The treaty allowed Russia to extend her Trans-Siberian railway across Chinese Manchuria to Vladivostok, and to use the railway to transport men and materiel through Chinese territory. It also gave Russia the right (once the 'dwarf men' had been expelled from Port Arthur) to harbour her fleet in that ice-free port, a concession that the Chinese would soon learn to rue.

The fabulous ransom exacted by the Japanese, and extensive acquisition of land, both excited the greed of the Western nations, and filled them with anxiety. With possession of Port Arthur, Japan was in danger of becoming the most puissant power in the region. Germany, France and Russia (whose massive eastern fleet was close by) together brought pressure on Japan to return Port Arthur and the Liaotung Peninsula to its original owners. In compensation, China was forced to part with a further thirty million taels for Japanese 'expenses'.

The easy Japanese victory began a feeding-frenzy among the Europeans over the moribund body of the Middle Kingdom. China did not have the cash to pay the Japanese indemnity, and there was intense rivalry among the Westerners to secure the right to loan the necessary funds. Not content with usury, each of the Powers now desperately cast about for pretexts that would allow them to take an even bigger slice of the Chinese melon. Japan had won land by force of arms; Britain had already extorted Hong Kong; with China in such a weakened condition, the other European powers were determined to take their share. A year after Li Hung-chang's return, Germany found her excuse in the murder, in Shandong Province, of two German missionaries. In reprisal, the Kaiser's forces seized the port of Kiaochow, close to Japanese-occupied Weihaiwei, and 'leased' the land for a distance of fifty kilometres around the port for a period of ninety-nine years. Anti-missionary disturbances in the southern province of Canton allowed France to force a similar ninety-nine-year 'lease' of the port-city of Kwangchowan. In 1897, the Russians took advantage of their secret agreement with the Chinese by sailing their warships into Port Arthur – and then refusing to leave. By the spring of 1898 Russia had 'leased' the fortress and a second port, Talienwan, until the year 1923.[9] Britain voiced concern that these rental agreements had undermined the balance of power in the region, and on this flimsy basis demanded the southern fortress and port of Weihaiwei – just as soon as the Japanese had been paid in full by the Chinese and had vacated the place. In the treaty ports, the press spoke openly of a division of China, as Africa had been portioned out to the colonial powers a few decades before.

Perhaps the only benefit from this degrading catalogue of national humiliation was the growing conviction among many Chinese intellectuals that the old way of interfacing with the world, the naive insular assumption of the superiority of all things Chinese, simply would not do. While the traditional mandarin scholar-gentleman might claim that excellence in all things violent did not prove Western superiority, others looked beyond the military and saw in the European model of governance many things that the Celestial Kingdom might incorporate to their advantage. Those Chinese who had latterly been sent as ambassadors and emissaries to the West often returned utterly in thrall to all things Western. Yehonala was more circumspect. Hearing one lady holding forth on the evils of foot-binding, she pointedly asked if the European practice of binding women's waists in whalebone corsets was not similarly barbaric.

If Yehonala was blind to the benefits of 'barbarian' technologies, the same could not be said of her nephew the Kuang Hsu Emperor. From his childhood interest in clockwork toys, Kuang Hsu had passed via his miniature train and Palace telephone to an unshakeable conviction that his Empire's survival depended upon drastic change to a Western model. The recent defeat at the hands of Japan and China's spineless 'leasing' of her territory to the aggressors only served to emphasise the gravity of the threat facing the Middle Kingdom. From around 1895 Kuang Hsu had ordered for his personal study every book on foreign learning that had been translated into Chinese. These he devoured with enormous speed, alone in his study, gradually adding to his knowledge of the outside world and its achievements. We should not make light of this solitary attempt: it was the first time any Manchu Emperor had ever concerned himself with a study of other nations, and it would have set his august and insular ancestors spinning in their ornate tombs.

It is easy to discern, and to sympathise, with Kuang Hsu's reasoning. The nations of the West were using the self-same technologies to carve 'spheres of influence' and (if Africa was a standard to judge them by) perhaps even colonies from his realm. Belief in tradition and the superiority of Chinese culture was no defence against these new invaders, and the time-honoured strategy of 'using one barbarian against another' had failed totally. True, each Western nation was jealous of the others and tried its utmost to gain the advantage. But only so far. These new barbarians understood that China was huge, big enough to allow everyone a 'slice of the melon'. Some slices would be larger, some smaller, but the Westerners realised that far more could be achieved if they did not go to war with each other, but acted in concert to swallow the Empire piecemeal. Thanks to the influence of the most militant reformers, the Emperor was introduced to the epic struggles of Russia's Peter the Great, and Japan's Hideyoshi, men who had achieved undying fame by sweeping away the old and modernising their nations. These tales undoubtedly had the most profound effect on the Emperor, at an almost visceral level. Japan's story was especially instructive: an Asian, tradition-bound nation, it had effected an almost overnight transformation from feudal state to an industrial society on the Western model. It possessed the most modern Western weapons, and had drilled its men and honed its fighting skills along 'barbarian' lines. With these accomplishments Japan, the reviled 'dwarf nation', had routed Chinese arms in an endless succession of defeats. Japan, an Asian state, now took its place among the great Western Powers, an accepted and equal partner of the Western barbarians. The solution was obvious. What Japan had achieved, China could also accomplish. To regain its former glory, China must follow the trail Japan had blazed.

There may well have been a further reason for Kuang Hsu's desire to lead the reform of China and to bring the nation to greatness – his impotence. The Emperor's inability to produce children of his own was well known and, in family-oriented Confucian society, would inevitably have left him secretly despised by the most of the nation he was set over. Indeed, children (and especially sons) were seen not so much as a natural consequence of biology but as a reward for virtuous behaviour in oneself or in one's ancestors.[10] Men who produced no offspring were known disparagingly as *t'ien yen*, 'natural eunuchs'.[11] This immense loss of face was undoubtedly a spur to his reformist zeal, if not *the* spur that pushed forward his thoroughgoing (and ultimately naive) purge of China's dead wood. If Kuang Hsu was sexually impotent, if he could not gain a degree of immortality by bequeathing living descendants to add their lustre to the Imperial line, then he would leave behind a deathless name in the consummation of his sweeping reforms.

Whatever the truth of this, Kuang Hsu was not alone in his assessment that Western learning was the key to regaining China's prestige, and indeed to its very survival as a sovereign nation. Throughout the empire many of the younger scholars had formed the same conclusion, and to a man they thirsted for information and guidance. When it was discovered which Western books the Emperor himself had begun to read, requests for the publications became so great that literary societies in the European treaty ports could not keep pace with demand. Pirated versions appeared, photographed by resourceful Chinese entrepreneurs, and sold for just a tenth of the cost of the originals. Reform clubs were set up in most of the big cities, where like-minded scholars and officials might meet to hear lectures, and to discuss how best the modernisation of China could be moved forward.

The chief guru of this movement was a charismatic young Cantonese scholar named Kang Yu-wei.[12] In his late thirties, Kang had spent his youth in rebellious rejection of the Confucian ways. For a while he had immersed himself in esoteric Buddhism, but after spending many months meditating in the mountains north of Canton, his brilliant and eclectic mind had been drawn towards barbarian knowledge. Kang's visits to the European enclaves inspired him, and by the age of twenty-two he had begun to imbibe Western learning via the translations to be found in southern Chinese bookshops. He seems to have formed a strange composite vision of himself as a Western-inspired Buddhist Bodhisattva – spiritually advanced human who, having attained enlightenment, forsakes the bliss of nirvana in order to lead other beings along the eight-fold path. But Kang Yu-wei saw himself as a Bodhisattva of a different kidney, one who was destined to redeem China using European learning. In the mid-eighteen-eighties he wrote that: 'My appearance in this world is solely for the purpose of saving all living beings. it is for this reason that I do not dwell in Heaven but enter into Hell.'

Kang's vigorous enthusiasm for Westernisation made him many converts, as did his copious literary output and perceptive analysis of China's predicament. As early as 1888 in a petition to the Emperor he had described how the Westerners had broken through China's ring of buffer states, and were 'now coming at the heart of the country. Japan plots in Korea; England is intriguing in Thibet; Russia is building railways in the north, threatening Beijing; and France is nourishing her ambition in the south-western provinces.' Reform he asserted, was essential. The traditional view that ancient institutions and traditions were inviolable must be swept away. If China emulated the root and branch reforms seen in Japan 'she will become strong and prosperous in ten years, and within twenty years she will become a powerful nation, able to recover her lost territories and to avenge her humiliations'.[13] The stirring call to arms never reached the Emperor – the petition was interdicted by conservatives and 'lost' within China's labyrinthine bueaucracy. But Kang was persistent. In April 1895 he was busily organising a petition of some thirteen hundred scholars against the proposed treaty with Japan, only to find his plan pre-empted when China signed the offending document early. Nothing daunted, he tried again with another petition in May and this time he was more fortunate. The defeat by Japan, and the humiliating Treaty of Shimonoseki, had produced a seismic change within some parts of the Chinese establishment. Kang's aspirations to incorporate the best of European ways, and to use the barbarians' own skills and weapons to prevent the dismembering of the Empire now found a ready ear among certain members of the Manchu hierarchy. Weng Tung-ho, the Emperor's tutor, having earlier been unconvinced by Kang's thesis, now made his approval public. The Viceroy of Hangzhou, Chang Chih-tung, sponsored the setting up of a Shanghai chapter of the Ch'iang Hsueh Hui (The Society for the Study of National Strengthening), of which Kang was a leading light. The Beijing branch had many influential members, including Yuan Shi-kai, who was later to play a ruinous role in the reform movement. With such influential friends to help him, Kang's second petition finally reached the Emperor.

Kuang Hsu was impressed by the reformer's analysis of the situation, which paralleled his own. Kang's petition did not play down the danger from Japan, but placed it in context, as part of a pattern; it saw the main threat as nothing less than the total dismemberment of China, the partition of the Empire among all the Powers, and concluded that 'China is confronted with the greatest danger in her history'. Kuang Hsu ordered three copies of the document made, and sent one to Yehonala. In July, an Imperial decree ordered the governors and viceroys of all Chinese provinces to modernise. This can only have had the tacit approval of the Empress Dowager and seems to indicate that, at that time, Yehonala too was a supporter of the reform process.

Unfortunately, the congenital inertia of the Chinese system meant that most governors did nothing, and the decree became just another worthless parchment in the mountain of pious words and exhortations that had issued intermittently from the throne since the Dynasty had come to power, some two hundred and fifty-one years before. The vested interest of the literati was too deeply entrenched in Chinese society to be diverted by mere words, and the river of bureaucracy continued to meander slowly along its accustomed and ineffective course. Disillusioned, Kang Yu-wei returned to Canton in 1896, where he continued to write and agitate for the reforms he believed were integral to China's survival.

Just two years later Germany's occupation of Kiaochow began the Powers' scramble to occupy Chinese land. Vindicated in his predictions, Kang returned to Beijing, having penned yet another memorial to the Throne. An Imperial decree was issued ordering that he be allowed to expound his views to the Tsungli Yamen (China's 'Foreign Office'). In addition, all Kang's books were to be collected and sent to the Emperor for his perusal. Kang's subsequent presentation before the Tsungli Yamen impressed its members, and piqued Kuang Hsu's interest anew. He wished to meet the man in person, but was dissuaded by Prince Kung, the old conservative war-horse, who argued on traditional grounds that it was beneath the Imperial dignity for Kuang Hsu to meet so lowly an official. Unwisely, Kuang Hsu acquiesced, but commanded instead that the reformer be given the unprecedented favour of memorialising the Emperor directly. Kang used this privilege to submit, on 29th January 1898, a detailed exposition of his reform plans. Only total reform would save the country, Kang insisted, half-measures would always fail. The Emperor must come out unequivocally for just such a root and branch programme. A loyalty pledge by all high officials, guaranteeing their support for the reforms, was a necessity; those refusing the oath must resign their offices. Once this was accomplished, a committee of 'Twelve Wise Men' (the Committee on Institutions) should be set up to block out the reform package for the Emperor's ultimate approval.[14]

Kuang Hsu was cautious. He knew that his formidable aunt seemed to be in favour of the reform process; but she would give no real indication of the scale or pace at which she wished modernisation to proceed. It is possible that Yehonala may have seen in Kuang Hsu a useful tool with which to experiment with the further remodelling of Chinese society. There is no doubt that she understood the need for reform as well as anyone; however, her power base lay not among the reformers, but with the conservative scholar-gentry and reactionary nobles, who were more concerned with their own perquisites and privileges than with China's place in the political firmament. She may have decided to remain purposely silent, and to keep her opinions blurred. Should matters go awry with Kuang Hsu's reforms, the Emperor would take the blame, and she could claim to be as shocked as anyone by the problems that had arisen. If everything progressed satisfactorily, then as 'overseer' of Kuang Hsu's attempts at governing the Middle

Kingdom, she would claim at least an equal share of the credit. In modern terms, Yehonala had a win–win situation, and her nephew was the fall guy.

In an Imperial proclamation on 11th June the Emperor gave Kang Yu-wei the first of his demands, and declared forthrightly for reform. On 16th June, ignoring the squeals of protest from the conservatives, he granted Kang a personal audience, conversing animatedly with the 'lowly official' for nearly three hours. What Kuang Hsu heard at that unprecedented meeting seems to have steeled his resolve: the Emperor embraced the whole of Kang's political philosophy. There would be no more delay, no more prevarication. The process of reform would begin in earnest.

Then began the almost continuous issuing of Imperial edicts that was to become known as the 'Hundred Days of Reform'. In the first two months Kuang Hsu issued twenty-seven decrees, all aimed at abolishing the worst of the old system of government and taking China into the modern era (see box).

It is hard to find fault with even a single one of Kuang Hsu's proclamations. Indeed, had they been implemented in their entirety, there is no doubt that they would have effected China's reawakening as a world power. The problem lay not so much in

EDICT

1. The establishment of a university at Beijing.
2. Imperial clansmen to visit foreign countries to study the forms of European and American government.
3. The encouragement of the arts, sciences and modern agriculture.
4. The Emperor willing to hear the objections of the conservatives to progress and reform.
5. The literary essay abolished as a prominent part of the governmental examinations.
6. Censure of those attempting to block the establishment of the Beijing Imperial University.
7. Construction of the Lu-Han railway to be expedited.

8. Advised the adoption of Western arms and drill for all Manchu troops.
9. Ordered agricultural schools established in all provinces to teach improved agricultural methods.
10. Ordered the introduction of patent and copyright laws to encourage inventors and authors.
11. The Board of War and Foreign Office both ordered to report on the reform of military examinations.
12. Special rewards offered to inventors and authors.
13. Officials ordered to encourage trade, and to assist merchants.
14. Ordered the establishment of school boards in every city in the Empire.
15. Ordered the establishment of the Bureau of Mines, and the Bureau of Railroads.
16. Journalists encouraged to write on all political subjects.
17. Naval academies and training ships were ordered.
18. A plea to all ministers and provincial authorities to make an effort to understand what the Emperor was trying to accomplish, and to help him in his efforts at reform.
19. Schools ordered at all Chinese legations in foreign countries for the benefit of Chinese children in those places.
20. Commercial bureaux ordered in Shanghai for the encouragement of trade.
21. Six bureaucratic boards in Beijing designated irrelevant and abolished.
22. The right to memorialise the Throne in sealed memorials granted to all who desired to do so.
23. Two presidents and four vice-presidents of the Board of Rites dismissed.
24. The Governorships Hubei, Canton and Yunnan abolished as being useless to the expense of the country.
25. Schools of instruction in the preparation of tea and silk were ordered to be established.
26. The traditional slow courier posts were abolished in favour of the Imperial Customs Post.
27. A system of budgets, as in Western countries, was approved.

the content of the edicts, but in the quality of the advisers who now counselled the Emperor. Like their leader, Kang Yu-wei they were to a man visionaries and theorists. Lacking the experience of practical government, and painfully conscious of both China's backwardness and the imminent danger of the Empire's dismemberment, they encouraged the avalanche of reform edicts. Isaac Headland, who was living in northern China throughout the 'Hundred Days', describes how a Chinese friend, a member of the prestigious Hanlin Academy, predicted unrest after only the sixth edict had been published, commenting that 'There is going to be trouble if the Emperor continues his reform at this rate of speed'.[15] It is a tragedy that none of the Emperor's advisers were able to view the future with such perspicacity. Had the nation's bureaucracy been given time to assimilate the changes (each of which, to the old-time literati, were epoch-making readjustments) the shock of the new might have been dissipated. But the very speed with which they were issued was guaranteed to stiffen resistance among the old guard. Nevertheless, while Kuang Hsu simply contented himself with creating new 'Western-style' offices, and their own interests remained immune, the conservatives were at first content to lie still, keeping a jealous, self-serving watch on his activities.

Unfortunately, the enthusiasts for reform compounded their errors with Imperial edicts 21, 23, 24 and 26. These were, in effect, an immediate, frontal assault on the perquisites and sinecures of the country's most powerful bureaucrats and nobles. The reactionaries began to stir. Things came to a head at the beginning of September, when Hsu Ying-k'uei, the President of the Board of Rites, blocked the passage of a memorial from a junior secretary, Wang Chao, to the Emperor in direct defiance of Imperial edict 22. Previously, several other high officials had ignored the Imperial decrees with impunity, and Hsu, no lover of the reform movement, no doubt believed his own disobedience would be similarly overlooked. He was wrong. To general wonderment, the Emperor acted with uncharacteristic ruthlessness: Hsu, together with all senior officials at the Board of Rites, were summarily dismissed from their posts. A few days later, on 5th September, Kuang Hsu appointed four young pro-reform secretaries to the Grand Council, 'practically to take over the duties of the Grand Councillors'. Two days afterwards he dismissed the veteran Li Hung-chang from his post at the Tsungli Yamen. The gauntlet had been thrown down before the old guard. They would not be slow to take it up.

CHAPTER SIXTEEN

Coup and countercoup

$\mathcal{T}$he dismissed members of the Board of Rites begged an audience with Yehonala. Accompanied by sympathetic members of the court, they laid out their complaint against the Emperor and pleaded on their knees for her to take up the reins of government. Yehonala listened to their request impassively, then closed the audience with no indication of her views. A pastmaster of intrigue, she was keeping her own counsel and none knew which way she might move.

Kuang Hsu, however, was convinced that he could divine his aunt's intentions, and the knowledge terrified him. On his ritual visits to perform his obeisance before Yehonala he had found her now implacably opposed to reform. Nothing he could say would move her. Rumours spread that Kuang Hsu's inspection of the Imperial troops at Tientsin, scheduled for 19th October, was the date set for his arrest and imposed abdication. On 13th September he sent a decree (written for safety in his own hand) via a trusted secretary to Kang Yu-wei:

> In view of the present difficult situation, I have found that only reforms can save China, and that reforms can only be achieved through the discharge of the conservative and ignorant ministers and the appointment of intelligent and brave scholars. Her Graceful Majesty the Empress Dowager, however, did not agree. I have tried again and again to persuade her, only to find Her Majesty more angry. You, Kang Yu-wie, Yang Jui, Lin Hsu and Tan Ssu-t'ung should deliberate immediately to find some ways to save me.
>
> With extreme worries and earnest hopes.[1]

The Emperor asked too much of his zealous, but naive, cadre of reformers. Theoreticians to a man, they were tiros in the game of power politics and unsuited to the subtle manoeuvrings of the court. But the Emperor had begged their aid and they sought desperately to devise some scheme to 'save' him, and the reform programme. From the Emperor's letter it was obvious that Yehonala was the reef upon which all their hopes would founder. Reasoned argument had failed to convince the Empress Dowager; force now seemed the only remaining option. After much discussion, it was decided that only a coup d'état, and Yehonala's confinement, could guarantee China's renewal.

Kang and his academic colleagues cast about them for a man of action to put their plan into effect. Increasingly desperate, they lighted upon Yuan Shi-kai, an army officer who had been a long-time member of the Ch'iang Hsueh Hui, the 'Society for the Study of National Strengthening', who now commanded the best-trained and most modern section of the Chinese armed forces. Short, shaven-headed and muscular, Yuan 'gave ... the appearance of great energy'[2] and by his exemplary record in Korea and his incorporation of the best of Western military techniques, had gained the admiration, and perhaps the trust, of the Emperor. It seems that Kuang Hsu was informed of the proposed plot and agreed to its implementation. On 16th September he granted Yuan Shi-kai an audience and promoted the general to honorary vice-president of the Board of War, a high rank for so young an officer. The next day Yuan saw the Emperor again, though it is not known for certain what passed between the two men at this meeting.

Ever watchful, Yehonala was certainly bothered by these events. Unsure of the junior officer's sympathies, she arranged for Jung Lu to telegraph Yuan Shi-kai from Tientsin, and to feed him a plausible, but completely fabricated, story of heightened tension in the area, which required Yuan's immediate return to the port (and would effectively isolate him from the Emperor). But the conspirators too were on the move. That same night, Yuan Shi-kai was visited by Tan Ssu-t'ung, one of the four men the Emperor had charged with finding 'some ways to save me'. The son of the Governor of Hubei, he had repudiated the easy life his family connections offered and, as often occurs when privileged youth turns revolutionary, of all the reformers his views were the most extreme. Tan boldly informed Yuan of the plot, and exhorted him to save the Emperor, 'eliminate the rebels, and discipline the palaces'. Tan suggested that Yuan should return to Tientsin as ordered, but he should immediately arrest and execute his superior officer, Yehonala's former lover, Jung Lu. His troops were then to march on Beijing, surround the Summer Palace, and isolate the Empress Dowager from her conservative allies. In some accounts, Tan explicitly states the need to execute Yehonala and offers to dispatch her himself. The Emperor would then be free to continue his programme of reforms.

It says much of the power and mystique of Yehonala that the plotters believed the key to the success of their scheme lay in confining, or killing, this diminutive sixty-four-year-old Manchu lady. She was still seen as the powerhouse, the dynamic brain, whose cool calculations and decisive actions were indispensable to the reactionaries. Kill the head and the anti-reformist body would die. Tan would allow Yuan Shi-kai no prevarication. He cut through the military man's temporising and demanded an instant answer: was Yuan with them or not? In his diary, Yuan Shi-kai records how a bulge in Tan's waistband indicated that his visitor was carrying a weapon. As it seemed unlikely the plotters would allow him to survive a negative response to their proposal, Yuan replied, 'In October the Imperial inspection will be held at Tientsin. At that time all troops will be assembled. If his Majesty issues an order, who dare disobey, and what cannot be accomplished?'[3] Apparently satisfied with this rather ambiguous response, Tan left to inform his co-conspirators that they had found their man – planning for the coup could now move forward.

The next morning the reform movement's chosen 'man of action' had a third brief audience with the Emperor, and then left by train for Tientsin. Some accounts relate that he had with him a small arrow, given by the Emperor as a symbol of Imperial authority, others that he carried a secret Imperial

decree, written in vermilion ink, and confirming in every particular the plan which Tan Ssu-t'ung had laid before him the
previous evening. Whatever the truth of this, there is little
doubt that the bullet-headed soldier had much to occupy him
as his carriage rattled eastwards towards the port city. Joining
with Kang Yu-wei would undoubtedly bring forward the
reforms which Yuan Shi-kai knew were essential for China's
survival. And, as he had commented to Tang, if the Emperor
commanded, it was his duty to obey – his training, his very
culture, demanded no less. But it was not so simple. If the
Emperor wished to move against his aunt, then the Emperor
himself was driving a coach and horses through Chinese traditional values, for it was to Yehonala, as the senior member of
the elder generation, that Kuang Hsu owed total respect and
complete obedience. Was it right to follow tradition and obey
his Emperor unquestioningly, if that same Emperor was intent
on committing sacrilege against these same sacred traditions?
At a more practical level, Yuan Shi-kai must have busily calculated the odds for and against failure of the enterprise. That it
was risky in the extreme was undeniable: Yuan commanded a
mere seven thousand troops (albeit better armed and trained)
against Jung Lu's massive force of a hundred thousand men.
Then again, if Jung Lu was removed, his men would be leader-
less and might well throw in their lot with the reforming movement. But they could just as easily tear to pieces the man
who had shot down their commanding officer. And yet, the
successful completion of his mission would, at a stroke, make
him the most powerful man in the Empire and win him the
undying gratitude of Kuang Hsu: he would drown beneath
the honours and wealth the Emperor would rain down upon
his head. On the other hand, the conservative faction was
strong, and Yehonala's wrath against traitors terrible to behold.
Even so …

By the time his train arrived at Tientsin station (where he
was greeted by a band sent to celebrate his recent promotion),
Yuan Shi-kai had made up his mind. Steeling himself, he made
straight for Jung Lu's headquarters. Once closeted with the old
Manchu warrior, he delayed no longer. The two men had sworn

an oath as blood-brothers some years before and Yuan now asked Jung Lu if he believed him faithful to that vow. 'Of course I do,' a mystified Jung Lu is reported to have answered. 'You well may,' Yuan replied, 'the Emperor has sent me to kill you, and instead, I now betray his scheme, because of my loyalty to the Empress Dowager and my affection for you'. He then exposed the reformists' plot in all its detail to an astonished Jung Lu, whose much-vaunted intelligence network had apparently been completely unaware of the conspiracy.

Jung Lu wasted no time. He bundled Yuan out of the office and together they took the train back to the capital, arriving just after 5 p.m. Casting aside all convention, Jung Lu burst into the Forbidden City, scattering bewildered guards, who did not dare impede the progress of so high an official, and pushing through the crowds of frightened eunuchs who, thanks to the Palace rumour-mills, were already aware that events of dire moment were afoot. He quickly ascertained Yehonala's location and, with Yuan at his side he strode rapidly through the shadow-filled corridors and halls, exiting the Forbidden City by a western gate and making for the ornate Altar of the Silk-worms on the north-eastern shore of Bei Hai lake. Here, for once unaware of the danger that threatened, Yehonala had completed the rites of the annual sacrifice to the God of Seri-culture. Falling to his knees and begging forgiveness for his presumption as he kowtowed, Yehonala's staunchest supporter laid bare her nephew's plot, how he planned to seize total power, how Jung Lu was to be murdered and she imprisoned, perhaps even killed.

It must have been very hard for Yehonala to come to terms with these revelations: not only had Kuang Hsu betrayed her and her followers, he had abandoned all the cultural traditions of filial piety which, or so the conservatives believed, set China apart from the barbarians. She had given Kuang Hsu's policy free rein as a means of pushing forward reform without risking a conservative backlash against her rule. But the ploy had backfired: now the puppet she believed she controlled was within an ace of taking from her the power and prestige she had fought all her life to retain. With that coolness under fire, the cold calculation, the remorseless will that marked her out from friend or foe alike, Yehonala immediately responded to the perils of the moment and reeled off her orders. In less than two hours she had assembled before her 'the whole of the Grand Council, several of the Manchu princes and nobles ... and the high officials of the boards, including the ministers whom the Emperor had cashiered ...'. To a man, they begged on their knees that she should resume command of the Empire. Nor was she in the mood to refuse their request. The countercoup had begun.

Under cover of night, Jung Lu's loyal Tientsin troops were brought up to replace the regular guards and secure the Forbidden City. Early the next morning the Emperor, apparently unaware of the discovery of the reformer's plot (if indeed he was ever truly privy to the conspiracy), visited the Chung Ho Hall to rehearse the rites for the autumnal sacrifice the following day. While Kuang Hsu went over the litany he was to recite, eunuchs loyal to Yehonala were silently moved into place. Guards were brought into their position. Moments later, as the Emperor left the hall, he was immediately surrounded by the soldiers and, with eunuchs in attendance, bundled out of the Forbidden City and taken to Nan Hai Hu, the southernmost of the Palace's trio of lakes. In the very centre of the lake lay a small island, and, nestling among its trees and rocks, a palace and pavilion, the Ocean Terrace, accessible only by a long causeway guarded by a drawbridge. The captive Emperor was marched into the Ocean Terrace and left there, his own familiar eunuch attendants denied him, to await the arrival of his august aunt.

Yehonala left Kuang Hsu to brood and worry over his fate for several hours. When she finally arrived (accompanied only by the Chief Eunuch, Li Lien-ying) she was in vindictive mood. She intended to spare his life, she informed a terrified Kuang Hsu, but he would be held here, at the Ocean Terrace, under the strictest scrutiny – his every action, his every word, noted and reported to her. 'How dare he forget the great benefits he owed her, his elevation to the throne and her generosity in allowing him to administer the government, he, a poor puppet, who had no right to be Emperor at all, and whom she could unmake at will?[4] Princess Te Ling's story of this meeting has Yehonala confronting the Emperor in his apartments. The dialogue too, is different, but the implacable sentiment behind it is identical in both accounts.

The Pearl Concubine, Kuang Hsu's favourite consort, pleaded with Yehonala to spare the Emperor further censure. Yehonala's response to what she must have regarded as unspeakable presumption was to order her to be carried away and imprisoned in another part of the Forbidden City. Years later she still harboured a bitter hatred of this lady, and when the opportunity arose, she was swift to exact an even more severe punishment than incarceration. Having removed his sole female friend, Yehonala now ordered her niece, Lung Yu, the Empress Consort, to attend on the Emperor, so ensuring that her primary information about his activities derived from an unimpeachable source.

With her nephew overthrown and safely locked away to await whatever fate she might consign him to, Yehonala turned her attention to his followers. Kuang Hsu's eunuchs had been dismissed when the countercoup began; fourteen were now put to death by Yehonala's express command. The rest were exiled to menial posts in the outer regions of the Empire. Weng Tung-ho, who had recommended the reformist Kang Yu-wei, was dismissed from all his posts, as was the Governor of Hunan, who had actually had the audacity to obey the Emperor and attempt to implement the reforms in his province. Chang Yin-huan, a Cantonese member of the Tsungli Yamen (whom Queen Victoria had created a Grand Commander of the Order of St Michael and St George) was banished to the deserts of the New Western Dominion (Xinjiang), turning down a British offer to rescue him,[5] and suffering a horrendous death in exile two years later. Nor did Imperial clansmen escape Yehonala's 'Divine Wrath': Tsai Ch'u whose reformist tendencies had led him to suggest to the Emperor that he put an end to Yehonala's meddling in government affairs, was sentenced to perpetual imprisonment in the 'Empty Chamber', the infamous jail of the Imperial clan court. Although she promised no general proscription, hundreds, perhaps thousands, of lesser officials were dismissed from their posts, many banished. But none of this sated Yehonala's craving for revenge. All the leading reformers' lives were forfeit as a matter of course, but above all she desired the capture and death of the ringleaders of the plot, Kang Yu-wei and Tan Ssu-t'ung.

Kang led a charmed existence during the perilous days of the countercoup. After trying and failing to find help for the Emperor from the Western Powers, he travelled disconsolately to Tientsin to catch a boat for Shanghai, blissfully ignorant of the price on his head. His friends had advised disguise for the journey, but Kang had refused, believing 'that death and life were predestined'.[6] Somehow, bare-faced, he moved unrecognised through Tientsin, escaping capture at Chefoo only because the arrest order which awaited him there had been sent in code, and no one at the port possessed the key to decipher what was undoubtedly the reformer's death warrant. On board the steamer to Shanghai he was told of the countercoup by a British official,[7] who then aided his escape to British-held Hong Kong, escorted by two ships of the Royal Navy. Kang eventually made his way to Japan, from which safe haven he continued to fulminate against the regime, and against Yehonala, whom he accused of the grossest indecencies.

Tan Ssu-t'ung, like the zealot he was, refused to flee the capital, and paid the ultimate price for his bravado. He was arrested with five others and arraigned before the Board of Punishments. Documents discovered at Kang's Beijing apartments left no doubt as to their guilt and the Grand Council declared for their immediate execution. Yehonala agreed, and not just for the sake of revenge – there were sound political reasons for the prisoners' early demise: the reformers were Chinese, not Manchu, and came mainly from the southern provinces. A lengthy trial would only exacerbate the tensions between the southerners and their Manchu overlords and may have precipitated a revolt. The Six Gentlemen of the Reform Movement, as they had come to be known, were taken to the execution ground outside the city where, before a multitude of onlookers they all bravely faced the headsman's sword. Tan retained his bravado to the end, shouting boldly, 'I am willing to shed my blood, if thereby my country may be saved. But for everyone that perishes today, a thousand will rise up to carry on the work of reform, and uphold loyalty against usurpation.'[8]

Kuang Hsu's great experiment was over. In a series of edicts, Yehonala systematically reversed every one of the Emperor's revolutionary decrees, to the delight of the reactionaries. The changes effected by the Hundred Days of Reform might have been a dream, so complete was the reversion to the old ways: the literati once more bent over their brush and ink, composing the onerous 'eight-legged essay' as the entrée to government service; the memorials of honest men were withheld or censored; the press was controlled; and the 'stupid people' continued to work the fields of the Middle Kingdom without benefit of modern agricultural techniques. The Manchu elite, freed from their obligation to foreign travel, returned to their favourite pastimes of intrigue, and growing their fingernails to obscene lengths. China was China once more. And Yehonala, gimlet-eyed and omnipotent, now sat even more securely upon the Dragon Throne.

CHAPTER SEVENTEEN

Self-strengthening

The reactionaries were everywhere victorious, but China's difficulties, internal and external, remained. Apart from the congenital self-serving nature of the ruling class, the problem really resolved itself into a single question: should China remain recognisably Chinese, with an age-old 'superior' culture that set it apart from the Western barbarians, or should it sweep the ancient law of the ancestors to one side and embrace the Western mercantile philosophy, with its alien systems of government and jurisprudence? Kuang Hsu had counselled change, but his blueprint for a stronger China – to emulate the social, educational and military mores of the West – had been rejected by Yehonala and her allies as totally unacceptable. The West might be superior in industry and weapons, but China's ascendancy in matters cultural and moral remained, for them, unchallengeable. Although she wanted, and could see, the pressing need for change, Yehonala, like most of the Empire she ruled, lived according to precedent and ancient decree – the mortar that held the Empire together. Without this social cement, or so it appeared to the reactionaries, the ship of state would be rudderless, adrift on a chaotic sea at the mercy of any wind of change, and the country must slide into anarchy. Yehonala could never countenance a society in which the laws of the ancestors were obsolete.

The challenge now was to protect China from the continued depredations of the Western nations and Japan while, at the same time, maintaining the Middle Kingdom's unique heritage. Just as in the late-twentieth century the Chinese government attempted to maintain its version of socialism while simultaneously preaching the doctrine of the free market. Yehonala and her ministers decided that China would pursue a similar schizophrenic policy: the country would maintain its ancient ways, but would emulate the West in one specific area only – in armaments. This decision was accompanied by a complete volte-face in foreign policy. From that moment on there were to be no more concessions to the foreign powers. On 28th September, Yehonala brought Jung Lu back from Tientsin to the capital and appointed him, in rapid succession, a member of the Grand Council, President of the Board of War,[1] and Imperial High Commissioner with command over the four army corps which defended the capital. He moved swiftly to reorganise the northern armies, forming a new Headquarters Army of ten thousand men under his direct orders and expanding and modernising the remainder so that, by 27th June the following year, Jung Lu was the head of a unified command of five armies numbering around sixty thousand men. A member of the Grand Council, the stern traditionalist Kang I, was sent to the Yangtse basin to modernise defences there, and to ensure that the taxes collected in the area found their way to Beijing to aid the rearmament process rather than lining the pockets of provincial governors. So successful was he in this task that Yehonala praised his commitment in a special edict, while the foreign press dubbed Kang 'The Lord High Extortioner'.[2] With the Russian Bear in mind, General Ch'ang Shun was directed to reorganise military defences in Manchuria, while at the same time commissioner Li Ping-heng was sent to the area on a mission that mirrored Kang I's Yangtse excursion.

The first indication of the melon's new determination to resist further slicing came in March 1899, when three Germans were attacked by villagers near the town of Jihchao in Shandong Province, close to their military base of Kiaochow. Characteristically, German troops responded by immediately invading the area, where they burned two villages and seized Jihchao. Uncharacteristically, the Chinese refused to accept this hostile act. Their Minister in Berlin assured the Kaiser's government that German citizens would be protected, while simultaneously lodging the strongest protest against German aggression. The Governor of Shandong was ordered to send an armed force to the region and not to 'accede unendingly to the aggressive demands of the Germans'. Thankfully, the Westerners withdrew in time, but the Chinese response made it obvious to all that, while they did not wish to be drawn into a conflict, any new foreign aggression would now be met with force.

With hideously bad timing, the Italian government chose this moment to demand from China the lease of Sanmen Bay in Chekiang Province, together with the usual package of railway and mining rights in the area. There was no real pretext for the Italian claim, nor any pressing economic reason. It was simply that Italy was a Great Power and, as all the other Great Powers had a piece of China, the Italians felt that their national prestige required them to have a concession too. Britain gave the Italians to understand that they would support the demand, leading *The Times* to telegraph its Beijing correspondent, George E. Morrison, with the cryptic message 'MORRISON PEKING REMEMBER MACARONI FRIENDSHIP TIMES', which must have caused much scratching of heads in the Chinese Intelligence Service.[3]

Unfortunately the Italian end of the negotiations was in the hands of the Italian Minister to Beijing, Signor de Martino, 'a highly strung, excitable and superstitious man, much dependent upon omens and portents. He had previously represented Italy in Japan and Brazil, where he had refused one day to sign an important convention because, on the way to the Foreign Office, he had encountered a squint-eyed man'.[4] Circumstances too conspired to turn the portentous Italian demand into a *commedia dell'arte* plot. Try as they might, the ministers of the Tsungli Yamen could not identify the bay the Italians demanded. Compounding the problem, the Chinese had no real knowledge of who or what the *Itali-ren* were, 'they had the vague impression that it was a minor state whose troops had been defeated by some black barbarians in Africa'. Not wishing make any decision, and in the misguided belief that it would somehow save Signor de Martino's 'face', they simply sent the Italian demand back to him without comment.

De Martino exploded, but the Chinese were granted an extra day's grace in the crisis, as the 13th of the month fell during the height of the confrontation, a day when the superstitious Italian minister would conduct no business for fear of the 'evil eye' (he would not so much as mention this date, always referring to it as 'the day of the fox'). Unfortunately, this delay only seemed to further agitate Signor de Martino. On his own authority he ordered Italian gunboats into the Yellow Sea and sent a terse ultimatum to the Chinese authorities requiring their immediate compliance with his demands. Alarmed by this unexpected turn of events, Britain quickly withdrew its promised 'diplomatic support'. But China refused to be coerced – they ignored the Italian warships and simply pretended the ultimatum had not been sent. Signor de Martino's wild bluff had been called – it was 'put up or shut up' now for the Italians. After several days of tension it was the Westerners who blinked first; de Martino was recalled to Italy in disgrace, and the demand for Sanmen Bay (wherever it might actually have been) was quietly shelved.

This colonial comedy of errors was to have far-reaching consequences. The Chinese success in facing down Italy persuaded Yehonala and many of her court that their new strategy was working, that once Western military superiority was neutralised, there was no reason why the barbarians could not be held in check, and ultimately expelled from the sacred soil of China. Such a day of reckoning could not come soon enough and, with Yehonala's blessing, the authorities pushed ahead with their military reorganisation and rearmament.

It was simply unfortunate that at this psychologically vulnerable moment, while her hopes ran so high, the fates conspired to bring to her notice a martial group claiming skills and supernatural powers that could sweep the 'big noses' into the sea. Playing equally upon her superstitious nature and her xenophobia, they convinced Yehonala that the time of retribution was at hand, and persuaded her to lead the Middle Kingdom into a conflict which, ultimately, destroyed the ancient dynastic system that had governed China for more than two thousand years.

CHAPTER EIGHTEEN

The Righteous Harmonious Fists

The martial arts have a long and illustrious history in the Middle Kingdom. Sword, axe, staff, fighting iron, halberd, and a myriad other weapons all had their different styles of combat, and different masters, who took in students and instructed them in the intricacies of attack and defence. In this, China was no different from, say, medieval Europe, with its cudgel-play and fencing masters. But China differed from Europe in two respects. There was an equal emphasis on unarmed combat in China, derived according to legend from the Buddhist missionary and master Bodhidharma, founder of the fighting monks of the Shaolin Temple. Striving to survive in a violent land, but denied weapons by their philosophy, the monks under Bodhidharma devised a system of fighting which turned 'the feet into spears and the fist to a mace'. When Japan took over Okinawa in the 1870s and forbade the inhabitants weapons, Chinese instructors were hired by the Okinawans to instruct them in unarmed combat. This 'boxing with the feet and hands' was eventually carried to Japan as *Kara-te*, 'empty-hand', fighting, whence it has since spread worldwide.

The Japanese term 'empty-hand' carries a nuance which is often lost to Westerners, who see the character for empty referring only to the weaponless hand of the fighter. But 'empty' refers also to the spiritual nature of the master's fighting technique.[1] Ordinary men go to fight with their minds in a state of agitation, stirred by fear, hatred, and hope of victory. Such emotions cloud the brain and produce possibly fatal errors during battle. But by virtue of the strict physical and mental training he has undergone, the *meijin* undertakes combat in

perfect calm, his mind empty of all preconceptions, unconcerned equally with life or death. In this state, called *Mushin*
(no mind) in Japan, the mind perfectly reflects reality just as
a still, calm lake mirrors the moon sailing in the heavens.
Nothing intervenes between the attack and the response, and
victory is inevitable.

This philosophy is itself a reflection of the original Chinese
technique derived from Ch'an (Zen) Buddhism. Over time,
numerous schools of fighting evolved, many of them taking a
particular animal totem and attempting to emulate its power
or speed: the white crane, the drunken monkey, the eagle
claw, the praying mantis and many other animal styles all had
their aficionados. Despite the plethora of techniques, all these
methods could be divided into two major groupings: the so-
called external and internal styles.

External styles emphasised muscular strength and speed.
The students trained with weights, and they spent much time
striking straw-covered wooden figures to strengthen their
knuckles and the balls of their feet for punching and kicking.[2]
Some schools favoured nail-pulling, hammering nails into
boards and dragging them out with the fingers to produce a
vice-like grip. Bizarre practices were indulged in to make the
body invulnerable to blows. The 'stone-hanging technique'
involved pinching and kneading the testicles with increasing
severity over a period of weeks and months until these most
sensitive areas of the male anatomy became relatively inured
to the torturous rites. Once this had been achieved, a string
was tied around the scrotum and a small stone hung from it,
the size of the stone increasing on a regular basis until skilled
practitioners of the art were capable of carrying a twenty-four-
pound weight suspended solely from the scrotal sac. The practice apparently made one immune to any attack on the groin
(whether it had the spin-off of making one impotent or infertile
is not recorded).

The followers of internal styles laughed such practices to
scorn. External schools relied on muscle power and the student's prowess would surely fail as he grew older and his body
wasted. The internal student believed that the secret of true

mastery lay in the cultivation of the *Qi*, the life force that flowed along the meridians of the human body and which was manipulated in normal humans by such devices as the acupuncturist's needles. Internal practitioners claimed that by special techniques a master could manipulate his own *Qi*, increasing its power a hundredfold and directing it at will. *Qi* could be concentrated in a particular area of the body to make that region invulnerable to blows from swords and other weapons. It could be projected from the master so that a single, gentle blow proved fatal, sometimes long after the victim had been struck. The practice of *Qi Gong*, now so popular in the West, derives directly from the internal styles of the martial arts such as Ba Gua, Hsing I, or Tai Qi Quan.[3]

Such arts were frowned upon by the authorities, especially when, as frequently occurred, they were amalgamated with occult worship of obscure deities. The Qing law code stated clearly: '... leaders of heterodox sects who worship concealed images and incite the people shall be sentenced to death by slow strangulation'. Martial arts groups who escaped the 'heterodox sects' category were still prohibited: 'Those who are self-proclaimed teachers of martial arts, practitioners, or students of these arts are all liable to a punishment of one hundred strokes and banishment to a distance of three thousand *li* (one thousand miles).[4] Such legislation did little to suppress these groups: many practised their skills in secret, or were so powerful in a given region that the local authorities baulked at implementing the required punishments.

At the end of the nineteenth century, Shandong Province, lying just south of Beijing, was the headquarters of two very powerful groups of magico-religious fighting societies – the Spirit Boxers and the Golden Bell. The former practised incantations and spirit possession:

The Boxer chief offered incense and recited incantations, and afterwards all his men would fall swooning to the ground. Then, getting up stiffly, they claimed to be possessed of gods. Their faces were not as before. They would jump and leap, holding swords and spears in their hands

and using them in a theatrical manner. Meaningless
sounds would come from their mouths as though they
were drunk with wine ... They said they could thrust
swords into themselves until the tips broke, and yet not
be wounded ... they named themselves the Righteous
Harmony Fists or the Righteous Harmony Society ... .[5]

Similar societies had flourished for centuries, and had made
equally wild claims of invulnerability. While these groups often
had as their avowed intention the overthrow of the Qing
Dynasty and the restoration of the Ming, in the late 1800s, a
new, vulnerable, and far more accessible enemy had appeared
in their midst – the Christians.

For decades now, thanks to the concessions extorted from
the Chinese authorities at the point of a gun, missionaries of
the various Christian denominations had been carrying the
faith deeper and deeper into China, often vilifying each other
in an embarrassing, and distinctly unchristian scramble for
souls. They had made some headway amongst segments of
the population, and Chinese Christians, and their churches,
were now a not-uncommon sight in all but the most remote
areas of the Middle Kingdom. Some of these were simply 'rice
Christians', converts who took on the new faith because of
the extra food provided by the missionaries to their flock;
but many found solace in the foreign faith and were sincere
in their beliefs. Unfortunately, because of the powers and privileges granted by various Sino-European treaties, it was
very easy for the missionaries to shield criminal elements
who were also members of the church from normal Chinese
justice, steadily feeding the resentment of the local population. As late as 15th March 1899 an official decree granted
official status to all Roman Catholic priests: missionaries
were placed on an equal footing with magistrates, archdea-
cons and deans with *tao-tai* (local governors), and bishops
were ranked with viceroys, and given permission to visit and
write to them as equals. The Christians' privileged position
bred resentment in the rest of the population, and when
floods and drought visited many parts of the country during

1898 and 1899, discontent swiftly turned to hatred against the new religion.

The fault lay, in large part, with the intolerant nature of the missionaries themselves, and their refusal to partake, even a little, of things Chinese. Other foreign religions had always adapted themselves to some degree to the indigenous culture. Even today, the Great Mosque of Xian, built in China's ancient capital during the fourteenth century, is outwardly indistinguishable from the more usual Buddhist temples of the region,[6] as is the Jewish synagogue at Kaifeng.[7] While early Christians did do their best to adapt to local conditions (the Jesuit fathers even petitioning the Pope – unsuccessfully – to permit ancestor worship) the typical nineteenth-century missionary saw Christianity purely in terms of a superior European civilisation. It was not sufficient that places of worship were established for Christian converts, the buildings had to be perfect facsimiles of European churches, built in stone, with romanesque arches and tall spires pointing straight towards Heaven.

What the missionaries failed to understand, or chose to ignore, was that such buildings, in themselves, were deeply offensive to Chinese beliefs. Chinese geomancy, *feng shui*, saw all nature as interrelated, part of an intricate web of energies, whose disparate elements must be kept in balance if the earth was to function harmoniously.[8] Just as a human possessed *Qi*, life energy, channelled along meridians in the body, so too in the body of the earth were there tides of vital energy flowing through telluric lines of force, the earth meridians. Human activity, especially buildings in inappropriate locations, could distort the flow of these energies and cause disruption to the natural cycles upon which all life depended. For the Chinese, the Christian churches, built without concern for the *feng shui* of the area, with their tall spires and deep foundations, were the equivalent of acupuncture needles driven heedlessly into the body of a healthy human – in both cases they must distort the flow of energy and result in disease. With such a worldview, it was inevitable that from now on, the fault for any of the natural disasters that periodically assailed China would be laid at the door of the 'foreign devil'.

With the advent of the 'forward policy' among the Great Powers, and the threat that China might be partitioned, a new layer of suspicion and hatred was added. The missionaries were now seen as advance elements of the conquering powers, as spies intent on the subjugation of the Sons of Han, and the destruction of the Empire. Western technologies further alienated the populace: steamships prevented boatmen from plying trade and 'the labourers from the countryside ... had lost their livelihoods from carts, boats and shops because of the railroads'.[9]

In the face of such 'provocations', xenophobia became patriotism, and the Righteous Harmonious Fists (nicknamed 'Shadow Boxers' or simply 'Boxers' by the missionaries and other foreigners), became a government-tolerated focus for all discontent with their slogan 'Uphold the Qing and exterminate the foreigners'. Many posters appeared, explaining the Boxers' grievances and their solution:

> Attention: all people in markets and villages in all provinces of China – now, owing to the fact that the Catholics and Protestants have vilified our gods and sages, have deceived our emperors and ministers above, and oppressed the Chinese people below, both our gods and our people are angry at them ... This forces us to practise the I-ho magic boxing so as to protect our country, expel the foreign bandits and kill Christian converts in order to save our people from miserable suffering.

By the spring of 1900, hundreds, then thousands of disaffected Chinese had rallied to the Boxers' scarlet banners, donning red headbands and jackets and enthusiastically practising the 'shadow boxing' and incantations which they fervently believed would render them invulnerable to the weapons of the foreign devils. They roamed across Shandong Province, then crossed into Chihli and Shanxi, burning churches, destroying Christian property and slaying as many missionaries and converts as they could find. As their numbers grew, bands of Boxers began drifting northwards, towards Beijing. still proclaiming their intention of ridding China of all foreigners and their hated religion.

Immured behind the high walls of the Forbidden City, Yehonala was thrilled and delighted when reports of the Boxers, and their anti-foreign sentiments, reached her. In her heart she was at one with them in their desire to rid China of the barbarians, by violence if necessary. But the politician in her was wary: worried that their much-vaunted occult powers might not be sufficient for the task. 'She does not approve of the Big Sword Society's proposed extermination of the foreigners,' wrote one Manchu official, a kinsman of Yehonala, 'because she does not believe they can do it.'[10]

Apart from the incessant depredations upon her Empire, there were several pressing reasons why Yehonala wished to vent her spleen against the foreigners. The arch-reformer Kang Yu-wei had been saved from her Divine Wrath by the British and escorted to the safety of their colony in Hong Kong. Despite setting an unprecedented one hundred thousand-tael price on his head, she had seen him chaperoned to Japan where he was allowed to continue his seditious activities. And most recently, Yehonala had been particularly angered by the response of the foreign legations to her new attempt to remove the Emperor Kuang Hsu permanently from the scene.

After the coup of 1898, her nephew had been held in the Ocean Terrace, the picturesque, island-bound nest of red-lacquered pavilions, halls and marble walkways, set in the South Sea, which Yehonala had herself embellished. In her first flush of anger at Kuang Hsu's attempted 'coup' she had ordered new 'improvements': many of the windows looking out over splendid views were bricked up, others were left open to the elements. The Emperor, already suffering from a variety of ailments, was kept half-starved and isolated, his quarters unswept, vermin-ridden and insufficiently heated. Such treatment could have only one motive. When persistent rumours spoke of the Emperor's illness and imminent demise, Sir Claude McDonald conveyed to the Chinese Foreign Ministry, the Tsungli Yamen, his belief that the death of the Emperor would not incline the European Powers to friendship and might have a disastrous effect on the Empire. Yehonala was incensed by this meddling in China's 'internal affairs', but she understood a veiled threat as well as anyone, and miraculously, from that time on the Emperor began to recover his health. On 24th January 1900, Yehonala tried another tack: Pu'n Chun, the son of the reactionary Prince Tuan, 'a boy of fourteen, very intelligent but violent-tempered',[11] was made the Ta-a-ko, the Heir Apparent to the throne. This was immediately understood by everyone at court to mean that Yehonala was setting the scene for Kuang Hsu's departure from this world. But again, her murderous plans were thwarted by the Westerners. Contrary to all diplomatic convention, none of the foreign legations sent in their congratulations on this grand occasion. 'The refusal on the part of the diplomatic corps to acknowledge the event deterred the reactionary party from carrying out their plan, and this particularly infuriated Prince Tuan, who was impatient to see his son enthroned'.[12]

As the first of the Boxers began trickling into the capital, Yehonala called urgent meetings of the Grand Council to determine what the Dynasty's policy should be. Many of the Princes of the Blood were Boxer enthusiasts, and believed implicitly in their powers. In part this may be due to their lack of education (the school for princes had been closed since the 1860s and many of the younger generation of nobles had little learning). Others took a less sanguine view of the Patriotic Bands' chances against Western artillery and musketry. Jung Lu and his colleague Yuan Shi-kai were both privately opposed to encouraging the Righteous Harmonious Fists phenomenon, though they seem to have kept their counsel when in the presence of Yehonala's pro-Boxer enthusiasms.

Some members of the foreign community were also becoming increasingly anxious about the perilous direction events seemed to be taking. Dr George Ernest Morrison, *The Times* correspondent in Beijing, confided to his diary on 17th April that '… the danger of the Boxers is increasing. The danger is *scarcity of rain* which is attributed to the disturbance of the feng shui by foreigners.' But Morrison was not unduly concerned at this time, adding, 'If rains come, the Boxers will soon disappear'. However, nine days later he was reporting, 'Antiforeign literature is being sold in the streets. There has been some serious Boxer fighting near Paoting fu, with an alarming account of a "battle" written by a missionary, Ewing, there.' By mid-May, and with the rains still awaited, Morrison was informed by his Chinese servant that eight million men were about to descend from heaven to destroy the barbarians. Two days later, on 18th May, rain did fall, but contrary to expectations, the Boxer depredations continued and moved ever-closer to the capital. 'French priests report 61 men women and children suffered death at Kaolo, midway between Paoting fu and Peking. Also trouble at Anshsien, from which people are fleeing by train into Peking. Some burned alive. The whole village of Kaolo is destroyed.' The rain or lack of it was irrelevant now – anti-foreign feeling had reached critical mass, it possessed a momentum of its own and appeared unstoppable without government intervention. But of this there was no real sign.

By 19th May, Bishop Favier, the Vicar-Apostolic of Beijing, wrote to the French Minister, M. Pichon, requesting a force of forty or fifty sailors to protect the Peitang, the Roman Catholic cathedral that lay about two miles to the north-west of the legations. The Boxers' known intention, declared Bishop Favier, was the destruction of all the Beijing churches: 'for us, in our cathedral, the date of the attack has actually been fixed', after which the Boxers were to lead an onslaught on the legations. M. Pichon was not impressed, telling Morrison that he considered Bishop Favier an alarmist. The British Minister, Sir Claude McDonald, shared Pichon's view, writing rather complacently to the Foreign Office, 'I confess that little has come to my knowledge to confirm the gloomy anticipations of the French Father'. Morrison was inclined to agree. 'We cannot feel this peril in the air,' he confided to his diary on the 21st, but added ominously that 'all knives and swords have doubled in value. Shops are working day and night to supply the demand.'[13]

Safe behind the high walls of the legations, and all but isolated from real events in China, the foreign community continued their round of parties and socialising, the British celebrating Queen Victoria's birthday on 24th May, and six days later enjoying an evening of dance and music courtesy of 'I-G's Own', Sir Robert Hart's Chinese orchestra. But the gaiety was becoming strained; the diplomats had already obtained permission for the deployment of foreign troops to guard the legations, and the military detachment duly arrived on the 3rd June, an American contingent of fifty-six marines being the first to march proudly up Legation Street to their embassy. The desire for troops was natural enough given the circumstances, but it served only to fuel Chinese resentment, especially when the number arriving, three hundred and eighty-nine men and sixteen officers from six different nationalities, turned out to be twice as many as had been agreed by the Tsungli Yamen. Sir Claude had by now changed his mind about Bishop Favier, commenting at the beginning of June that he was 'very much alarmed'. The Chinese officials did not seem to share his concern. When, on 4th June, Henry Cockburn attended a crisis meeting at the Tsungli Yamen, one of the mandarins nodded off while the Englishman was making an important point. Cockburn swept out in high dudgeon: 'There you have China ... What are you to make of such a people? The Empress Dowager is giving a theatrical performance while the country is in serious stress and strife.'

Tension in the capital increased day by day until 9th June 1900 when a rumour swept the city that the Imperial Government had decided to murder all foreigners in Beijing. Fearing the worst, Sir Claude McDonald telegraphed the head of the British Naval Force, Admiral Sir Edward Seymour, requesting additional troops to guard the legations; he later rescinded his request after speaking to the heads of other legations, only to change his mind once more and beg for reinforcements on hearing further horrendous news: not confirmation that a massacre of foreigners was planned, but that a mob had invaded the Westerners' Beijing racecourse – and had actually burned down the grandstand! With unconscious irony Sir Claude asserted that, more than any other incident, this act of desecration had brought home 'more vividly ... to the minds of all Europeans in Peking, a sense of the perilous position in which they stood'.

The British Consul in Tientsin called a meeting of all foreign ministers that same evening. The next day, at 9 a.m., an international force of over fifteen hundred men was en route for Beijing, carried in five separate trains. With hindsight, this 'Seymour expedition' was probably a mistake and it may have precipitated the very crisis it was intended to prevent. News of the 'invasion' by foreign troops spread rapidly and it galvanised the Chinese population all along the Tientsin–Beijing rail-track. Within hours of the relief force leaving Tientsin the telegraph line to the capital was cut. And support for the Boxers blossomed. On 10th June the British Summer Legation on the Western Hill was put to the torch. The diplomatic staff watched the mounting violence with increasing alarm, looking to the approaching Seymour relief column to save the day, and very possibly their lives. So impatient were they that, on the 11th, several diplomats ventured out to Ma Chia Pu station to await the expected arrival of the relief column. But the hours slipped by, morning turned to afternoon, and the promised trains never arrived. One by one the diplomats returned to their respective legations until only Mr Sugiyama, the Japanese Chancellor, remained. Eventually, with night drawing on, even he gave up, riding back the way he had come in a small Chinese cart. As he passed the main gate of the southern city, the Muslim braves of Tung Fu-hsiang (who earlier that day had allowed him to pass out of the city unmolested) suddenly surrounded the cart, their faces sullen and full of menace. Within moments Sugiyama had been dragged from his seat and flung to the ground. Using their rifle butts, Tung's men beat out his brains and left his body sprawled in the dusty road. According to some reports, his heart was cut from his chest and presented to general Tung as a souvenir. Sugiyama was the first of the foreign officials to die.

The sad fact was that Sugiyama's journey had been in vain from the beginning – the troop trains were nowhere near Beijing. While the Japanese minister lay dying, the foreign soldiers of the relief column were themselves fighting for their own lives, beating off an attack by the Boxers at Lang-fang, just half-way to Beijing, that left at least fifty of the Chinese combatants dead. A railway advance is always vulnerable. The Chinese destroyed the tracks and simply pulled up more as each damaged section was repaired. The Seymour expedition, surrounded by increasing numbers of Boxers and facing a hostile populace, could think only of its own survival.

The Beijing legations were left isolated and, for the moment, abandoned to an uncertain fate.

CHAPTER NINETEEN

Siege at Beijing

The news that the foreigners were attempting to send an 'army' to the heart of the Middle Kingdom only served to fan the flames of Yehonala's ever-present xenophobia. On 11th and 12th June, officials from the Tsungli Yamen had called on Sir Claude McDonald in an attempt to dissuade him from his request for military assistance, but the British Minister was adamant, the troops must come. The following day a decree was issued with the Empress Dowager's blessing which, in its bellicose intransigence mirrored the edict promulgated the year before against the Italian attempt to seize a Chinese concession. Yuan Shih-kai was ordered to send his troops to Beijing for the capital's defence. And that same day a large force of Boxers was allowed to enter within the walls of the capital. Yehonala and the court were preparing for war.

The Boxers, of course, were already at war with the foreigner. Almost as soon as they entered the capital, the burning of churches and murdering of Chinese converts (the 'secondary hairy ones') began in the west of the city. Morrison of *The Times* described 'Awful cries ... all through the night. The roar of the murdered. Rapine and massacre'. As Bishop Favier had reported, the extermination of the 'primary foreign devils' was planned for later. The next day, the 14th, the army of the 'Righteous Harmonious Fists' penetrated into the Tartar or Manchu City, where the legations were located. They entered by the Hata Men Gate, and immediately burned the church that stood nearby, searching out Christian converts and putting all they found to the sword or throwing them alive into the flames.

One group of Westerners found a Chinese woman, bound hand and foot, who had been soaked in petrol and set aflame to act as a human torch on a darkened pathway. For *The Times* correspondent, it was more than he could stand:

> At two in the afternoon Dr Morrison, who has a nobler heart than many of the selfish refugees, on hearing that many of the Christian converts were still at the mercy of the Boxers near Nan-tang Church, applied to Sir Claude McDonald for guards to rescue them. Twenty British were given him, and were joined by a force of Germans and Americans. Morrison guided them to the spot, and it will ever be a bright spot in the record of the Doctor's life that he was the means of saving from atrocious tortures and death over a hundred helpless Chinese.[1]

The Chinese survivors were housed in 'The Fu', a high-walled palace of Prince Su, a Manchu noble, which lay just to the east of the British legation, with a street and small canal between. As the day wore on, more and more converts found their way to the comparative safety of The Fu 'laden with their pots and pans, their beds and their bundles of rice'. Eventually there were over two thousand Chinese sheltering in the legation's compounds. For these desperate souls, the future looked bleak indeed; their only hope of succour lay with the legations; but the foreigners might yet negotiate safe passage out of the capital, and then, unless the Empress Dowager changed her mind and decided to suppress the Boxers, the converts could look for no quarter from the Righteous Harmonious Fists.

At that exact moment, Yehonala was still undecided in her policy towards the Boxers. On 16th June she called a full Imperial Council – all the Manchu nobles and the high officials of the boards and ministries were in attendance – to discuss the issue. An initial suggestion that the Boxers be chased from the capital was swamped by pro-Boxer protests, led by Prince Tuan, the head of the reactionary party. The Emperor, Kuang Hsu, whose opinion was not actively sought by anyone, was for conciliating the Powers, but his brief statements were ignored by everyone. When Yuan Ch'ang, of the Tsungli Yamen, the Chinese Foreign Ministry, declared that the Boxers were not patriots but rebels and that they still died from foreign bullets despite their magic formulas, Yehonala interrupted from her dominant position on the dais. 'If we cannot rely on the supernatural formulas, can we not rely upon the heart of the people? China is weak: the only thing we can depend upon is the heart of the people. If we lose that, how can we maintain our country?' Yehonala's preference was clear, and as ever, she carried the day. In the end it was decided that two officials should be sent towards Tientsin to dissuade the foreign powers from attempting to advance on Beijing. That same day an edict commanded that 'young and strong Boxers' should be recruited into the army. It seems that Yehonala had taken on board some of the moderates' views and that she was attempting to assimilate the potentially dangerous Boxer mob by drawing off the best of their number into the armed forces, where they could be subject to military discipline.

It was, on the face of it, a reasonable strategy. But by the next day everything had changed. Unexpectedly, a second Imperial Council was summoned, where Yehonala, black-faced and tight-lipped, announced that she had now received a four-point demand from the foreign governments. The Powers now required that the Emperor be given a special place of residence; that all revenues should be gathered by the foreign ministers; and that all military affairs be overseen by foreign representatives. Yehonala omitted the fourth and last demand. There was deathly quiet in the council chamber. These demands amounted to the destruction of the regime, at very least its total subservience to the Powers. At last Yehonala broke the silence, and all the old vehemence, the courage and fighting spirit were at once evident: 'Now they have started the aggression,' she declared, 'and the extinction of our nation is imminent. If we just fold our arms and yield to them, I would have no face to see our ancestors after death. If we must perish, why not fight to the death?'[2]

What had added oxygen to Yehonala's already incandescent xenophobia was the fourth demand, which she had kept secret from the Imperial Council. This had required her to step down as head of government and 'to restore the rule to the Emperor'. The first three demands had been hateful enough, but to give up her power? She would rather die, and see the Middle Kingdom a barren wasteland, than acquiesce to the barbarian. Nothing better could have been devised to increase the Empress Dowager's belligerence and will to fight than this. And with good reason, for the document was more than just a case of barbarian insensitivity and bad timing. The 'Four Demands' had been carefully drawn up, specifically designed to infuriate the Empress Dowager. The document was a fraud, a forgery concocted by Prince Tuan with the express purpose of enraging Yehonala and spurring her towards war with the foreigners.

It worked. Orders were issued to the provinces, commanding that troops be dispatched for the defence of Beijing. Three ministers were sent to the foreign legations to inform them that, should they wish to begin hostilities, they must leave Beijing. The ministers met with Sir Claude the following day and, as he mentioned nothing of the four demands during a long conversation, the Chinese officials became convinced the document Yehonala had brandished so angrily the day before was false. But the damage had already been done, and Sir Claude's steadfast refusal to rescind the request for more troops, while understandable from the Westerners' perspective, simply played into the hands of the reactionaries at court. At the same time, the allies at Tientsin and on the coast were forced by circumstances into actions which could only strengthen the case of the war-party.

Two days before, on 16th June, and long after the ill-fated Mr Sugiyama and the rest of the *corps diplomatique* had vainly awaited their rescuers at Ma Chia Pu station, the Seymour relief column remained stuck half-way between Beijing and Tientsin, under heavy attack, taking many wounded and with ammunition running dangerously low. Realising the imminent danger that his force might be encircled and cut off, Seymour first decided to fall back on Tientsin, but after receiving reports that a strong force of Chinese and Boxers might lie between him and safety, he made instead for the Taku forts. In a brief ultimatum to the Chinese commander, he stated his intention of occupying the bastions 'provisionally, by consent or by force' before 2 a.m. on the following morning. The Chinese refused and commenced firing on the allied force, but they were outgunned by the rapid advance of two Western warships and capitulated the same day.

The Viceroy of Chihli, Yu-lu, described the allied ultimatum in a memorial which was received at Beijing on the 19th June. Fearful of reporting bad news, he described the fighting but omitted the fact that the Taku forts had actually fallen. For Yehonala and the Imperial court, the news merely confirmed the allies' intention to attack, and an official made the journey once more to the foreign legations to inform them of a break in diplomatic relations and to allow them 24 hours in which to vacate the capital, after which time their safety could not be guaranteed. Knowing nothing of the failure of the Seymour expedition, or of the hostilities at the Taku forts, the diplomats assembled to discuss the Chinese ultimatum and to decide if a retreat to Tientsin was necessary, or safe. The German Minister, Baron von Ketteler, a short-tempered aristocrat of the old school, was adamant that the Chinese could not be trusted and that the legation staff would be murdered en route to Tientsin. Many were inclined to agree, until both M. Pichon and the American Minister, Major Conger, spoke in favour of a withdrawal from the capital. George Morrison, *The Times* correspondent, was appalled that Minister Pichon, the 'Protecteur des Missions Catholiques en Chine' should recommend leaving Beijing when this retreat would inevitably result in 'the immediate abandonment to massacre of thousands of native Christians who had trusted the foreigner and believed in his good faith'. Nevertheless, self-interest prevailed and almost all of the foreigners voted to put their trust in the Chinese safe conduct, to fly with their own skins intact and to leave the Chinese converts to their fate. A message, signed by the Spanish Consul, Señor Cologan, was sent to the Tsungli Yamen just before midnight, asking for a meeting to discuss transport, security and provisioning of the foreign convoy to Tientsin. Morrison protested to the Spanish Minister that the Chinese would be 'massacred to a man', only to be told by Cologan, 'That does not regard us.' *The Times* man was disgusted by the craven attitude of his fellow Europeans; throughout the crisis this Australian journalist stands head and shoulders above most of the ineffectual diplomatic staff whose actions at this critical time would reflect, for better or worse, upon their individual countries. Morrison again took the floor. 'He looked the ministers square in the eyes and said: "if you men vote to leave Peking tomorrow, the deaths of every man, woman and child in this huge unprotected convoy will be on your heads, and your names will go down to history, and be known for ever as the wickedest, weakest and most pusillanimous cowards who have ever lived."' His plea fell on deaf ears. If the Chinese replied with an acceptable itinerary, the legation staff were set upon a rapid retreat from Beijing.

Everyone rose early the next day, and the hours ticked by slowly as they awaited the response from the Chinese to their midnight letter. Nine o'clock came without word from the Tsungli Yamen. At nine-thirty there was still no news. The hot-tempered von Ketteler was for visiting the Yamen to extract an answer from the mandarins, but most decided it was wiser to go on waiting, agreeing with Sir Claude McDonald that 'it would be undignified to go to the Yamen and sit there waiting for the Princes'. Von Ketteler disagreed, hitting the table with his fist and declaring that he would go alone and sit there all night if he had to. He stalked out with his secretary, Herr Cordes, and soon they were being carried in their scarlet and green sedan chairs out of the legation in the direction of the Chinese ministry, leaving the rest of the ministers to kick their heels and damn the Chinese for their tardiness.

Just twenty minutes later one of von Ketteler's Chinese grooms crashed through the door yelling, 'Any man speakee have makee kill German Minister'. He was disbelieved, but the story proved to be horribly true.[3] A Chinese bannerman in full uniform had approached von Ketteler's sedan chair and shot the minister repeatedly at short range. His secretary, Herr Cordes, had somehow managed to escape, despite being shot in both legs as he fled. Concern was also being expressed for Professor Hubert James, a kindly old man, the epitome of the absent-minded academic, who had gone out beyond the legation buildings to help Chinese converts, and had simply disappeared. It was to be a further three days before his horrific fate was finally known to the foreign community. By now, even the most optimistic among the foreigners admitted that the Chinese would certainly have massacred them all had they left for Tientsin. More than two months later, when the crisis had abated, this was confirmed by an unimpeachable source. Morrison recorded that the president of Civil Appointments, Hsy Fu, confided to one of the Europeans that 'there was a plot to murder all the ministers that morning, and the murder of one minister only was a premature accident, deplorable from the Chinese point of view, for it prevented a general massacre'. That the killing of von Ketteler had been ordered from on high was confirmed by the murderer himself. Just before he was beheaded for the crime, the Manchu bannerman responsible bemoaned the fact that he had been promised a promotion and a reward of seventy taels for killing the barbarian, but had received just forty pieces of silver.

The diplomats' last escape route had been closed. Come what may (and they can only have looked on the future with trepidation), they were now confined to the capital, trapped within the legation perimeter while outside, chanting and brandishing their swords, halberds and rifles, the mass of Boxers swirled through the streets of Beijing, crying vengeance (see Map 2). At the exact hour the Chinese ultimatum to leave Beijing expired, at 4 p.m. on 20th June, the first fusillade of shots crashed into the legation buildings, wounding an Austrian soldier and killing a French marine. The siege had begun.

In the Forbidden City the mood was grim but resolute. No one really knew where the road Yehonala had chosen would lead. But the atmosphere lightened the next day when a memorial from Yu Lu, the Chihli Viceroy, arrived detailing a series of victories against the Powers: two foreign warships had been damaged by fire from the Taku forts; the allied troops had been repulsed in Tientsin; and the Boxers were cooperating well with the Imperial Chinese regular troops in withstanding the allied attacks. Once again, mention that the Taku forts had fallen was conspicuous by its absence from the memorandum, and the viceroy forebore to inform the court of any of the other reverses he had suffered. Buoyed up with this good news, elated by the 'victories' and filled once more with the ancient hauteur of her caste, on 21st June Yehonala issued an Imperial edict declaring war on an astonishing nine of the most powerful countries on the globe: Great Britain, France, the United States of America, Germany, Japan, Italy, Austria-Hungary, Belgium and Holland. The next day the Boxers were formally organised as adjuncts to the government troops. Prince Chuang and Kang I were given overall command of the Boxers, and vast quantities of rice were released from government stores and distributed to the hungry auxiliaries. Two days later, one hundred thousand taels were dispensed among the Boxers and other military personnel in the capital.

The game plan that Yehonala and the reactionaries had devised seems to have been coloured from the start by a primitive urge for revenge. Militarily, the diplomats in Beijing posed no threat at all to China. So small a number of ill-armed foreigners could easily have been cooped up indefinitely within the legations by a small detachment of Chinese troops. They were certainly in no position to mount an incursion or in any way materially affect the outcome of the war that Yehonala had declared on the Powers. The real danger, the true threat to Yehonala and her reactionary allies, lay at Tientsin, in the form of modern, highly-drilled and battle-hardened allied troops, who were already preparing for a second assault on Beijing. If they could have been dislodged from Chinese soil before they were ready to begin their advance on the capital, the Chinese would have been in a much stronger position to face any further threat. Yet for some reason, Chinese troops who could have helped mount such an attack were held back in Beijing, for the express purpose of exterminating the strategically irrelevant legations. Though (purposely) vaguely worded, an Imperial decree issued on 23rd June makes the Chinese policy plain:

> The work now undertaken by Tung Fu-hsiang should be completed as soon as possible, so that troops can be spared and sent to Tientsin for defence.[4]

The motive behind this 'legation first, Tientsin after' strategy can only have been Yehonala's revenge, a desire to vent the pent-up anger and frustration and humiliation that had festered in her breast since Lord Elgin and Baron Gros had marched on Beijing, burnt the Summer Palace and forced the Hsien Feng Emperor and herself on their ignoble flight to Jehol forty years before.

Not everyone was overjoyed with the high-risk strategy China was following. The southern viceroys and governors, perhaps because they were further from the scene of the crisis, came to a much more realistic appraisal of their country's chances in a fight against all the major world powers. They at first requested Li Hung-chang to memorialise against hostilities and the Boxers, but, canny politician that he was, Li declined to put his head so obviously above the parapet. He did, however, agree with the other officials that China south of the Yangtse should try, if possible, to dissociate itself from events in the north. Fortunately, an edict issued on 20th June commanded that the viceroys 'should be united together to protect their territories',[5] a phrase which the southerners decided to interpret, not as a call to arms against foreign aggression, but as requiring them to use their own initiative to protect their areas. Such protection, they decided, was best achieved by guarding the foreigners from harm and by crushing the Boxers. They also agreed, quite illegally, to suppress the Imperial edicts declaring war on the Powers, and commanding the organisation of the Boxers into quasi-official militias. The foreign consuls in Shanghai were approached, and it was agreed with them that the foreign concession there should be protected by foreign troops, while the Yangtse valley would be controlled by the respective viceroys in the area. These actions did much to prevent the conflagration spreading and also, by the obvious differences in policy between north and south, later allowed the Throne to claim that the Boxer insurgency and the ensuing atrocities were the result of a 'rebellion' beyond the control of the Imperial power.

The foreigners and the Chinese converts were now firmly shut up in the legation quarter; at the beginning of the siege they numbered 473 allied civilians, 409 military, 400 Chinese servants and around 2,750 Chinese Christians. A second far more exposed group, consisting of Bishop Favier, twenty-two nuns and around three and a half thousand Chinese Christians, including eight hundred children, were surrounded by Yehonala's troops at Peitang Cathedral. They were defended by a small crew of sailors, just forty-three men, that the prescient clergyman had requested before the storm broke. Ranged against them were thousands of Boxer recruits, ill-equipped and indisciplined red-sashed troops, together with general Tung Fu-hsiang's white-turbaned, veteran Muslim warriors, and men of Jung Lu's Headquarters Army, Western-drilled and equipped with modern foreign rifles, most of whom had been deployed around the legations. 'There were jackets and tunics of every colour; trouserings of blood red with black dragons; great two-handed swords in some hands, men armed with bows and arrows mixing with Tung Fu-hsiang's Kansu horsemen, who had the most modern carbines slung across their backs. There were blue banners, yellow banners embroidered with black, white flags and red ... Men from all the Peking banners seemed to be there, with their plain and bordered jackets showing their divisions.'[6]

The allied defensive position was extremely poor. As soon as firing started the Austro-Hungarian legation had been relinquished by its garrison, which had in turn put those defending the customs building at risk and so it too was given up to the enemy. George Morrison regarded the Austro-Hungarian withdrawal as a very poor show indeed: 'No sufficient reason has been given for its abandonment,' he wrote later. At first, the foreigners attempted to hold on to every square yard of the legation quarter, but it soon became clear that the perimeter was too large for their limited firepower (four pieces of light artillery, together with rifles and carbines and less than three hundred rounds per man), so they were forced to yield both the French and the Italian legations to their Chinese attackers. On the 23rd June their most prized vantage point, a bastion on the high walls of the Tartar City was carried by a Chinese assault and, amid a sandstorm that blew loess from the Ordos desert into every house in Beijing, they were forced to fall back upon the last strong defensive position they had – the three-acre compound of the British legation.

That day's storm persuaded the Chinese to commit an act of sacrilege against their own nation that has rightly gone down in history as a crime against all humanity. Adjoining the British legation to the north, and separated in places by just a few feet, was a building which, if fired (and given the prevailing wind), would almost certainly carry the blaze into the foreigners' final defensive position. The building was the famed centre of academic brilliance, the Hanlin Yuan, the Forest of Ten Thousand Pencils, the omphalos of all Chinese learning.[7] That it housed the oldest library in the world, containing priceless, unique manuscripts dating back over a thousand years, seemed to bother the Chinese not at all. Firebrands were thrown into the broken windows and through the open doors, and the Forest of Ten Thousand Pencils went up like matchwood. But no sooner had the flames taken hold than the north-west wind suddenly dropped, leaving the fire centred in the library, while the efforts of a bucket-chain of volunteers at the legation prevented the conflagration spreading to the British building. The destruction of this matchless store of knowledge (an act of vandalism comparable with the loss of the library of Alexandria in AD 391 or the burning of the two hundred thousand volumes in the library of Pergamum) achieved nothing and served only to forever diminish Chinese cultural heritage.

Paradoxically, it was the foreigners who made an effort to rescue the surviving treasures of the Hanlin Academy. Even before the flames from the library had died away, Sir Claude had sent a note to the Tsungli Yamen informing them that certain manuscripts had been saved and requesting that Chinese officials supervise the salvage. There was no reply. 'Other great libraries ... had been destroyed by the victorious invader, but what can we think of a nation that sacrifices its most sacred edifice, the pride and glory of its country and learned men for hundreds of years, in order to be revenged upon foreigners?'[8]

The Chinese renewed their efforts to storm the legation, and both rifle and artillery fire were more or less continuous over the first few days. There were some lucky escapes: as Mrs Bredon and her daughter lay asleep, a four-pounder cannonball crashed through the window of the bedroom and dropped harmlessly between them; a shot meant for one of the defenders missed and instead smashed off the neck of a liquor bottle he was holding; a musket-ball grazed Captain Strout's neck; an army sergeant had his razor shot from his hand as he made ready to shave. But not every bullet was so obliging, and every day brought reports of men wounded, or dead. As the weeks wore on the defenders drew more closely together as casualties steadily reduced their ranks. But national rivalries continued to rankle. When the siege finally ended, Morrison recorded the following summation of national characteristics: 'I sent my servant on a message. He was robbed by a Russian, buggered by a Frenchman, killed by a German. In my dismay, I made complaint to a British officer. He looked at me, put his eye-glass into his eye, and said, "Was he really? What a bore!"'

The sarcasm, the bravado, the black humour, all acted as a defence against the intolerable strain of living under the constant threat of death. Early in the siege, news had come in of the fate of kindly Professor James. He had been captured by Tung Fu-hsiang's Muslim braves on the day of von Ketteler's murder, and taken to Prince Chuang's palace, his captors goading him forward with their bayonets. The Prince had held him in chains for three days, and according to some had tortured the old man, before ordering his decapitation. The severed head was displayed to the populace, one Chinese diarist recording:

> his head is now exhibited in a cage, hanging from the main beam of the Tung An Gate. It had to be put in a cage, as there was no queue to hang it by. The face has a most horrible expression, but it is a fine thing, all the same, to see a foreigner's head hung up at our palace gates.[9]

That a similar fate might befall each foreigner within the legations must have been a source of constant anxiety to everyone caught up in the siege. On 22nd June, Yehonala directed Professor James's murderer, Prince Chuang, to issue a proclamation offering fifty taels for the head of every male barbarian, forty taels for a foreign woman, and incredibly, thirty taels for the head of a child. In that lay the strength of her hatred against the foreign devils, or perhaps her fear that they might depose her. She wanted them dead. All of them.

By 16th July it appeared Yehonala had obtained her desire. The *Daily Mail* reported 'The Peking Massacre' of 7th July in heroic and distressing detail. After suffering a sustained artillery barrage, the story detailed how the Chinese had attacked in human waves, and how, '... standing together as the sun rose fully, the little remaining band, all Europeans, met death stubbornly ... and finally, overcome by overwhelming odds, every one of the Europeans remaining was put to the sword in the most atrocious manner'. The tale was repeated in the House of Commons, a memorial service was organised for 28th July at St Paul's Cathedral, and *The Times* joined in the universal grief writing, 'The time has now come when hope must be abandoned. It would be foolish and unmanly to affect to doubt the awful truth.' Pages of obituaries were printed, including that of Sir Claude McDonald, Sir Robert Hart, and *The Times'* own 'devoted correspondent', George Morrison. Rising to the occasion with true journalistic passion, the 'Thunderer' described how 'The Europeans fought with calm courage to the end against overwhelming hordes of fanatical barbarians thirsting for their blood ... When the last cartridge was gone their hour had come. They met it like men ...' and so on in similar vein, making the account curiously reminiscent of the accepted version of Custer's Last Stand.

And just as accurate. The whole story was bunkum from first to last, thought up by an anonymous 'special correspondent' and datelined Shanghai. On such stories were the myths of Empire maintained. To be fair, there was nothing intrinsically impossible about the tale. If the Chinese had succeeded in breaking through the defence perimeter there is no doubt that a general massacre would have taken place, and it is more than likely that the defenders would have fought to the last round and beyond, and even, as some of the later stories claimed, would have shot their women and children rather than leave them to the mercies of the Boxers. But the plain fact was that, on 16th July, the legation perimeter was holding, just, though the defenders were under severe pressure from their Chinese attackers. However, for at least one European, the day of the 'massacre' did bring death. At about seven o'clock in the morning of the 16th, George Morrison, Captain Strouts of the Royal Marines Light Infantry and the Japanese Colonel Shiba were making a round of inspection, which entailed their crossing an area of The Fu notorious for its exposure to fire. As they doubled across, Strouts was hit in the thigh, severing the femoral artery. Morrison was also hit in the leg and Colonel Shiba took a bullet through his coat which fortunately left him untouched. They carried Strouts to the hospital but he died of shock and blood loss soon after. Morrison was laid up by his wound and remained bedridden for almost a month.

Strouts was buried that same afternoon, alongside Harry Warren, a student who had been shot the day before while on watch. To the remaining defenders the deaths and wounding were a cruel loss; Strouts and Morrison especially had been towers of strength throughout the siege, and their absence was keenly felt. The general belief was that things could only get worse. However, the defenders were about to receive an unlooked-for respite from their troubles.

Unknown to them, Tientsin had fallen to the allies on 13th July, the defeat made worse by the death of one of China's best commanders, General Nieh, just before the battle. Within a few days of this disaster, Yehonala had received a memorial from thirteen viceroys and governors of most of the southern provinces, citing four requests: protection of foreign merchants and missionaries; an Imperial letter of regret for Baron von Ketteler's death to be sent to Germany; a list detailing Boxer-inspired destruction of foreign property, so that proper compensation could be made by the Imperial Government; and an express decree that any disturbances by 'bandits' or troops in Chihli Province should be suppressed by force. A further spur to such requests came in the form of warnings from the allied governments that Yehonala and her Grand Council would be held to account for any harm that might befall the staff of the legations. Jung Lu had already concluded that a massacre at the legations would bring down such retribution from the Powers that the Dynasty must fall. Quietly he worked to prevent the success of the siege. The defenders noticed that far fewer assaults were made by the sectors held by Jung Lu's troops, and that it was from this part of the perimeter that messengers appeared and extra rations could sometimes be purchased. Jung Lu also controlled the only battery of heavy artillery in Beijing, guns which, had they been used against the legations, would have reduced the defences to rubble within hours. When the Muslim general Tung Fu-hsiang demanded access to these weapons, Jung Lu, risking the displeasure of his mistress, refused point-blank.

But Yehonala too, had begun to read the writing on the wall. It was evidently time to 'adjust policy' and in typical fashion, she was not slow to do what had to be done. By 17th July an edict had been issued complying with all four 'requests' of the southern mandarins. Li Hung-chang, the old warhorse who, Yehonala knew, had the respect of the foreigners, was deputed to inform the allied governments that their people in the legations were safe and would be protected.

Even before this, Yehonala had been playing a double game. On 3rd July, while the battle around the legations raged, she had sent a decree to her ministers abroad, commanding them to tell the foreign governments that the Imperial Government would 'strictly order the commanders to protect the legations to the best of their ability and to punish the rebels so far as circumstances permit'. From an autocratic Empress with enormous military might at her command, this was pure sophistry; and it implied that, if their best was not good enough, or circumstances did not permit, then the foreigners might perish. Appeals were also made by the August Mother to the Czar, Queen Victoria and the Emperor of Japan, requesting their help in settling the crisis peacefully. Yet on the same day that all these missives were sent, an edict was posted to the Chinese governors and commanders stating that 'there is absolutely no possibility that we will immediately negotiate for peace ... The generals, viceroys, and governors must sweep the word "peace" from their hearts; they will then feel emboldened and strong.'[10]

It may be that such diplomatic posturing reveals that Yehonala was carefully balancing her relations with the war and peace factions within her government. But there is no doubt that she herself wanted to see the legations taken, and that she was furious that the foreigners not been crushed. Nevertheless, she felt it expedient to hold off from attempting the complete annihilation of the Beijing diplomats. Worrying news was received that the Chinese army had tried to hold the line at Peichang, but had been dislodged and had retreated to Yangts'un. Perhaps the foreigners might win after all. And if so, the death of their people in Beijing would certainly result in reprisals that could mean the destruction of the Dynasty. And the end of her power. On 17th July, Yehonala declared a truce and, for a time, all firing ceased on the Chinese side of the legation perimeter.

Three days before this armistice, the legations had received a letter, purportedly from 'Prince Ch'ing and others', requesting in courteous terms that the foreign community leave the legations and go in groups to the Tsungli Yamen, 'pending future arrangements' for their return home. Unsure of the true authors of the note, the ministers answered cautiously, declining the Chinese offer and stating that the foreign community was acting only in self-defence. While these negotiations continued, the truce began and relations between the combatants became positively surreal. Chinese soldiers, who hours before had been intent on extermination, now approached the legation barricades to chat warmly with the defenders. The legation garrison bought eggs and staples from their Chinese opponents, and the Japanese even managed to purchase a number of rifles from their attackers. One of I-G's Own, a trumpeter in Robert Hart's orchestra, who had since been fighting on the Chinese side, asked for treatment for a damaged ear. Blindfolded, he was taken into the legation hospital, cared for, and released, fit and ready to fight the foreigner again. Just a few days before this chivalrous cameo took place, eighteen captured Chinese had been put to death in cold blood in the French legation, bayoneted one at a time 'by a French corporal to save cartridges'.[11]

Expressions of amity continued to increase on the Chinese side. On 20th July, with Yehonala's blessing, the Tsungli Yamen sent four cartloads of vegetables and watermelons across no-man's-land as a gesture of good faith. The carts were warmly welcomed and the food appreciated, but all requests by the Tsungli Yamen to vacate the legations, and to trust in Chinese goodwill were laughed to scorn. There is much evidence that the Chinese offer was genuine − given the military reverses on the coast even Yehonala and many reactionaries were desperate for a way out of the impending catastrophe, and yielding up the besieged could well have paved the way to a cessation of hostilities. But after such prolonged suffering, and so many deaths, the defenders were in no mood to abandon the one place in all Beijing that offered them some small shred of protection, transitory though it might be. And so the chance of a peaceful solution slipped away.

By late July the pendulum had swung back to war with the appearance in Beijing of a renowned military hero. Li Ping-heng had made a name for himself in the Sino-French War of 1885, and more recently as Yehonala's 'Lord High Extortioner' in Manchuria (see p. 204). Li was vehemently anti-foreign, opposed to railways, paper currency, post offices, mining and modern schools.[12] But his patriotism, efficiency and integrity were undoubted. When he had offered his services as an army commander at the end of June he was immediately ordered to the capital. So necessary was his presence deemed that two decrees commanded him to speed his journey to Beijing, to travel day and night so as to arrive at the earliest possible moment. Li entered the city on 26th July and, after conferring with the two arch-conservatives, Kang I and Hsu T'ung, he was granted an audience with the Empress. Li stiffened Yehonala's wavering resolve, telling her that 'only when one can fight can one negotiate for peace'. Such warlike words were music to her ears and as a mark of her favour, Yehonala granted Li the right to ride within the Forbidden City and to be carried by sedan chair at the Winter Palace. More importantly, she gave Li command of four of the army groups at present ranged before Beijing. Yehonala's mercurial temperament now swung behind Li's policy of negotiating from strength. With war again her chosen policy, the Boxers and reactionaries took their moment of Imperial favour to orchestrate the execution of five outspoken liberal ministers. So complete was Yehonala's volte-face that Yuan Shi-kai telegraphed a friend on 2nd August with the terse message: 'It is hopeless. Better say less.' The Empress again dreamed of victory; she had relinquished all hope of immediate reconciliation with the Powers and ordered the complete annihilation of the legation defenders.

Yehonala's hero Li Ping-heng left Beijing for the front on 6th August, dressed, according to some reports, as a Boxer chieftain, in a red turban and with a red sash around his waist. Just before he set out he had visited the court and boasted, 'These few foreign soldiers – it is not necessary for me to fight them. They will run away.'[13] He immediately suffered a string of defeats at allied hands. The town of Peichang had only recently fallen to the foreigners and the Chinese forces had retreated to Yangts'un. An assault on the 6th left Yangts'un in allied hands. The Viceroy of Chihli, Yu Lu (whose optimistic war reports at the start of the crisis had encouraged Yehonala's bellicose tendencies), committed suicide. Three days later Li's army was defeated before the town of Hosiwu and the following day the town itself yielded to the victorious foreign troops. Li fell back on Ma'tou, only to relinquish the town the next day. His report, submitted to Yehonala on the 11th August, shows none of Li's former arrogance and reveals a man close to despair:

> I have retreated from Ma'tou to Changchiawan. For the past few days I have seen several tens of thousands of troops jamming all the roads. They fled as soon as they heard of the arrival of the enemy; they did not give battle at all. As they passed the villages and towns, they set fire and plundered, so much so that there was nothing for the armies under my command to purchase, with the result that men and horses were hungry and exhausted. From youth to old age I have experienced many wars, but never saw things like these ... As all the armies are taking to flight, the situation is getting out of control. There is no time to regroup and deploy. But I will do my utmost to collect the fleeing troops and fight to the death ....

That same afternoon, Li Ping-heng was dead. As the Chinese army again collapsed before the allied assault, Li committed suicide, taking poison rather than face the shame of successive defeats by the barbarians he despised.

Even before this final disaster Yehonala seems to have realised that the game was up. Unaware of her hero's death, on the same day he took his life she appointed her old champion Li Hung-chang as Minister Plenipotentiary to treat with the Powers. The next day news reached the Palace of the defeat at Hosiwu and Yehonala immediately ordered the Tsungli Yamen to send some of its ministers to the legations to open negotiations for a ceasefire. The mandarins wrote to Sir Claude McDonald and were informed by letter that the Chinese officials could be received the following morning, at 11 a.m. This was the last best chance for a peaceful solution to the crisis. Just three days before, an allied messenger had won through to the legations bearing a message from General Gaselee, commander-in-chief of the relief force, informing them: 'Strong force of allies advancing. Twice defeated enemy. Keep up your spirits.' Colonel Shiba had also received a dispatch from General Fukushima, which was far more detailed, giving the planned line of march of the allies, and their projected arrival in Beijing on the 13th or 14th of August. The news had buoyed up the besieged 'everyone went about beaming with delight',[14] and the defenders felt certain that they would now be negotiating from strength when the officials of the Tsungli Yamen arrived. But it was not to be. The mandarins lost their nerve, fearing that anyone who entered the legations would be held hostage, or worse, should the negotiations break down. On the 13th August, the morning of the meeting, a note arrived bemoaning the firing from the legations and claiming that none of the ministers could come as they 'all have important engagements'. Incomprehensibly, a second note arrived later, during the height of a bombardment by the Chinese, proposing that '… dating from today, neither Chinese nor foreigners shall, if possible, again hear the sound of a rifle' and that even now, provisions were being bought for the aid and succour of the legation inhabitants. As Sir Claude read the note a Chinese shell crashed into the room where he was sitting. It was all too much, even for an inveterate diplomatist like Sir Claude, well-versed in the art of talking softly while waving a big stick. The Chinese message went unanswered. The siege would go on.

Just prior to the arrival of the mandarins' note, the Chinese had begun to attack with increased vigour in a final attempt to overrun the legation. On the 11th the French and German legations were assaulted with unequalled ferocity, and the following day a constant fusillade from the Chinese embrasures left two of the defenders dead and several wounded. At around the same time, in an area known to the legation inhabitants as the Mongol Market, a Chinese officer was shot down as he attempted to lead a charge on the barricades. The presence of an officer in the vanguard, leading from the front, was so unusual that the rumour went round that he had sworn to capture the legation in five days, and having failed over the first four, had attempted this rash manoeuvre as his time ran out. Though the ordinary Chinese soldier fought bravely enough, the faint-heartedness of their officer class was a by-word among the defenders. One participant commented that the Chinese word commanding attack could be given with the sense of either 'go and attack!' or 'come with me and attack' and that while 'we often heard the command "go", we never heard the word "come"'. Rather than depress their spirits, the desperate nature of these assaults served to cheer the legation garrison. It was taken as confirmation that the relief force was not far away. Spirits rose, and the defenders, firing from newly strengthened barricades and embrasures constructed during the lull in hostilities, held the Chinese at bay. Confidence in their eventual rescue was now so high that the committee organising the defence offered a prize for the best medal commemorating the siege. Various designs were submitted, including one showing three figures, American, Japanese and European, standing hand-in-hand on the head of a dragon with the legend: *Ex ore draconis liberati sumus.*

But a final crisis was yet to come. At around 9 p.m. the bell in the legation tower rang out in a general call to arms, as a furious rifle and artillery attack was mounted by the Chinese on several sides of the defence line. Every man in the legation was sent to his post (except the Norwegian missionary Nestergaard who had lost his reason early in the siege and had been left firmly bound in the stables). Even the two priests (who had never before been asked to bear arms) were handed revolvers. But the looked-for general assault never materialised and the firing dropped in intensity around midnight. Just two hours later the crash of allied artillery could be heard echoing across the night sky, and a little after this the defenders heard the unmistakable sound of the tap-tap-tap of Maxim guns, and knew their rescue was imminent – 'whatever happens, we have got / the Maxim gun, and they have not'. The word ran round the lines that the allies were just outside the eastern wall of the capital. As if in response, the Chinese firing intensified anew and to the ringing of the alarm bell, every soldier and volunteer again raced for his appointed position in the defence. Over the din, the besieged could hear the Chinese commanders exhorting their men, but no enemy soldiers appeared willing to expose themselves above the parapet, and gradually, the storm of firing died away to its normal, background intensity, and the volunteers were stood down.

When dawn broke that day everyone in the legation was convinced their day of deliverance had come. But firing continued unabated, and it was not until around two o'clock in the afternoon that the first allied soldiers, from the British Sikh regiments, made their way cautiously across the lawn of the British legation. Pandemonium ensued, everyone rushing forward, 'cheering, clapping, waving handkerchiefs, shaking hands'. General Gaselee and his staff appeared, surrounded by more Sikhs and Rajputs, and the rejoicing redoubled. 'We were all dancing for joy, and some could scarcely restrain their tears.' The tumult roused the Chinese, many of whom still held their posts, and they poured in an angry fusillade of rifle fire, slightly wounding a legation lady, the first and only female in the siege to be shot. A Rajput soldier was less lucky; just after arriving at the legation he peered out through a loophole and was immediately shot in the face and killed.

In their wild joy at being rescued, the inhabitants of the legation somehow forgot their fellow-besieged who were still surrounded by Chinese forces in the Peitang Cathedral. This omission is perhaps understandable in a group of people who had suffered such privations and terrors for fifty-five days. But no such excuse remains for the allied soldiery, whose express purpose was to rescue all foreign personnel from danger. It is doubly inexplicable for the French and Italian contingents, who both had countrymen in dreadful danger just two miles to the north of the legations. Yet the fact remains that for two days nothing was done to help these unfortunates. Instead, as the remnants of the Chinese force fell back, the allied armies turned their attention from conquest to rapine and looting, the different national contingents 'pressing out to clear the Tartar City, to capture the Imperial City, to guard the palace, in jealous fear lest any other nations should be first to win places of importance.[15] As the foreigners spread through the city, the few inhabitants who had not already fled the city did whatever they could to ingratiate themselves with the conquerors. Seeing the turbans of the Indian troops, Muslim Chinese began wearing the same headgear; most houses put up notices declaring that the inhabitants were the obedient subjects of whichever foreign power they could write down (Japan – written in Chinese ideograms – was the most common, but USA was seen also, often scrawled upside-down); those with a little English pleaded in that language for mercy: 'Most noble great man, sir, I hope you will not kill us; we are all good men here.' One *Beijing-ren* had a placard on his door 'covered with a lot of unintelligible characters. When asked what they meant, he said he did not know – he had copied them off a Japanese matchbox.'

On many occasions, the capital's inhabitants pleaded in vain. There was much looting and killing in the first few days by all the foreign contingents, though the time was not without its black humour:

'That is a fine sable coat! Bring it along.'

'But there is a Chinaman inside.'

'Give it a shake. He will fall out.'[16]

'Russians looting, ravishing the women in a (legation) bandboy's house, when the Chinese seized a cornet and played the Russian national anthem; and at once the soldiers jumped to their feet, and when the notes were finished, saluted and walked out.'[17]

It was left to the only non-Christian contingent among the allies, the Japanese, to lift the siege at Peitang, which they did on 16th August. But the delay brought about perhaps the most tragic and unnecessary of all the deaths among the besieged. Padre d'Addosio had survived the legation siege unscathed. Now, anxious about his countrymen at the Peitang Cathedral, he decided to leave the legation defence line and ride over on his donkey to learn their fate. It was just two short miles, and most of the Chinese army had fled, but the route he chose was guarded by the die-hard Muslim troops of Tung Fu-hsiang. Somewhere between Peitang and the legations, Padre d'Addosio was stopped, dragged from his donkey and carried to Prince Tuan's palace, where he was savagely put to death.

The priest's murder was the last violent death among the besieged. All surviving foreigners were safe, the Chinese army was routed, and the Imperial City was in the hands of the allies. The siege of the legations was over. Just one question remained – where was the prime instigator of the attack? Where was Yehonala?

CHAPTER TWENTY

Flight ... and return

When the legation siege was lifted on the 14th August, Yehonala was still in the Forbidden City. The isolation of the Empress behind the walls of the Great Within was so complete that she was not even aware of the relief force's advance. Weeks later, she described her rude awakening to a provincial official:

> We heard bullets flying, making noises like the cries of cats ... I wondered how there could be so many cats. I was dressing my hair at that moment. Another 'maiow' was heard and a bullet flew in through the window. It dropped to the floor and bounced and rolled. We examined it closely. Just when I had decided to inquire into the matter, Tsai-lan was seen outside the curtain at the door. He said with a shaking voice, 'the foreign soldiers have entered the city. Go quickly Old Buddha' ... The Emperor was even more frightened than I, and wanted to run away with me at once. I said, 'Look at your dress; how could you go out this way?' Then with frantic haste we threw away his dress of pearls and his red tasselled hat and pulled off his official gown. He put on another long coat.

Yehonala had earlier claimed she would commit suicide rather than leave the Imperial City. Now she made the humiliating decision to escape as a commoner. She shed her jewellery and took the green jade nail casings from her hands before cutting the six-inch-long nails of her little and ring fingers, the grotesquely long fingernails that Manchu nobles affected to show themselves a leisured class. Her immaculately coiffured hair was shorn, and what remained was tied up with a scarf. Then, with her court ladies and eunuch attendants bustling and panicking around her she put on the dark blue tunic of a peasant:

> I disguised myself as a maidservant. We escaped immediately. We had no time to take any clothing, but went with empty hands. We walked until we reached the north gate of the Forbidden City, where we saw a mule cart, the only cart we had seen since we left the Palace ... I entered it with the Emperor and ordered the carter to drive quickly forward. Others with us hired their carts as they walked along. When we got out of the north-west gate of the city, we gathered together; but we dared not stay there, fearing the foreign soldiers might come after us. We travelled day and night ....[1]

Yehonala omitted one incident from her account of the flight. And with good reason, for it reflects no glory on her and reveals the Empress Dowager's high state of agitation, and the power of life and death she still wielded over all her subjects. As the procession made to leave, Kuang Hsu's favourite consort, the Pearl Concubine, repeatedly begged the Empress Dowager, on her knees, not to to flee, not to besmirch the honour of the Dynasty, for to flee was humiliating and would imperil the Empire. Other accounts claim that she begged only to be taken with the Emperor in his flight. Whatever the reason, whether Yehonala saw herself in this young girl when, forty years before, she had demanded defiance, and had counselled so eloquently against the flight of Hsien Feng to Jehol, or whether she was simply incensed by the concubine's presumption, her response was fatal. She barked a command to the eunuchs and, before the horrified eyes of Kuang Hsu and the rest of the court, the Pearl Concubine was seized by the eunuchs and cast down a nearby well and left to drown. Yehonala commanded the cart to proceed and, terrified and chastened, the broken remnants of the Manchu court scurried from their capital.

Yehonala had left with the ineffective Prince Ch'ing the onerous burden of negotiating with the victorious allies. Long before this, she had ordered Li Hung-chang, the veteran of a score of international conferences, from southern China to Beijing in order to support the Prince in his discussions. But Li had dragged his feet, at first ignoring the summonses, then moving to Shanghai, where he settled for several weeks, brooding on the disaster in the north, before finally, after eleven edicts demanding his presence, landing at Tientsin on 19th September, well after the debacle at the legations and the fall of Beijing. He managed to find excuses to remain in the port city for a further three weeks, before eventually making his way to the capital to take up his duties.[2]

Li Hung-chang and Prince Ch'ing were faced with an almost impossible task. Though riven by international jealousies, the Powers were astute enough to know that a united front would be the best way for each of them to extract maximum benefit from the Middle Kingdom. Their initial dreams of partition of China had long since been consigned to oblivion – despite the undoubted advantages of such a situation, it was recognised that China was simply too vast, its population too large (and most importantly, too *coherent*) for partition to work. Likewise, deposing the Manchus and attempting to install a puppet dynasty or republican government was fraught with too many unknowns. The only remaining option, as the canny Irishman, Sir Robert Hart, pointed out, was to treat with Yehonala and the Manchu. But while the Dynasty might be safe from the barbarians, the Powers were determined to exact punishment and reparations from the Chinese nation. There was more than one way to slice a melon.

The Russians had already gone their own route and effected the de facto partition of one part of China. They used the pretext of Boxer unrest to seize Manchuria, rapidly defeating the Chinese forces there, and on 1st October marched victoriously into Mukden, the Manchu's ancient capital. Japan let it be known, through unofficial channels, that if the Chinese fought the Russian occupation, Japan would supply materiel and officers to train the Chinese army. But the Russians were playing a subtle game, wresting land from China while at the same time offering to broker a truce with the Great Powers in Beijing.[3] Li

Hung-chang ignored the Japanese proposal: he had already declared that the Russian advance had no permanent territorial designs. To Li's mind, it was better to have a reasonable peace agreed in Beijing and to negotiate Russian withdrawal at a later date, than to begin yet another war with exhausted, demoralised troops and no real certainty of victory.

The Powers' proposals were not long in coming. On 4th October 1900, the French put forward a six-point note as a basis of negotiation. It required: punishment of those responsible for the recent attacks on foreigners; the continued prohibition of arms imports; indemnities for nations, societies and individuals harmed during the hostilities; the strengthening of legation fortifications and establishment of a permanent foreign military presence in Beijing; destruction of the Taku forts; and military occupation of two or three points on the Taku–Tientsin road. This constellation of demands effectively left China humiliated, penniless and helpless. Foreigners would decide the punishment of Chinese, even Princes of the Blood. Indemnities (as the Chinese already well knew) would siphon off resources that might otherwise have been used for self-strengthening. And with a permanent bastion within the capital, the Taku forts gone, and the road to Tientsin under barbarian control, foreign troops could be landed at will – the Chinese would be powerless to resist further demands, reasonable or otherwise, by the Powers. Which was, of course, the reason for the demands in the first place.

The remaining Powers were not satisfied with the French proposal and the final eleven-point Joint Note presented to the Chinese included additional impositions, including the erection of 'expiatory monuments' apologising for the deaths of Baron von Ketteler and Mr Sugiyama, military occupation 'of certain points ... to maintain communication between the capital and the sea', the death penalty for joining an anti-foreign society, changes to commercial treaties to 'facilitate' commercial relations, and the modification of 'Court Ceremonial relative to the reception of foreign Representatives in the manner which the Powers shall indicate'.[4] China was on the floor, and the foreign community was intent on giving it a good kicking.

News of the various stages of the negotiations was conveyed to Yehonala and the court as they continued their flight from the vengeful foreign armies. At first the 'Sacred Chariot' had travelled north. Additional carts had been commandeered, and in an unspoken symbol of their relative positions, Yehonala rode in a cart alone, while Kuang Hsu, the Emperor, was forced to share his conveyance with others. Two days after leaving the capital, Yehonala and the court arrived in Huai lai, where the district magistrate Wu Yung, beside himself with worry at the visit of the 'Two Palaces', could only offer green bean and millet porridge to break their two-day fast. He apologised profusely, but Yehonala, tired, dirty and careworn, was pragmatic: 'In time of distress this is enough. Can I at this time say what is good and what is not good?' Wu Yung was taken to greet the Emperor, who was 'standing by a chair. He was wearing a half-worn black silk wadded coat, wide in the skirt and sleeves, and he had no outside coat or waistcoat, nor had he a sash. His hair, where it should have been shaved, was an inch long, and his pigtail was disordered. His face was covered with dust, through which his skin showed yellow and dry.' He too was feasted with green bean and millet porridge, and a little later the Two Palaces joyfully shared five eggs which Wu had found in the drawer of an abandoned house.

Yehonala's initial plan was to cross the Great Wall and head for the safety of the Manchu homeland, just as she had done forty years before when Hsien Feng's court had first fled the wrath of the barbarians. But the Russian invasion and 'annexation' of Manchuria thwarted her designs, and at Hsuan Hua the caravan turned south-west towards Ta-t'ung in Shanxi Province, then south on a five-hundred-mile journey through Taiyuan to Tung-kuan, where the long line of carts and horses turned due west for the final seventy-mile march through Shanxi province to arrive at Xian, the ancient capital of China (see Map 3).

It was here Yehonala heard of the final terms that Li Hung-chang had managed to wrest from the Powers. They now comprised 'Twelve Articles' but were, in essence, unchanged from the Joint Note presented earlier. Li counselled acceptance of the articles in their entirety. The terms had already been submitted for comment to the Grand Councillors, and Jung Lu, Wang Wen-shao and Lu Ch'uan-lin had all telegraphed Li requesting substantial changes, but the Chinese negotiator was unmoved. On 27th December he memorialised the Imperial court pointing out that the attitude of the Powers was stern and that they would brook no argument. He again advised acceptance, warning that the allies might break off negotiations, and move troops forward, imperilling the existence of the nation. That same day the Imperial court promulgated an edict commanding acceptance, and requiring only that, within the framework of the Twelve Articles, the negotiators strive to cut the best deal possible. Another notable, Chang Chih-tung, held out against the agreement, even suggesting that the negotiations be moved to Nanking, a proposal that the aged Li Hung-chang, now so ill that he had to be helped by servants to the negotiating table, called 'a nonsensical idea and a distorted view'. Li must have known that his time was short; exasperated by the Imperial court's indecision, on 6th January 1901 he sent in another memorial exhorting the Grand Councillors to agree to the signing of the Twelve Articles, the contents of which 'are not open to discussion; any argument would only lead to the rupture of negotiations ... A decree has been issued ordering acceptance [that of 27th December]; if we do not sign they would consider the Court breaking its word and the plenipotentiaries possessing no authority. In that eventuality not only would it be impossible to request them to withdraw their troops, but also impossible to stop their military advance.'[5] On 10th January the Imperial court reluctantly took Li Hung-chang's advice and ordered the signing of the Twelve Articles. China, and the Manchu elite, had come a long way from the arrogant appraisal of 'barbarians' that had so tainted the negotiations with Lord Elgin and Baron Gros just fifty years before.

Sitting safe in Xian, with her Grand Eunuch Li Lien-ying already organising tribute and 'squeeze' sufficient to support her in the manner to which she (and he) had become accustomed, Yehonala was not too displeased with the progress of the peace process. She had been mortally afraid that the allies would blame her for the attack on the legations, for the murder of von Ketteler and Sugiyama, and for the whole Boxer madness. She had also believed that partition of the Empire was a possibility, that the Dynasty might be dispossessed, and that, at the very least, her own powers would be commandeered and handed over to the Emperor. Discovering that none of this applied, and that the Powers had decided a stable China under the Manchu, headed by the Old Buddha was the least of all possible evils, she was quite prepared to endorse the decision of her Grand Councillors. For her there were only two sticking points: the amount of reparations to be paid; and who was to be punished for what George Morrison, with a grand sense of hyberbole, called 'crimes unprecedented in human history, crimes against the law of nations, against the laws of humanity, and against civilisation'.[6]

The indemnity question turned out to be just as much a negotation between the Powers as between them and the Chinese. The Chinese could not pay the huge sum, four hundred and fifty million taels, that was finally agreed, and there was money to be made in loaning such an enormous sum, though the allies could not agree an appropriate percentage for the loan. There was also the question of which part of Chinese government revenue could be seconded to cover the annual repayments: raising import duties was favoured by many of the Western nations, but Britain (which enjoyed more trade with China than all the other nations combined and would therefore pay the lion's share of import duties) refused to agree. Taxation of presently duty-free merchandise was suggested, or appropriation of the tax on salt (part of this had already been earmarked by the Chinese to pay off earlier foreign loans). Much horse-trading went on; at one point the Germans (who at first had demanded an increase in Chinese import duties to ten per cent), changed their stance and acceded to a British proposal of half that amount, provided that the British support a German proposal for a four per cent interest rate on the loan the Chinese would need to pay the indemnity.

The question of punishment was equally complex. In an attempt to head off demands for the death penalty for a large number of pro-Boxer ministers, Yehonala and her ministers had issued a decree on 13th November 1900, in which nine officials and Princes of the Blood were given a variety of sentences, ranging from life imprisonment, through degradation and banishment, to simple house arrest. It was not enough for the Powers. They handed their own 'black list' to Li Hung-chang, with the names and crimes of a dozen men who, they claimed, 'deserved death'. Three of the twelve, Hsu Tung, Li Ping-heng and the arch-conservative Kang I, were already dead, having either committed suicide or succumbed to illness. The rest comprised three nobles, Prince Chuang, Prince Tuan and Duke Tsai Lan; five mandarins, Ying Nien, Chao Shu-ch'iao, Yu Hsien, Hsu Ch'eng-yu and Ch'i Hsiu; and one army commander, the Muslim general Tung Fu-hsiang. On 5th February the two sides met at the British legation, where the Chinese informed the foreign ministers that their demands had been forwarded to Xian and a decree had been issued which increased punishment to the very maximum the Chinese would allow. Two people, Prince Chuang and Yu Hsien, were sentenced to die. Six others were given sentences ranging from life imprisonment in Xinjiang (Prince Tuan) to degradation and exile. The three ministers who had predeceased the indictment, could suffer posthumous degradation should the allies insist. The Chinese insisted that the Muslim general, Tung Fu-hsiang, a major player in the legation siege, could not be sentenced at this time, because of his popularity and the number of men under his command. But they agreed that he would be punished as soon as circumstances permitted.

Again, it was not enough. The allies were intent on preventing a repetition of the turmoil and massacres of the past year. The foreign ministers were adamant that an example be made, so that such atrocities would never again be contemplated by any inhabitant of the Middle Kingdom. They wanted more blood, more executions. After a swift consultation, the allies responded the following day with demands that essentially reiterated their position, with the exception that they would make no objection if the death sentences on Prince Tuan and Duke Tsai Lan were to be commuted to perpetual imprisonment in the wilds of Xinjiang, 'no commutation of the punishment being subsequently pronounced in their favour'.[7] They also accepted the Chinese position regarding the Muslim general, Tung Fu-hsiang, but insisted that he be immediately relieved of command pending his punishment. For the rest, only death would suffice to placate the Powers.

The Chinese were appalled at the extent and severity of the retribution demanded and attempted to mitigate the punishments for Ying Nien and Chao Shu-ch'iao, neither of whom, they believed, deserved the death penalty. They also demanded the return of the two ministers held captive by the Japanese, Ch'i Hsiu and Hsu Ch'eng-yu, claiming that only China had the right to punish Chinese high officials. A capital sentence for Chao Shu-ch'iao was thought especially unjust, and great efforts were made to save him. Chinese records showed that, early in the crisis, he had been sent to investigate the Boxers, and had returned to Beijing after two days spent with the Righteous Harmonious Fists. His subsequent memorials to the Throne had contained nothing that might be construed as commending or protecting the Boxers. No fewer than twenty-one officials, and the representatives of four provinces, composed a joint telegram demanding that everything possible be done to save Chao's life. The Chinese pulled all the strings they could find, even asking the foreign consuls in Shanghai, Nanking and Hangzhou to ask their ministers to reconsider. The response was unequivocal. The allies were implacable, and the British, Japanese and Germans gave notice that delay could adversely affect the rest of the peace negotiations. Nevertheless, Prince Ch'ing and Li Hung-chang received further instructions to enquire if Ying and Chao might be permitted to commit suicide, and requesting the return of Ch'i Hsiu and Hsu Ch'eng-yu so that they may be executed by their fellow countrymen. On 21st February the allies agreed to release the two mandarins, but insisted that suicide was not an option and that death by strangulation must be administered. There is something deeply disquieting in this squalid, vindictive and relentless seeking after revenge, in the spectacle of supposedly

civilised Victorian gentlemen baulking at allowing a man the
right to die by his own hand and persisting in demands that
he suffer a slow, humiliating death by the garrotte. Did the circumstances, and the need to set an example, truly require such
barbarity?

In the end, the Chinese decided unilaterally that suicide by
hanging was equivalent to death by strangulation. A proclamation was issued the same day which acceded to all the allies
demands, save only that Ying Nien and Chao Shu-ch'iao were
given leave to hang themselves. Unfortunately, this act of clemency backfired on the one man who was almost certainly guiltless of the crimes attributed to him by the foreigners, Chao
Shu-ch'iao.

Chao was in Xian when notice of his sentence was pronounced, and he seems to have accepted his fate with typical
Confucian stoicism. Unfortunately, the official designated to
oversee his suicide was Ts'en Ch'un-hsuan, a warrior noted as
much for his savagery as for his acts of bravery. According to
the magistrate Wu Yung, who was in Xian at the time: 'Chao
was physically strong and could not die although he tried
many means. He tied his throat and took medicine. Tsen was
no longer patient enough to wait and urged him on roughly.'
Eventually, tiring of these attempts, Ts'en ordered Chao's own
servants to do away with him in a singularly barbaric manner.
Under Ts'en's direction, they 'pasted Chao's mouth, ears, nose
and eyes with cotton paper over which they poured wine. He
died and recovered many times, until he died at last. It was
very deplorable. Ts'en was too inhuman.'[8]

However deplorable and barbaric, these executions of the
ostensible 'ringleaders' of the Boxer uprising did effectively
remove the last major obstacle to peace between the belliger-
ents. Together with the beheadings of several minor officials
named by the allies (a number of whose executions were
attended by European 'observers'), they left the way clear for
the normalisation of relations, and this, in turn convinced
Yehonala that she might now return safely to Beijing. On
the 6th October 1901, after a number of false starts and
delays, the Sacred Chariot was again on the move, the

Two Palaces making their slow and arduous return to the
capital.

> Cartloads of baggage went first, setting out early in the
> morning. Then the first group, the horse soldiers, went out
> of the city; these were followed by the eunuchs, then the
> princes, and then the high officials on horses or in carts.[9]
>
> Suddenly, there sounded three cracks of the Imperial
> whip and several yellow sedan chairs came out from the
> palace. The people in the street all knelt and were silent.
> In the yellow sedan chairs were the Emperor, the Empress
> Dowager, and the young Empress.
>
> Princes and high officials came next, and then the Ta
> Ah-ko, the Heir Apparent, followed by a large number
> of carts heavily loaded with archives of the different
> yamens. It was mid-morning before they had all passed
> through the South Gate of the city.[10]

The imperial caravan travelled due west, and into a tragedy
that was soon to rob Yehonala of her strongest support. As
they approached the city of Hua-chou, Jung Lu's only son,
who was travelling with the caravan, died of an unknown illness. The death of his heir left the Grand Secretary, now
seventy years of age, a broken man. Worse still, protocol
demanded that Jung Lu remain with the procession, and so
the old nobleman was unable to arrange his son's funeral,
but had instead to leave its organisation in the hands of
another official, Hu Yen-sun. The Sacred Chariot continued
its journey westward, but bad news continued to dog them.
Word was brought that Li Hung-chang, the veteran of scores
of battles and a hundred diplomatic combats, had died. The
news shattered everyone, especially Yehonala. Of all her
counsellors, Li was the most experienced by far in foreign
diplomacy, and now, at the time of greatest crisis, he was
gone. 'All the Court officials, eunuchs and guards, looked at
each other as if the beams and posts of the house had fallen
and they had no one to depend upon ... Even those who used
to slander him were sorry.'[11] Yehonala did what she could. The
respected official Wang Wen-shao was given Li's appointment

as plenipotentiary, and the loyal Yuan Shi-kai was made Viceroy of Li's old province, Chihli.

The sombre caravan plodded on, following the course of the mighty Huang He, the Yellow River, to the city of Kaifeng, where Yehonala sojourned for a month. In characteristic style, the Old Buddha's earlier gloom and anxiety quickly dissipated, and she found the Kaifeng interlude 'as pleasant as the hunting trips of the Han Dynasty'. But happy though she was, she did not flinch from unpleasant duties. It was while in Kaifeng that she let the axe fall on the last prominent pro-Boxer at her court. In an edict promulgated on 30th November, Prince Tuan's son, the coarse, arrogant Ta Ah-ko, the Imperial Heir Apparent, who in happier times had strutted about the Forbidden City dressed in the red uniform of the Righteous and Harmonious Fists, was stripped of his rank and became a simple commoner, banished forever from the court.

From Kaifeng the procession turned north towards Beijing, some four hundred miles distant. The departure ceremony followed that of Xian 'except that high officials had come from various provinces ... and so the crowd was larger. The procession was more uniform. It was especially delightful that the weather was good. The sun was shining and the wind was soft. It was not dusty. Banners flew in the air. Everyone was silent, the only sounds were the steps of the horses and the grinding of the wheels of the carts in the sand. A city of silk stretched for miles along the riverbank and the accoutrements of a thousand soldiers flashed like fire. It was like ten thousand peach trees in full bloom in the springtime'.

A story current at that time had Jung Lu asking Yehonala what she would do if the legation siege failed and the barbarians took Beijing. She is said to have quoted the Machiavellian advice of a classic of the Han Dynasty: 'If the Emperor wishes to gain the allegiance of other countries, he can only do so by convincing their rulers that he possesses the three cardinal virtues ... to simulate affection, to express honeyed sentiments, and to treat one's inferiors as equals.'[12] From the time of her return, it became obvious that Yehonala intended to put this ancient admonition to good use.

Breaking with precedent, and perhaps as a first gesture to placate foreign opinion and symbolise her new acceptance of things Western, Yehonala made the last stage of her journey by train, travelling with her retinue in a carriage newly upholstered in Imperial yellow, complete with throne. At a time and date calculated as auspicious by the court astrologers, 7th January 1902, the Sacred Chariot arrived at a newly constructed terminus, complete with a gorgeous pavilion and stocked with gold-lacquer thrones, cloisonné jars and enormous vases of fine porcelain. Here Yehonala and the rest of the royal party transferred to traditional sedan chairs for their approach to the Great Within, along roads scattered with Imperial yellow sand and lined with troops, all of whom fell to their knees in homage as the Two Palaces passed by. In compliance with the terms of the peace agreement, all foreign soldiers (with the exception of the new legation guard) had long since vacated the capital. Beijing belonged once more to Yehonala.

The foreign ministers remaining in Beijing had issued directives against any Westerner's obvious attendance at this exclusively Chinese ceremony. But such was the interest, and the infamy, that attached to Yehonala's name, most of the foreign residents of the capital made their way onto the wall of the Tartar City, above the Chien Men Gate. It was here, according to ancient custom, that the returning Emperor and his suite must leave their sedan chairs to worship at a small temple built against the wall, containing a shrine to the tutelary deities of the Manchu race. An Italian sailor, Don Rodolfo Borghese, has left us a description of the Sacred Chariot's arrival, and of Yehonala's genius at public relations:

> We could not have chosen a better place to watch from. First to arrive were the Manchu bannermen on their fiery little horses. Next came a group of Chinese officials in gala robes, and finally the imperial palanquins, which advanced at an almost incredible speed between the two lines of kneeling soldiers ... When they reached the enclosure between the wall and the outer lunette the chairs halted and the Emperor and Empress stepped

down ... As she got out of her chair the Empress glanced up and saw us: a row of foreigners, watching her arrival from behind the ramparts. The eunuchs appeared to be trying to get her to move on, as it was not seemly that she should remain there in full view of everybody. But the Empress was not to be hurried ... At last she condescended to move, but before entering the temple, where the bonzes were all ready to begin the ceremony, she stopped once more and, looking up at us, lifted her closed hands under her chin, and made a series of little bows.

The effect of the gesture was astonishing. We had all gone up on the wall, in the hopes of catching a glimpse, as she passed, of the terrible Empress, whom the West considered almost an enemy of the human race. But we had been impressed by the magnificence of the swiftly moving pageant, and in our breathless interest we forgot our resentment against the woman who was responsible for so much evil. That little bow made to us who were watching her, and the graceful gesture of the closed hands, took us by surprise. From all along the wall there came an answering, spontaneous burst of applause. The Empress appeared pleased. She remained there for a few moments longer, looking up and smiling. Then she disappeared within the Temple

Yehonala had judged the mood of the barbarians to a nicety. She had 'simulated affection' and treated her inferiors as equals, and they had loved it. From that moment, and for no better reason than a few simple bows given at just the right moment, the declaration of war, the legation siege, the price for the heads of 'barbarian' children, all memory of past sins was flushed from the collective psyche of the foreigners. Yehonala was forgiven.

CHAPTER TWENTY-ONE

Reluctant departure

*O*ver the next few months Yehonala's charm offensive went into overdrive. Just eight days after returning to the capital, the August Mother received the foreign ministers at audience. Within two weeks, the ladies of the diplomatic community had been invited to a similar audience, a formal but nevertheless unprecedented reception – where the Empress sat aloof on the Dragon Throne, whispering her comments to Prince Ch'ing who acted as her spokesman. This was just the beginning. The meetings with the ladies became far more intimate, Yehonala walking among them, smiling at the once-hated foreign devils (for whose heads, the year before, she would cheerfully have paid forty taels apiece), holding their hands and announcing with every sign of sincerity that they were 'all one family, all one family'. Many times, to the shock and surprise of her strait-laced, Victorian guests, the Old Buddha would weep when speaking of the legations siege: 'I deeply regret all that occurred during those troublous times. The Boxers for a time overpowered the government, and even brought their guns in and placed them on the walls of the palace. Such a thing shall never occur again.'[1] Facing Yehonala in tears, at once an Empress and a sad old lady, it was surprisingly easy for the ladies to believe that she had never intended harm to any foreign visitor, the bloodthirsty edicts and rewards for barbarian heads notwithstanding. Possibly because the diplomatic community knew how indispensable Yehonala was to China's stability, her version of events came to be accepted as the party line in both Occident and Orient. The Western histories to this day speak of the Boxer 'rebellion', despite the fact that the event was an uprising against foreign domination not Manchu rule, and the Boxers were officially seconded as auxiliaries in the Manchu's attempt to kill all foreigners, or drive them into the sea.

Nor did the August Mother shrink from stealing the Emperor's reform clothes. Edict after edict now appeared (some issued as early as her stay in Xian), in which Kuang Hsu's reforms, which Yehonala had so violently and comprehensively destroyed in 1898, were reinstated with the Empress Dowager's explicit imprimatur. Succeeding where several Emperor's had failed, she now organised the suppression of the opium trade, though she allowed those over sixty to smoke a pipe in moderation. She even dispatched a commission of eminent Chinese abroad, to study the possibility of giving China a constitutional government. And yet even here there was deception. Many of the reform decrees were pure window-dressing; no attempt was made to implement them, and it is hard to avoid the conclusion that they were, like much else in Yehonala's last years, designed to ingratiate herself with the foreign community, to ensure their high regard and, in consequence, Yehonala's continued hold on power.

But no amount of artifice could hide the simple, obvious fact that Yehonala and her confidants were growing old. Early in 1903 Jung Lu, her friend and counsellor, and love-of-her-life, crushed by the death of his only son, was seized with a bout of his old affliction, asthma, from which he never recovered. The Russians continued to hold Manchuria and in despite an agreed Sino-Russian deadline for Russian withdrawal from the region, that date came and went without any sign that the homeland of the Manchu would be returned to the Middle Kingdom. Katherine Carl was an American artist at the Chinese court during the twilight of Yehonala's reign. She had been commissioned to produce a portrait of the Empress, and spent many hours with Yehonala, labouring under horrendous artistic constraints owing to the wide divergences between Chinese and Western artistic conventions. She was able to observe Yehonala at first hand over several months and, to some degree at least, to see the private

woman behind the Imperial mask. Though her finished portrait of Yehonala is stilted and, to Western eyes, dissatisfying,
the word-picture she paints of the Empress in her late sixties
reveals a tired, lonely, and perhaps disillusioned old lady, fated
now to ride her own personal tiger until she could ride no
more: 'Her Majesty was looking tired and anxious these
days. She would often go to the gardens immediately after
the [morning] Audience, for solitary walks unattended by
the ladies, and when she went for a walk, accompanied
by the Empress and the Princesses, she would sit distraught
and abstracted before the finest views and those she loved
most. She seemed absent-minded ... Her strong face looked
tired and worn. Her arms hung listlessly by her side, and she
seemed almost to have given up. I saw her furtively brush
away a tear.'[2]

But despite this, much of the old iron-willed Yehonala
remained. Notwithstanding her many disappointments, her
loss, and the cares of old age, still she could not bring herself
to hand on the sceptre to the Emperor. While she lived, she
was adamant, Kuang Hsu would never hold power.

For his part, the Emperor seems to have been playing a
waiting game. He was just thirty-two, and despite several ailments, it was in the way of things that he should eventually
survive his ageing, formidable aunt. Katherine Carl appraised
him with an artist's eye and found him a

slight and elegant figure, not more than five feet four in
height. He has a well-shaped head, with the intellectual
qualities well developed, a high brow, with large brown
eyes and rather drooping eyelids, not at all Chinese in
form and setting. His nose is high and, like most members
of the Imperial Family, is of the so-called 'noble type'. A
rather large mouth, with thin lips, the upper short with
a proud curve, the lower slightly protruding, a strong
chin a little beyond the line of the forehead, with not an
ounce of superfluous flesh on the whole face, give him an
aesthetic air and, in spite of his rather delicate physique,
an appearance of great reserve strength.

Carl also sensed the quiet brooding nature of Kuang Hsu, and was perceptive enough to divine the reason that lay behind this 'sphinx-like quality'.

> The Emperor dresses with extreme neatness and great simplicity, wearing few ornaments and no jewels except on state occasions. His face is kindly in expression, but the glance from his rather heavy-lidded eyes is shrewd and intelligent ... Does he dream of future greatness for his Empire? Does he feel that though his first efforts at governing have failed, he can bide his time – that all things come to him who waits? It almost seems so! He appears to fully realise, now, that he made a mistake in the choice of his instruments and time, in his efforts for progress. But the look of eternal patience in those large eyes seems to show that he will yet try to accomplish China's salvation – that he is but waiting his opportunity.[3]

The Japanese victory over the Russians in 1904 was a defining moment between the Eastern and Western nations of the world. Foreshadowing the events of Pearl Harbour thirty-seven years later, Japan attacked the Russian Fleet in Port Arthur without warning, and destroyed it. On land, the Japanese annihilated the eighty-three thousand poorly led Russian troops in Manchuria, losing over a hundred and thirty thousand men in the process. It had been a costly victory, but Japan had conquered. For the first time in over two hundred years, an oriental country had comprehensively vanquished an occidental power. The Russo-Japanese War taught the Chinese elite an important lesson – it emphasised the fact that Western technology was essential to save China from its enemies. What Japan could do today, China might achieve tomorrow. It was now plain to all that Kuang Hsu's 1898 strategy had been essentially correct. These events boosted the Emperor's status at court, and it became obvious that, with youth on his side, he and the reformers must eventually win out in the long battle against Yehonala and the reactionary old guard.

There were many at court who had come to the same conclusion, and were terrified at the prospect. They foresaw personal disaster if Kuang Hsu succeeded the Old Buddha. As the Chinese say, 'When the tree falls, the shade is gone', and should Yehonala 'mount the dragon' before Kuang Hsu, the protective shade she spread over those who had betrayed the Emperor, and made Kuang Hsu's life a living hell for so many years would be removed. As Emperor, he could deal with them as he wished. Chief among these was Yuan Shi-kai, now the rich and powerful Viceroy of Chihli, who had informed Jung Lu and the Empress of the reformist plot and sent Kuang Hsu to his Ocean Terrace prison, and Li Lien-ying, the Grand Eunuch, who had delighted in humiliating the Celestial Prince, keeping him ill-clad, cold and hungry throughout the period of his confinement. Neither could expect mercy if Yehonala should predecease the Son of Heaven. For both, it was essential that Kuang Hsu should die young. Nor would his aunt, determined that he should never rule without her, shed many tears.

With so many powerful foes – Yehonala, Yuan Shi-kai and Li Lien-ying – ranged against him, it came as no surprise that, when Yehonala was taken ill in 1908, Kuang Hsu should also suddenly sicken, becoming so ill that he was forced to take to his bed. Somehow, Yehonala knew the Emperor's malady was fatal. On 13th November – though Kuang Hsu still lived – she was well enough to preside over a council to appoint a new Emperor. Yuan Shi-kai upheld the candidature of Prince Pu Lun, Prince Ch'ing's son, who had already reached the age of majority. Yehonala would have none of it. She rejected the nomination out of hand, and named as her choice Pu Yi, the son of Prince Ch'un and grandson of Jung Lu. Perhaps Pu Yi's nomination was a final act of affection towards her faithful friend and lost love. Perhaps more important, Pu Yi was a child of tender years, not yet three. Yehonala had lost none of her old cunning: Pu Lun as Son of Heaven would have meant her immediate retirement; with a child Emperor, she could continue as before. As ever, she carried all before her at the council and Pu Yi was designated the new Emperor. It seems that, despite her illness, Yehonala was planning on yet another long regency. But it was not to be.

The day after she had decided on his successor, Yehonala went to visit Kuang Hsu on what was now, undoubtedly his deathbed. Three days before, he had been visited by a physician, Dr Chu, who had some time earlier examined the Emperor and diagnosed Bright's disease. Dr Chu now found the Emperor sleepless, thrashing about his bed, tormented with agonising stomach cramps: 'he could not urinate, his heart beat grew faster, his face burned purple, his tongue had turned yellow – symptoms which had no connection with his previous illness.'[4] The implication was clear – Kuang Hsu was not dying from the effects of any of his known illnesses. This 'disease' was new and sudden. Kuang Hsu was being poisoned.

During a brief respite from his agony Kuang Hsu is said to have asked for paper and written his own uncompromising valedictory message:

> We were the second son of the Prince Ch'un when the Empress Dowager selected Us for the throne. She has always hated Us. But for Our misery of the past ten years, Yuan Shi-kai is responsible and one other. When the time comes, I desire that Yuan be summarily beheaded.[5]

It was a tragic, pathetic, and ultimately vain request. The Son of Heaven had long since ceased to wield any effective power in his kingdom. Nothing was done and the message itself, if it ever existed, has disappeared. But even during his last moments, when he could no longer speak, Kuang Hsu persisted. It was noticed that he was slowly moving the index finger of his right hand in a continuous circle. In Chinese calligraphy, *Yuan*, the first character of Yuan Shi-kai's name, means 'round' or 'circle'. At the hour of the cock (some time between 5 and 7 p.m.) on 14th November 1908, while Yehonala, his wife Lung Yu, and the Lustrous Concubine stood watching at his bedside, the circling finger faltered, then failed to move, and the unhappy and unfortunate spirit Kuang Hsu left on its final journey to the Nine Springs.

Yehonala spent little time in mourning. After a good night's sleep, next day she was hale enough to resume her normal routine, rising at six o'clock and breakfasting on a bowl of hot milk and *congee*, rice porridge with a little added lotus root. Morning was always devoted to business, and she spent the hours before noon chairing a meeting of the Grand Council which considered the steps that needed to be taken as a result of the late Emperor's demise, and Pu Yi's accession. Decrees were prepared, under the new Emperor's imprimatur, by which Yehonala passed on her honorific of Empress Mother to Kuang Hsu's widow, and was given a more prestigious new title (and a further hefty stipend) that of Great Empress Mother. Her work over, and confident of a regency that would last until the new Emperor's majority (at least fourteen years, when she would have reached the grand old age of eighty-seven) Yehonala laid aside the duties of government and retired for lunch. One account has her indulging in a large helping of crab apples and clotted cream, an unlikely and rather irrresponsible repast for someone said to be recovering from a bout of dysentery. But whatever the midday menu, shortly after partaking of the meal, Yehonala felt suddenly ill, and within minutes had fainted away. When she came to, she seemed suddenly convinced that her end was near. Why this should be has never been satisfactorily explained. Any natural illness, especially one with such a sudden onset, always brings with it the possibility of recovery, at least until the disease has progressed somewhat and medical science can come up with a prognosis. Yet Yehonala remained convinced that she would soon die and that no remedy would avail. This conviction has strong echoes of both her cousin Sakota, the Empress of the Eastern Palace, and of the Kuang Hsu Emperor, each of whom was, almost certainly, poisoned.

Twenty years earlier Yehonala had been accused of poisoning her cousin, and in 1908, the capital's gossips were certainly convinced that the Emperor had been given poison. The rumour-mill ground out at least three versions of Kuang Hsu's death. In one Yuan Shi-kai, terrified (rightly) that with Yehonala dead a resurgent Kuang Hsu would wreak vengeance upon the man who had so comprehensively betrayed him, had bribed one or several Eunuchs of the Presence to poison the Emperor. Another tale pointed the finger of guilt at Yehonala, who, it was said, could not abide the thought of her hated nephew ruling in her stead and, fearing posthumous reprisals on her name and reputation, had commanded the eunuchs to administer the toxin. Yet another story blamed the eunuchs themselves, especially the Grand Eunuch, Li Lien-ying, who had mistreated the Emperor for years. Knowing of the bad blood between the Emperor and his aunt, Li had been the instigator of the poisoning, confident that the murder would be given a plausible gloss by the Empress.

But now it was the Empress herself who was carried to her room, and dressed in the traditional costume of death, the Robes of Longevity, vestments which less than a day before, in his final act of defiance, Kuang Hsu had refused to wear. Yehonala ordered her valedictory message prepared, to which she added in her own hand a final platitudinous paragraph:

> Looking back upon the memories of the past fifty years, I perceive how calamities from within and aggression from without have come upon Us in relentless succession. The new Emperor is an infant, just reaching the age when wide instruction is of the highest importance ... His Majesty must devote himself to studying the interests of his country and refrain from giving way to grief. It is my earnest prayer that he diligently pursue his studies and that he may hereafter add fresh lustre to the glorious achievements of his Ancestors.
>
> Mourning to be worn for twenty-seven days only.
> Hear and obey![6]

− this from a woman who had allowed her own son (if son he was) to slowly destroy himself in brothels and opium dens, and who had savagely imprisoned her nephew for 'studying the interests of his country' when those interests conflicted with her own. It seemed that, even in death, Yehonala held the mask of deceit firmly before her face.

But as the eunuchs turned her face to the south, the traditional direction in which the sovereign must die, her final words betrayed a knowledge that her constant striving for supreme power had caused irreparable harm to her nation:

'Do not allow eunuchs to meddle in government matters,' she whispered, 'the Ming Dynasty was ruined by eunuchs and its fate should be a warning to my people.' The rest of her speech was even more telling: 'Never again allow a woman to hold the supreme power in the State. It is against the house-laws of our Dynasty and should be forbidden.'

Yehonala said no more. Facing south, her breathing slowed, then stopped. 'Her mouth remained fixedly open, which the Chinese interpret as a sign that the spirit of the deceased is unwilling to leave the body.'[7] She was seventy-three years old. The Great Empress Mother of China, the author of so many others' violent deaths, had finally 'mounted the dragon'; and left the Dynasty, and China, to chaos – as she, perhaps, had always planned.

Epilogue

*W*as Yehonala poisoned? Clearly, the death of the Emperor and the Great Empress Mother within the space of twenty-four hours can only be regarded as horribly suspicious, a coincidence of monumental proportions. That Kuang Hsu was deliberately put to death seems incontrovertible. His death was too convenient and, leaving aside the (often well-founded) rumours that unanimously assigned his death to poison, the medical evidence of Dr Chu is damning. That accepted, it is the indisputable fact that Yehonala's death followed immediately upon that of Kuang Hsu's that gives us the best evidence that her own demise was not natural. The pro-Emperor faction would have been credulous in the extreme had they not envisaged an early-death scenario for the Emperor, and planned their response. Yehonala's own certainty of her imminent dissolution adds strength to this hypothesis – none knew better than Yehonala the symptoms and results of the many poisons available to a clandestine assassin. One would have to be terminally naive to believe that each faction, reformers and conservatives, would fail to take steps to protect itself, should the worst happen. Whether as an act of vengeance, or for their own protection, it seems clear that Yehonala's death was a direct reprisal by the reformers for the poisoning of the Emperor.

Whatever hatreds simmered below the ornate, ritual-bound surface of the Great Within, they did not debar the Great Empress Mother from a funeral befitting her exalted status. In the September following her death, a special ceremony was performed, 'a magnificent barge made of paper and over a hundred and fifty feet long was set up outside the Forbidden City on a large empty space adjoining the Coal Hill. It was crowded with [paper] figures of attendant eunuchs and handmaidens, and contained furniture and viands for the use of the illustrious dead in the lower regions. A throne was placed in the bow and around it were kneeling effigies of attendant officials, all wearing their robes of state as if the shade of the Western Empress were holding an audience'. Once everything was in place and the requisite rites had been performed, this unique 'paper Court' was consigned to the flames 'in order that the Old Buddha might enjoy the use of it at the Yellow Springs'.[1]

The Emperor Kuang Hsu was buried before his aunt, at a cost of half a million taels. Reflecting the true status of the relationship between the Emperor and his 'august aunt', Yehonala's own funeral was a far more sumptuous affair and cost around three times as much. Almost a year after her death, on 5th November 1909, following the long and involved funerary rites that preceded burial, Yehonala's body was transported in glory from the Great Within to her final resting place, the Eastern Tombs. Her cortège, led by innumerable horsemen and eunuchs uncountable, and officials swathed in white, the mourning colour of the East, 'offered a gorgeous spectacle: red robes of bearers, yellow robes of Lamaist priests, silver and gold of rich embroideries'. A troop of musicians blew forth mournful dirges as the Grand Eunuch, Li Lien-ying, plodded sorrowfully before the coffin of his mistress, carrying Moo-tan, her favourite pekingese. The dog was said to have died of grief at the tomb entrance (emulating the tale of T'ao Hua, another faithful canine in the Sung Dynasty, who had similarly given up the ghost for the Emperor T'ai Tsung), and to have been buried alongside Yehonala's corpse. A more prosaic tale recounted that Moo-tan was spirited away after the ceremony by the eunuchs and sold at a good profit. Whatever the truth of this, on 9th November, at the astrologically propitious time of seven in the morning, the coffin containing the body of the Great Empress Mother was finally shut up within its Jewelled Chamber.

Yehonala's coffin contained much more than her body. The always-careful Grand Eunuch, Li Lien-ying, meticulously catalogued the fabulous treasures that accompanied his mistress to the grave:

A mattress seven inches thick, embroidered with pearls, lay on the bottom of the coffin, and on top of it was a silk embroidered coverlet strewn with a layer of pearls. The body rested on a lace sheet, with a figure of Buddha woven in pearls.

At the head was placed a jade ornament formed as a lotus, and at the foot a jade ornament carved into leaves. She was dressed in ceremonial clothes done in gold thread, and over that an embroidered jacket with a rope of pearls, while another rope of pearls encircled her body nine times and eighteen pearl images of Buddha were laid in her arms ... Her body was covered by a sacred Tolo pall, a chaplet of pearls was placed upon her head, and by her side were laid 108 gold, jade and carved-gem Buddhas. On each of the feet were placed one watermelon and two sweet melons of jade, and two hundred gems made in the shape of peaches, pears, apricots and dates. By her left side was placed a jade cut like a lotus-root with leaves and flowers sprouting from the top: on the right hand was a coral tree. The gaps were filled with scattered pearls and gems, until the whole was spread level, and over all was spread a network covering of pearls.

As the lid was being lifted to place in position, a Princess of the Imperial house added a fine jade ornament of eighteen buddhas and another of eight galloping horses.[2]

The Dynasty did not long outlast the funeral of the Great Empress Mother. Since the death of Yehonala, the Empire had been administered in Pu Yi's name by his father Prince Ch'un, Kuang Hsu's younger brother, who had been named Regent. But he possessed none of the authority, the charisma of power, that had animated the small frame of the Empress, and as Lady Townley had presciently asked, after Yehonala who could 'resist the tide of foreign aggression and stem the torrent of inward revolt'?[3] Within two years of her being laid to rest the country was in chaos, with insurrections against the Dynasty breaking out all over the Empire. On the 12th February 1912, the Manchus abdicated power, handing over executive power to Yehonala's faithful servant Yuan Shi-kai, who, self-interest to the fore as ever, attempted almost immediately to found his own dynasty on the still-warm body of the Manchu. He failed, and China entered a dark night of warlords and lawlessness from which it took decades to recover.[4]

The ancient prophecy had been fulfilled. After more than two hundred and fifty years a 'ten-mouthed woman with grass on her head' had ruled the Middle Kingdom and had wrought vengeance upon the Imperial clan of the Aisin Gioro. A female of the Yeho-Nala tribe had established dominion over the Manchu, and she had brought both the Dynasty, and her nation, to ruin and destruction.

Postscript

Nineteen years after Yehonala had been laid to rest in her vault with such pomp and ritual, a huge explosion echoed through the pine-clad valley of the Eastern Tombs, shattering the sombre silence of her mausoleum. The gateway to the 'Jewelled Chambers' of the Emperors had been dynamited by desperate men intent on plunder, and Chinese grave robbers crawled through the shattered entrance to despoil the sarcophagi of those who had once held the Mandate of Heaven.[1] The Emperor Ch'ien Lung's body was desecrated and dismembered, along with his wives. Yehonala's tomb was ransacked, the coffin violated, and all its priceless gold, jade and jewelled treasures taken. The sacred Tolo pall was ripped from the corpse and the pearl-encrusted, cloth-of-gold vestments torn away, leaving the pitiful cadaver naked to the waist, her undergarments half-removed. The earthly remains of Yehonala, once the most powerful female ruler on earth, were dumped unceremoniously on the floor of the tomb, face down, her sunken eyes staring sightlessly at the dark earth of the Middle Kingdom.

References and notes

Chapter 1

1. Hughes, E. R. *Two Chinese Poets: vignettes of Han life and thought.* Princeton University Press, 1960.
2. Chang, Jolan. *The Tao of Love & Sex.*
3. Gulik, R. van. *Sexual Life in Ancient China.*
4. *Dynastic History of the Later Han,* quoted in Read, D. *The Tao of Health, Sex and Longevity.*
5. *Straits Times,* July 14th, 2002.
6. 453–221 BC by modern dating. From the time of the dissolution of the kingdom of Chin. Orthodox scholars, however, preferred 403 BC, the year when the King of Chou legitimised the action taken fifty years earlier by the Han, Wei and Chou clans.

Chapter 2

1. Michael, F. *The Origin of Manchu Rule.*
2. Bland J. O. P. and Backhouse, E. *China Under the Empress Dowager.*
3. Yun Yu-ting. *The True Story of the Kuang-Hsu Emperor.*
4. Michael, F. *The Origin of Manchu Rule,* p. 82.
5. Freedman, M. *Chinese Lineage and Society.*
6. Mungello, D. E. *Curious Land, Jesuit Accommodation and the origins of sinology.* Steiner, 1985.
7. Bland, J. O. P. and Backhouse, E. *China Under the Empress Dowager.*
8. Sun Tzu. *The Art of War,* p. 63.
9. *Wiles of War, The,* p. 303.
10. Bland, J. O. P. and Backhouse, E. *China Under the Empress Dowager.*
11. Bland, J. O. P. and Backhouse, E. *China Under the Empress Dowager.*
12. Struve, L. S. *The Southern Ming, 1644–1652,* p. 15.
13. Bland, J. O. P. and Backhouse, E. *China Under the Empress Dowager.*
14. Bland, J. O. P. and Backhouse, E. *China Under the Empress Dowager.*

15. Struve, L. S. *The Southern Ming, 1644–1652*, pp. 177–178.
16. Balm, A. J. *The World's Living Religions*, p. 156.
17. Huang, R. *1587, a Year of No Significance*, p. 28.

Chapter 3

1. Bernbaum, E. *Sacred Mountains*.
2. Chung, S. F. *The Much Maligned Empress Dowager*, p. 3.
3. Pa. *An Unofficial History ...* . Quoted in Vare, D. *The Last Emperor*, p. 3.
4. Fairbanks, J. K. *Chinabound*, p. 38.
5. Keswick, M. *The Chinese Garden*.
6. Swann, N. L. *Pan Chao, foremost woman scholar of China*.
7. Fielde, A. *Pagoda Shadows*.
8. Jackson, B. *Splendid Slippers*.
9. Beahan, C. *The Woman's Movement and Nationalism in late Ch'ing China*, 1976, p. 22.
10. Beahan, C. *The Woman's Movement and Nationalism in late Ch'ing China*, 1976, p. 23.
11. Parker, E. H. *John Chinaman*.
12. Warner, M. *The Dragon Empress*, p. 18.
13. Te Ling. *Two Years in the Forbidden City*.
14. Te Ling. *Two Years in the Forbidden City*.

Chapter 4

1. Dreyer, E. L. *Early Ming China*.
2. Hu Chui. *The Forbidden City*.
3. Chang Hsin-pao. *Commissioner Lin and the Opium War*.
4. Balazs, E. *Chinese Civilisation and Bureaucracy*, p. 16.
5. Mencius (trans. Lyall, L. A.). Longmans, 1932.
6. Worswick, C. and Spence, J. *Imperial China in Photographs 1850–1912*.
7. Balazs, E. *Chinese Civilisation and Bureaucracy*.
8. Backhouse, E. and Bland, J. O. P. *Annals and Memoirs of the Court of Peking*.
9. Anderson, M. M. *Hidden Power*.
10. Mitamura, T. *Chinese Eunuchs*, p. 29ff.
11. Mitamura, T. *Chinese Eunuchs*.
12. Ayalon, D. *Eunuchs, Caliphs and Sultans*.
13. Collis, M. *The Great Within*, p. 19ff.

14. Han Fei Tzu. *The Complete Works of Han Fei Tzu.*
15. Hinsch, B. *Passions of the Cut Sleeve*, pp. 142–143.
16. Vare, D. *The Last Empress.*

Chapter 5

1. Shelley, P. B. *Ozymandias.*
2. Cary-Elwes, C. *China and the Cross*, p. 215.
3. Spence, J. *God's Chinese Son*, p. xix.
4. Medhurst, H.W. *Pamphlets Isuued by the Chinese Insurgents at Nanking*, 1853.
5. Medhurst, H.W. *Pamphlets Isuued by the Chinese Insurgents at Nanking*, 1853.
6. Bland, J. O. P. and Backhouse, E. *China Under the Empress Dowager.*
7. Cheng, J. C. *Chinese Sources for the Tai Ping Rebellion.*
8. Hirth, F. *China and the Roman Orient*, pp. v–vii.
9. Roberts, F. M. *Western Travellers to China.*

Chapter 6

1. Wakeman, F. E. *The Great Enterprise: the Manchu reconstruction of imperial order in seventeenth-century China*, p. 2.
2. Geiss, J. P. *Peking Under the Ming*, pp. 157–158.
3. The situation has strong parallels with today's drug problems. Like the pros and cons with regard to present-day legalisation of 'hard drugs', it is beset with exactly the same imponderables.
4. Marshall, P. J. *East Indian Fortunes: the British in Bengal in the Eighteenth Century.*
5. Rockhill, W.W. *Diplomatic Audiences at the Court of China*, p. 5.
6. Hurd, D. *The Arrow War.*
7. Deng, S. and Fairbank, J. K. *China's Response to the West*, p. 48.
8. Hurd, D. *The Arrow War*, p. 166.
9. Armitage, A. H. *The Storming of the Taku Forts.*
10. Lane-Poole, S. *The Life of Sir Harry Parkes Sometime Her Majesty's Minister to China and Japan.*
11. Bland, J. O. P. and Backhouse, E. *China Under the Empress Dowager*, p. 12.
12. Bland, J. O. P. and Backhouse, E. *China Under the Empress Dowager*, pp. 25–26.
13. Vare, D. *The Last Empress.*
14. *Wiles of War, The*, p. 303.
15. Swinhoe, R. *Narrative of the North China Campaign of 1860.*
16. Herrison, Comte de. *Journal d'un Interprète en Chine.*

Chapter 7

1. Barrow, J. *Travels in China.*
2. Swinhoe R. *Narrative of the North China Campaign of 1860.*
3. Loch, H. *Personal Narrative of Occurrences during Lord Elgin's Second Embassy to China, 1860.*
4. This was very much an empty threat – there was no heavy artillery with which to attack the capital's massive walls.
5. Waldron T. *Letters and Journals of James, Eighth Earl of Elgin.*
6. Saved by Père David transferring several to Great Britain where the species thrived and was eventually returned to China in the late 1970s.
7. Spence, J. *The China Helpers*, pp. 74–75.
8. La Gorce, quoted in Vare, D. *The Last Empress*, p. 47.

Chapter 8

1. Vare, D. *The Last Empress*, p. 64.
2. Chung, S. F. *The Much Maligned Empress Dowager.*
3. Bland, J. O. P. and Backhouse, E. *China Under the Empress Dowager.*
4. Bland, J. O. P. and Backhouse, E. *China Under the Empress Dowager.*
5. Bland, J. O. P. and Backhouse, E. *China Under the Empress Dowager.*

Chapter 9

1. Bland, J. O. P. and Backhouse, E. *China Under the Empress Dowager.*
2. Dillon, E. J. *Fortnightly Review.*
3. Curwen, C. A. *Taiping Rebel*, p. 145.
4. Cahill, H. *A Yankee Adventurer.*
5. Cheng, J. C. *Chinese Sources for the Tai Ping Rebellion*, p. 99.
6. Curwen, C. A. *Taiping Rebel.*
7. Cheng, J. C. *Chinese Sources for the Tai Ping Rebellion*, p. 104.
8. Wilson, A. *The Ever Victorious Army.*
9. Cheng, J. C. *Chinese Sources for the Tai Ping Rebellion*, p. 111.
10. Cheng, J. C. *Chinese Sources for the Tai Ping Rebellion*, p. 126.
11. Michael, F. *The Tai Ping Rebellion.*
12. Cheng, J. C. *Chinese Sources for the Tai Ping Rebellion*, p. 130.
13. Wilson, A. *The Ever Victorious Army.*

14. Curwen, C. A. *Taiping Rebel.*
15. Bland, J. O. P. and Backhouse, E. *China Under the Empress Dowager,* p. 65.
16. Curwen, C. A. *Taiping Rebel.*
17. Bland, J. O. P. and Backhouse, E. *China Under the Empress Dowager.*

Chapter 10

1. Bland, J. O. P. and Backhouse, E. *China Under the Empress Dowager,* p. 81.

Chapter 11

1. Bland, J. O. P. and Backhouse, E. *China Under the Empress Dowager,* p. 104.
2. Te Ling. *Imperial Incense,* p. 161.
3. Bland, J. O. P. and Backhouse, E. *China Under the Empress Dowager,* p. 105.
4. Wu Yung. *The Flight of an Empress,* p. 200.
5. Bland, J. O. P. and Backhouse, E. *China Under the Empress Dowager,* p. 106.
6. The vote was seven in favour of Pu Lun, with three votes cast for Prince Kung's son.
7. Bland, J. O. P. and Backhouse, E. *China Under the Empress Dowager,* p. 112.
8. Wolf, M. *Women and Suicide in China.*

Chapter 12

1. Cordier, H. *Historie des relations de la Chine avec les puissances occidental,* p. 486.
2. Bland, J. O. P., quoting Sir Valentine Chirol, in *Li Hung Chang,* p. 284.
3. M. B. Jansen (ed.) *Cambridge History of Japan,* vol. 5, *The nineteenth century.*

Chapter 13

1. Bland, J. O. P. and Backhouse, E. *China Under the Empress Dowager.* p. 117.
2. Bland, J. O. P. and Backhouse, E. *China Under the Empress Dowager.*

Chapter 14

1. Bland, J. O. P. and Backhouse, E. *China Under the Empress Dowager.*
2. Sergeant, P. *The Great Empress Dowager of China.*
3. Johnston, R. F. *Twilight in the Forbidden City.*
4. Johnston, R. F. *Twilight in the Forbidden City*, p. 369.

Chapter 15

1. Vare, D. *The Last Empress.*
2. Carl, K. A. *With the Empress Dowager of China.*
3. Dulles, F. R. *China and America.*
4. Chaiken, N. *The Sino-Japanese War.*
5. Tyler, J. *Pulling Strings in China.*
6. Tyler, J. *Pulling Strings in China.*
7. Bland, J. O. P. *Li Hung Chang.*
8. Bland, J. O. P. and Backhouse, E. *China Under the Empress Dowager*, pp. 168–169.
9. According to the Russian diplomat, Count Witte, Li Hung-chang and another colleague were paid 500,000 taels each in order to hurry this process forward.
10. Waltner, A. *Getting an Heir.*
11. Gulik, R. van. *Sexual Life in Ancient China.*
12. Lo Jung-pang (ed). *Kang Yu Wei, a biography and symposium.*
13. Kang Yu-wei. *Nan Hai Hsien Sheng Ssu Shang Shu Chi* (The four petitions of Mr Kang Yu-wei), 6–114. Shanghai, 1895.
14. Shen Tung-sheng *et al.* (eds). *Kuang Hsu Cheng Yao,* 24/16–17. Shanghai, 1909. Quoted in Tan, C. C. *The Boxer Catastrophe,* p. 19.
15. Headland, I. *Court Life in China.*

Chapter 16

1. Liang Ch'i-chao. *Wu Hsu Cheng Pien Chi* (The coup d'état of 1898). In Yun Shih Ho Chi. *A Critical Study of Li Hung Chang.* Shanghai, 1936.
2. Ch'en J. *Yuan Shih Kai.* Allen & Unwin, 1961.
3. Tan, C. C. *The Boxer Catastrophe.*
4. Bland, J. O. P. and Backhouse, E. *China Under the Empress Dowager.*
5. Pearl, C. *Morrison of Peking,* p. 90.

6. Lo Jung-pang (ed) *Kang Yu Wei, a biography and symposium.*
7. This official was J. O. P. Bland, co-author of the classic *China Under the Empress Dowager.*
8. Richard, A. *Forty-five Years in China,* p. 267.

Chapter 17

1. Tan, C. C. *The Boxer Catastrophe.*
2. Mayers, *China No. 1,* 1900, p. 352, quoted in Tan, C. C. *The Boxer Catastrophe.*
3. Pearl, C. *Morrison of Peking.*
4. Pearl, C. *Morrison of Peking,* p. 95.

Chapter 18

1. Plée, H. *Karate.*
2. Smith, R. W. *Shaolin Temple Boxing.*
3. In 1998 I spoke with a WWF official who swore that he had seen a demonstration in Sichuan Province in which a bottle was broken, a newspaper set on fire, solely by the concentrated 'thought-power' of three wandering monks. He could see no way in which the objects burned or destroyed could have been tampered with during the demonstration.
4. Buck, D. D. (ed.). *Recent Chinese Studies of the Boxer Movement.*
5. Wu Yung. *The Flight of an Empress.*
6. National Geographic Authors. *Journey into China.*
7. Goldstein, J. *The Jews of China.*
8. Eitel, E. J. *Feng Shui.*
9. Yuan Yong, in Buck, D. D. (ed.). *Recent Chinese Studies of the Boxer Movement.*
10. Bland, J. O. P. and Backhouse, E. *China Under the Empress Dowager,* p. 225.
11. Bland, J. O. P. and Backhouse, E. *China Under the Empress Dowager,* p. 226.
12. Tan, C. C. *The Boxer Catastrophe.*
13. Pearl, C. *Morrison of Peking.*

Chapter 19

1. Savage-Landor, H., quoted in Pearl, C. *Morrison of Peking.*
2. Bland, J. O. P. and Backhouse, E. *China Under the Empress Dowager,* p. 225.

3. Allen, R. *The Siege of the Peking Legations, being the diary of R. Allen.*
4. Bland, J. O. P. and Backhouse, E. *China Under the Empress Dowager,* p. 225.
5. Tan, C. C. *The Boxer Catastrophe.* p. 78.
6. Putnam Weale, B. L. *Indiscreet Letters from Peking.*
7. Lui, Adam Yuen-chung. *The Hanlin Academy.*
8. Pearl, C. *Morrison of Peking,* p. 118.
9. Bland, J. O. P. and Backhouse, E. *China Under the Empress Dowager.*
10. Tan, C. C. *The Boxer Catastrophe,* p. 98.
11. Pearl, C. *Morrison of Peking,* p. 119.
12. Tan, C. C. *The Boxer Catastrophe,* p. 104.
13. Wu Yung. *The Flight of an Empress,* pp. 49–50.
14. Allen, R. *The Siege of the Peking Legations, being the diary of R. Allen,* p. 260.
15. Allen, R. *The Siege of the Peking Legations, being the diary of R. Allen,* p. 276.
16. Vare, D. *The Last Empress,* p. 248.
17. Pearl, C. *Morrison of Peking,* p. 118.

Chapter 20

1. Wu Yung. *The Flight of an Empress,* p. 210.
2. Bland, J. O. P. *Li Hung Chang.*
3. Tan, C. C. *The Boxer Catastrophe,* p. 162.
4. Tan, C. C. *The Boxer Catastrophe,* p. 151, n. 142.
5. Tan, C. C. *The Boxer Catastrophe,* p. 156, n. 155.
6. Pearl, C. *Morrison of Peking,* p. 215.
7. Tan, C. C. *The Boxer Catastrophe,* p. 220, n. 12.
8. Wu Yung. *The Flight of an Empress,* p. 227.
9. More than two thousand carts were needed to transport the court.
10. Wu Yung. *The Flight of an Empress,* p. 231.
11. Wu Yung. *The Flight of an Empress,* p. 242.
12. Vare, D. *The Last Empress.*

Chapter 21

1. Headland, I. *Court Life in China,* p. 98.
2. Carl, K. A. *With the Empress Dowager of China.*
3. Carl, K. A. *With the Empress Dowager of China.* pp. 65–67.
4. Pelissier, R. *The Awakening of China, 1793–1949* (edited and trans. M. Kieffer). Secker & Warburg, 1967, p. 245; quoting *The Gospel of Chung Shan,* pp. 51–52.

5. Bland, J. O. P. and Backhouse, E. *China Under the Empress Dowager*, p. 460.
6. Bland, J. O. P. and Backhouse, E. *China Under the Empress Dowager*, pp. 468–469.
7. Bland, J. O. P. and Backhouse, E. *China Under the Empress Dowager*.

Epilogue

1. Collis, M. *The Great Within*.
2. Vare, D. *The Last Empress*, 1938, quoting Moore, Bennet, *Illustrated London News*.
3. Lady Susan Townley. *My Chinese Notebook*.
4. Semblance of Dynasty carried on in part of the Forbidden City till 1924 when the 'child-Emperor', Pu-yi, now eighteen years old, was forced to leave the Palace.

Postscript

1. MacAleavy, H. *A Dream of Tartary*, p. 186, quoting commission of enquiry report.

Bibliography

A

Allen, R. *The Siege of the Peking Legations, being the diary of R. Allen.* London, 1901.
Anderson, M.M. *Hidden Power: the palace eunuchs of Imperial China.* Prometheus Books, 1990.
Armitage, A.H. *The Storming of the Taku Forts.* 1896.
Ayalon, D. *Eunuchs, Caliphs and Sultans: a study in power relationships.* Magnes Press, Hebrew University, 1999.

B

Backhouse, E. and Bland, J.O.P. *Annals and Memoirs of the Court of Peking.* Heinemann, 1914.
Balazs, E. *Chinese Civilisation and Bureaucracy: variations on a theme.* Yale University Press, 1964.
Balm, A.J. *The World's Living Religions.* Dell Publishing Co., 1964.
Barrow, J. *Travels in China.* 1804.
Beahan, C.L. *The Woman's Movement and Nationalism in late Ch'ing China.* 1976.
Bennet, Moore. *Illustrated London News.* 1909.
Bernbaum, E. *Sacred Mountains of the World.* Sierra Club Books, San Francisco, 1990, p. 41.
Bland, J.O.P. *Li Hung Chang.* Constable, 1917.
Bland, J.O.P. and Backhouse, E. *China Under the Empress Dowager.* Constable, 1910.
Buck, D.D. (ed.). *Recent Chinese Studies of the Boxer Movement.* M.E. Sharpe, 1987.

C

Cahill, H. *A Yankee Adventurer: the story of Ward and the Tai Ping Rebellion.* New York, 1930.
Carl, K.A. *With the Empress Dowager of China.* Eveleigh Nash, London, 1906.
Cary-Elwes, C. *China and the Cross: a survey of missionary history.* P.J. Kennedy & Sons, New York, 1956, p. 215.
Chaiken, N. *The Sino-Japanese War, 1894–1895.* Venthone, 1983.
Chang Hsin-pao. *Commissioner Lin and the Opium War.* Harvard University Press, 1964.
Chang, Jolan. *The Tao of Love and Sex: the ancient Chinese way to ecstasy.* Wildwood House, 1997.
Cheng, J.C. *Chinese Sources for the Tai Ping Rebellion.* Hong Kong University Press, 1963.

Chung, S.F. *The Much Maligned Empress Dowager*. Ph.D. thesis, University of California, Berkeley, 1979, p. 3.

Collis, M. *The Great Within*. Faber & Faber, 1941.

Cordier, *Histoire des relations de la Chine avec les puissances occidental*. 1902.

Curwen, C.A. *Taiping Rebel: the deposition of Li Hsiu Cheng*. Cambridge University Press, 1977, p. 145.

D

Deng, S. and Fairbank, J.K. *China's Response to the West*. Harvard University Press, 1954.

Dillon, E.J. *Fortnightly Review*.

Dreyer, E.L. *Early Ming China*. Stanford University Press, 1982.

Dulles, F.R. *China and America: the story of relations since 1784*. Greenwood Press, 1981.

Duus, P. *The Abacus and the Sword: Japanese penetration of Korea 1895–1910*. University of California Press, 1995.

E

Eitel, E.J. *Feng Shui*. Lane, Crawford & Co., 1873.

F

Fairbanks, J.K. *Chinabound*. Harper & Row, 1932, p. 38.

Fielde, A.M. *Pagoda Shadows: studies from life in China*. W. G. Corthell, 1890.

Freedman, M. *Chinese Lineage and Society*, Oxford University Press, 1966.

G

Geiss, J.P. *Peking Under the Ming*, pp. 157–158.

Goldstein, J. *The Jews of China*. M.E. Sharpe, 2000.

Gulik, R. van. *Sexual Life in Ancient China*. E.J. Brill, Linden, 1974.

H

Han Fei Tzu, *The Complete Works of Han Fei Tzu* (trans. W.K. Liao). Probsthain, London, 1930.

Headland, I. *Court Life in China*. Fleming H. Revell Co., 1909.

Herrison, Comte de. *Journal d'un Interprète en Chine*. Paris, 1886.

Hinsch, B. *Passions of the Cut Sleeve: the male homosexual tradition in China*. University of California Press, 1990, pp. 142–143.

Hirth, F. *China and the Roman Orient: researches into their ancient and medieval relations as represented in old Chinese records*. Leipzig. 1885.

Hu Chui, *The Forbidden City* (trans. Yang Aiwen, Wang Xingzheng). China Photographic Publishing House, Beijing, 1996.

Huang, R. *1587, a Year of No Significance*. Yale University Press, 1981.

Hurd, D. *The Arrow War: an Anglo-Chinese Confusion 1856–1860*. Collins, 1967.

J

Jackson, B. *Splendid Slippers.* Ten Speed Press, Berkeley, 1997.

Jansen, M.B. (ed.). *The Cambridge History of Japan,* vol. 5, *The nineteenth century.* Cambridge University Press, 1989.

Johnston, R.F. *Twilight in the Forbidden City.* Victor Gollancz, 1934.

K

Kanazawa, Hirokazu. *Shotokan Karate.* London, 1972.

Keswick, M. *The Chinese Garden: history, art and architecture.* Academy Editions, 1978.

L

Lane-Poole, S. *The Life of Sir Harry Parkes Sometime Her Majesty's Minister to China and Japan.* Macmillan. 1894.

Lo, Jung-pang (ed.). *Kang Yu Wei, a biography and symposium.* University of Arizona Press, c.1967.

Loch, H. *Personal Narrative of Occurrences during Lord Elgin's Second Embassy to China, 1860.* London, 1869.

Lui, Adam Yuen-chung. *The Hanlin Academy: training ground for the ambitious, 1644–1850.* Archon Books, 1981.

M

MacAleavy, H. *A Dream of Tartary.* George Allen & Unwin, 1963.

Marshall, P.J. *East Indian Fortunes: the British in Bengal in the eighteenth century.* Clarendon Press, 1976.

Michael, F. *The Origin of Manchu Rule in China.* Johns Hopkins Press, 1942.

Michael, F. (in collaboration with Chung-li Chang). *The Tai Ping Rebellion.* University of Washington Press, 1971.

Mitamura, T. *Chinese Eunuchs.* C.E. Tuttle & Co., 1970, p. 29ff.

N

National Geographic Authors. *Journey into China.* National Geographic Society, 1982.

P

Pearl, C. *Morrison of Peking.* Angus & Robertson, 1967.

Pa. *Unofficial History of the Empress Dowager.* 1911.

Parker, E.H. *John Chinaman and a few others.* John Murray, 1901.

Plée, H. *Karate.* London, 1969.

Putnam Weale, B.L. *Indiscreet Letters from Peking.* Hurst & Blackett, 1907.

R

Read, D. *The Tao of Health, Sex and Longevity.* Fireside, 1989.

Richard, T. *Forty-five Years in China.* T. Fisher Unwin, 1916.

Roberts, F.M. *Western Travellers to China.* London, 1932.

Rockhill, W.W. *Diplomatic Audiences at the Court of China.* Luzac & Co., 1905.

S

Sergeant, P. *The Great Empress Dowager of China*. Hutchinson & Co., 1910.

Smith, R.W. *Shaolin Temple Boxing*. C.E. Tuttle & Co., 1964.

Spence, J. *The China Helpers*. Bodley Head, 1969.

Spence, J. *God's Chinese Son*. Flamingo, 1997, p. xix.

Straits Times, 14th July 2002.

Struve, L.S. *The Southern Ming, 1644–1662*. Yale University Press, 1984.

Sun Tzu. *The Art of War* (trans. Samuel B. Griffiths). Oxford University Press, 1971, p. 63.

Swann, N.L. *Pan Chao, foremost woman scholar of China*. Russel & Russel, New York, 1968.

Swinhoe, R. *Narrative of the North China Campaign of 1860*. London, 1861.

T

Tan, C.C. *The Boxer Catastrophe*. Columbia University Press, 1955.

Te Ling. *Two Years in the Forbidden City*. Moffat, Yard & Co., 1911.

Te Ling. *Imperial Incense*. S. Paul & Co., 1934.

Teng, S. and Fairbank, J.K. *China's Response to the West*. Harvard University Press, 1954, p. 48.

The Complete Works of Han Fei Tzu (trans. W.K. Liao). Probsthain, London, 1930.

Tyler, W.T. *Pulling Strings in China*. Constable & Co., 1929.

V

Vare, D. *The Last Empress*. John Murray, 1938.

W

Waldron, T. *Letters and Journals of James, Eighth Earl of Elgin*. 1872.

Waltner, A. *Getting an Heir*. University of Hawaii Press, 1990.

Wakeman, F.E. *The Great Enterprise: the Manchu reconstruction of imperial order in seventeenth-century China*. University of California Press, 1985, p. 2.

Warner, D.A. and P. *The Tide at Sunrise: a history of the Russo-Japanese War 1904–1905*. Angus & Robertson, 1975.

Warner, M. *The Dragon Empress*. Vintage, London, 1993.

Wiles of War, The (trans. Sun Haichen). Foreign Languages Press, Beijing, 1991, p. 303nb.

Wolf, M. 'Women and Suicide in China', in *Women in Chinese Society* (M. Wolf and R. Witke, eds). Stanford University Press, 1975.

Wolsley, G.J. *Narrative of the War with China in 1860*. 1862.

Worswick, C. and Spence, J. *Imperial China in Photographs, 1850–1912*. Scolar Press, 1979.

Wilson, A. *The Ever Victorious Army*. Blackwood, Edinburgh, 1868.

Wu Yung. *The Flight of an Empress*. Faber & Faber, 1937.

Y

Yun Yu-ting. *The True Story of the Kuang-Hsu Emperor*. In Chung-kuo chin-pai, nien-shih tzu-liao, ch'u-pien (Tso Shun-sheng, ed.). Shanghai, 1931, p. 484).

Index

About the author

Keith Laidler is an anthropologist, author and filmmaker. He is the author of seven books and producer of a large number of films, for some of which he did his own camera work. Originally concentrating on nature films, Dr Laidler worked with Sir David Attenborough on *The Living Planet*. His production company, Wolfshead Productions has made a number of highly acclaimed documentaries for a variety of broadcasters. He holds a PhD in Anthropology from Durham University.

Dr Laidler has a strong interest in China, which he visits regularly as founder of The Panda Trust, an organisation formed to protect the panda. He has, over recent years, turned his investigative techniques towards history and religion.